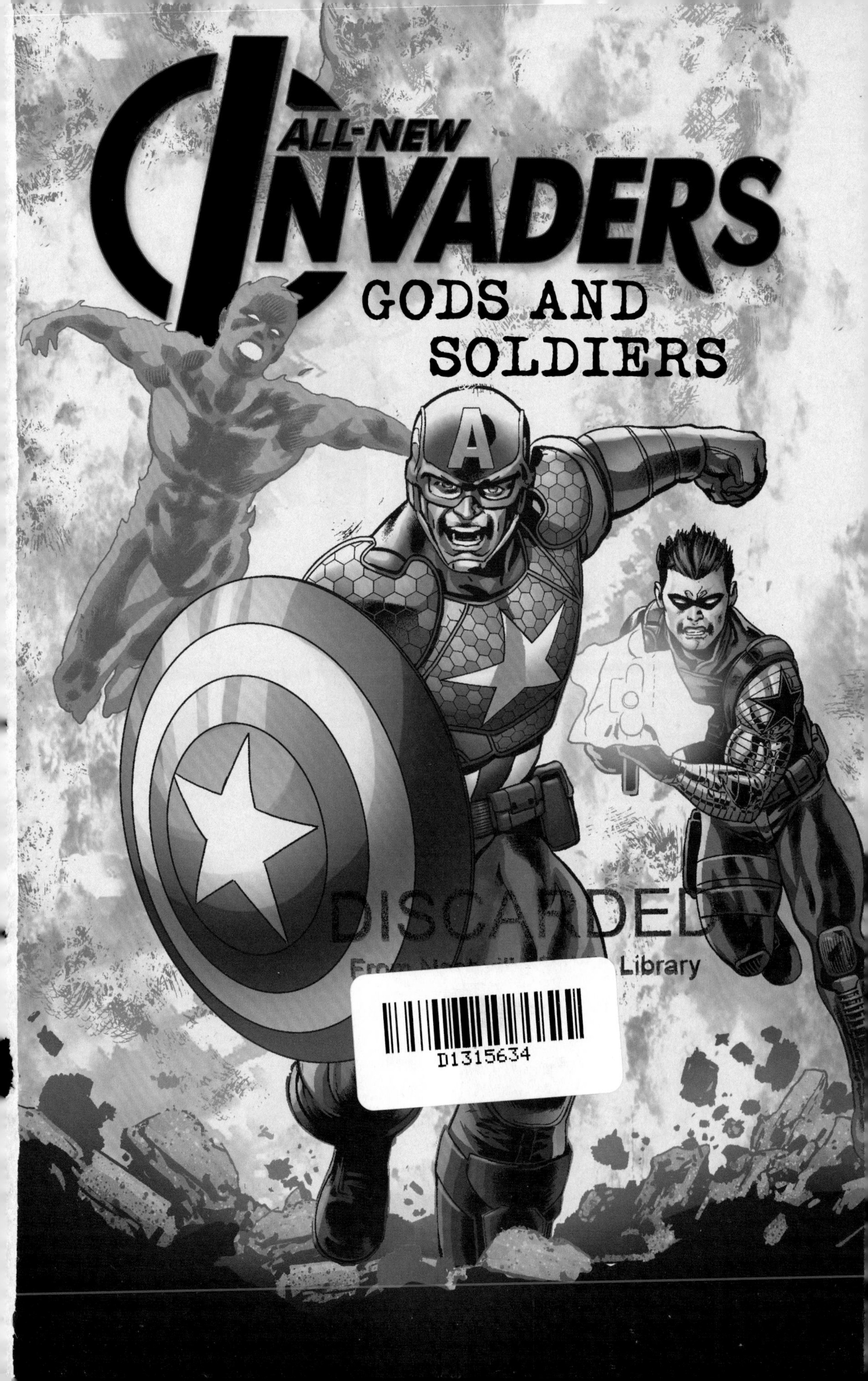
ALL-NEW
INVADERS
GODS AND SOLDIERS

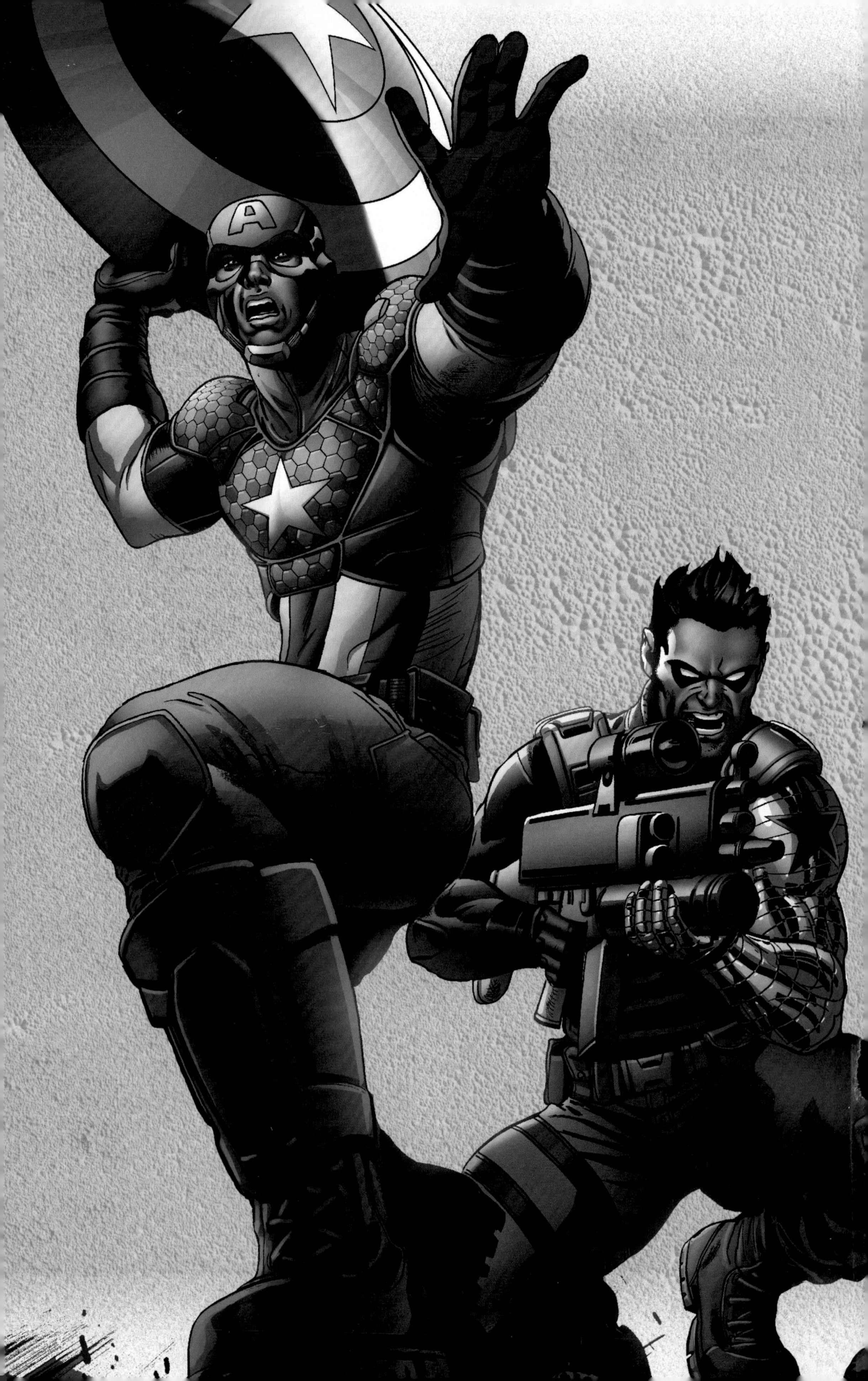

WRITER
JAMES ROBINSON

ARTIST
STEVE PUGH

COLOR ARTIST
GURU-eFX

LETTERER
CORY PETIT

COVER ART
MUKESH SINGH

ASSISTANT EDITOR
EMILY SHAW

EDITOR
MARK PANICCIA

COLLECTION EDITOR
JENNIFER GRÜNWALD

ASSISTANT EDITOR
SARAH BRUNSTAD

ASSOCIATE MANAGING EDITOR
ALEX STARBUCK

EDITOR, SPECIAL PROJECTS
MARK D. BEAZLEY

SENIOR EDITOR, SPECIAL PROJECTS
JEFF YOUNGQUIST

SVP PRINT, SALES & MARKETING
DAVID GABRIEL

BOOK DESIGN
NELSON RIBEIRO

EDITOR IN CHIEF
AXEL ALONSO

CHIEF CREATIVE OFFICER
JOE QUESADA

PUBLISHER
DAN BUCKLEY

EXECUTIVE PRODUCER
ALAN FINE

ALL-NEW INVADERS VOL. 1: GODS AND SOLDIERS. Contains material originally published in magazine form as ALL-NEW INVADERS #1-5 and ALL-NEW MARVEL NOW! POINT ONE #1. First printing 2014. ISBN# 978-0-7851-8914-5. Published by MARVEL WORLDWIDE, INC., a subsidiary of MARVEL ENTERTAINMENT, LLC. OFFICE OF PUBLICATION: 135 West 50th Street, New York, NY 10020. **Printed in Canada.** ALAN FINE, EVP - Office of the President, Marvel Worldwide, Inc. and EVP & CMO Marvel Characters B.V.; DAN BUCKLEY, Publisher & President - Print, Animation & Digital Divisions; JOE QUESADA, Chief Creative Officer; TOM BREVOORT, SVP of Publishing; DAVID BOGART, SVP of Operations & Procurement, Publishing; C.B. CEBULSKI, SVP of Creator & Content Development; DAVID GABRIEL, SVP Print, Sales & Marketing; JIM O'KEEFE, VP of Operations & Logistics; DAN CARR, Executive Director of Publishing Technology; SUSAN CRESPI, Editorial Operations Manager; ALEX MORALES, Publishing Operations Manager; STAN LEE, Chairman Emeritus. For information regarding advertising in Marvel Comics or on Marvel.com, please contact Niza Disla, Director of Marvel Partnerships, at ndisla@marvel.com. For Marvel subscription inquiries, please call 800-217-9158. **Manufactured between 6/6/2014 and 7/14/2014 by SOLISCO PRINTERS, SCOTT, QC, CANADA.**

10 9 8 7 6 5 4 3 2 1

PREVIOUSLY...

During World War Two, a group of Allied super heroes known as the Invaders banded together to fight the Axis in the name of freedom. But that was then...

These heroes lived on into the present day by one means or another — fluke or luck or fate. Now, their lives are very different from the honor and glory they shared as their own unique "Band of Brothers" back during the war.

Although these men fought side by side in the fire of war, they have rarely been together since.

That's about to change.

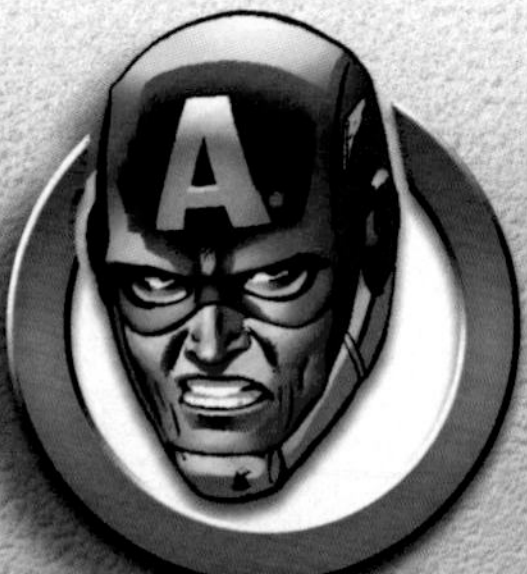

CAPTAIN AMERICA, the super-soldier, living legend, and sentinel of liberty remains the epitome of a national/world hero, with links to both the Avengers and S.H.I.E.L.D. and a continued history of doing good.

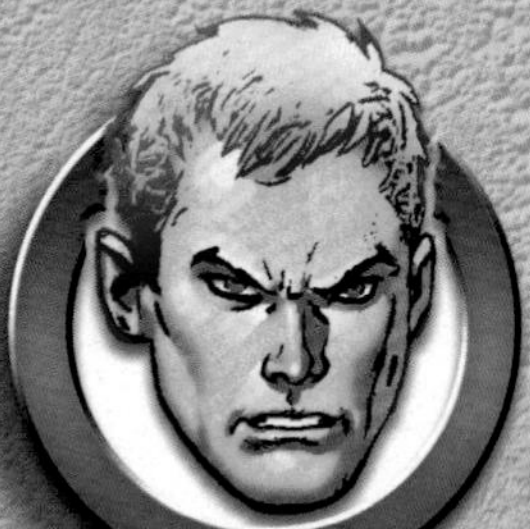

JIM HAMMOND, THE ORIGINAL HUMAN TORCH and the world's first synthetic human, is perhaps the least known of the heroes. Recently a cadre of robots and androids planned to take over Earth, a plan that Jim betrayed and helped defeat for the sake of humanity.

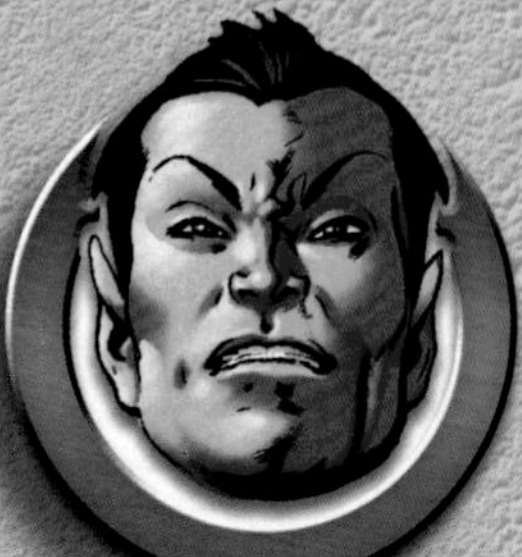

NAMOR THE SUB-MARINER, aquatic ruler of the undersea kingdom of Atlantis has been a hero too since the war, but at other times, humanity's greatest foe. Currently his place in the world is somewhere between the two.

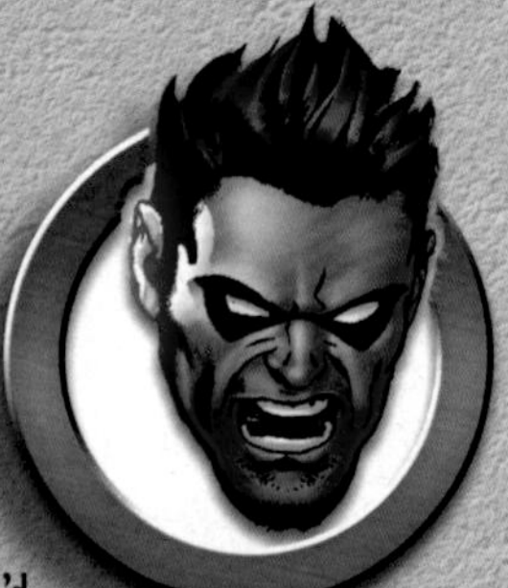

JAMES "BUCKY" BARNES, one-time sidekick of Captain America, was long thought to have died in the closing months of the war. Actually he'd survived and was brainwashed by the Russians into becoming the assassin and super-spy known as the Winter Soldier. He remains a wanted man for his crimes as a Russian killer and was forced to fake his death. The Winter Soldier now lives in the shadows.

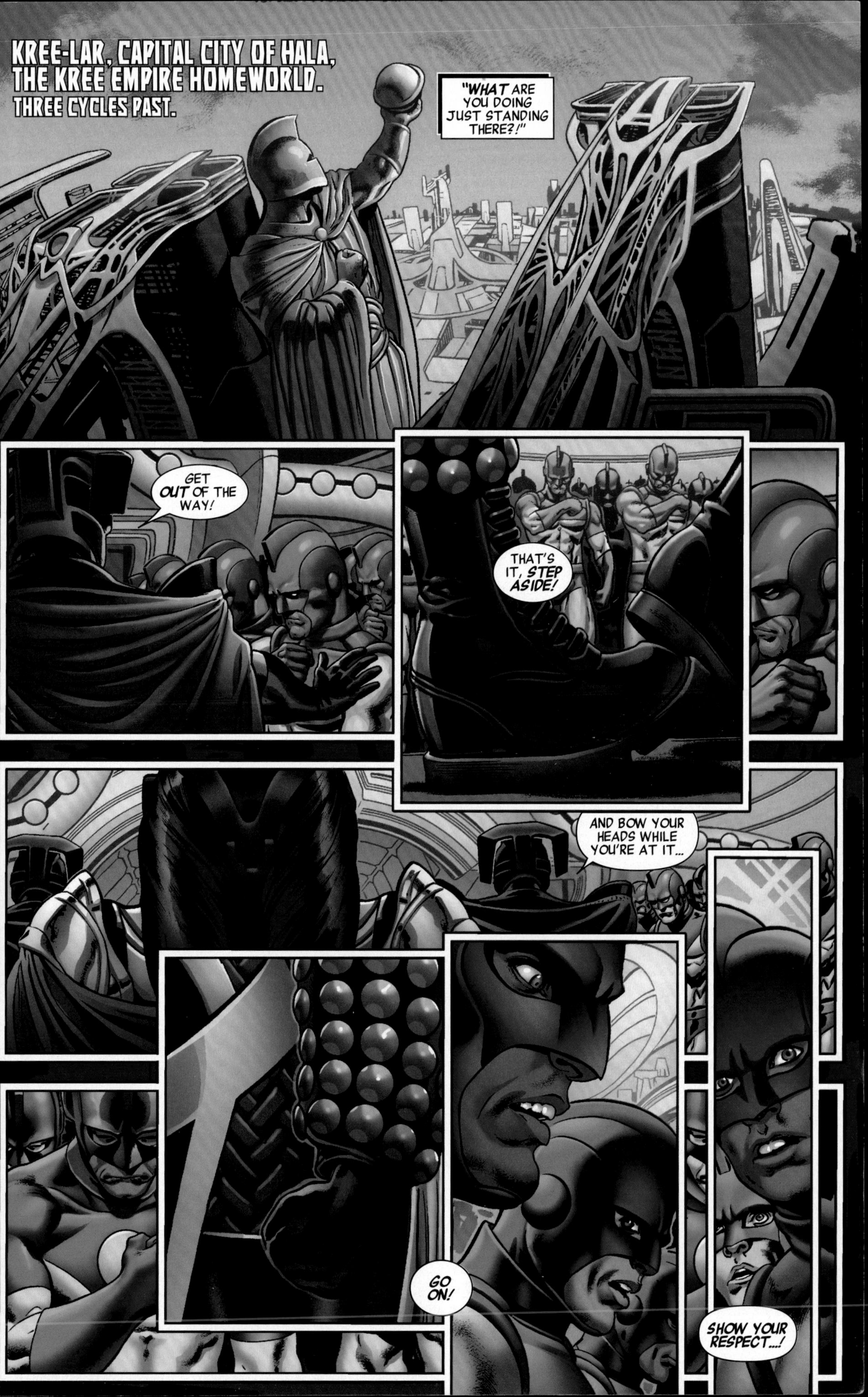
KREE-LAR, CAPITAL CITY OF HALA, THE KREE EMPIRE HOMEWORLD.
THREE CYCLES PAST.
"WHAT ARE YOU DOING JUST STANDING THERE?!"
GET OUT OF THE WAY!
THAT'S IT, STEP ASIDE!
AND BOW YOUR HEADS WHILE YOU'RE AT IT...
GO ON!
SHOW YOUR RESPECT...!

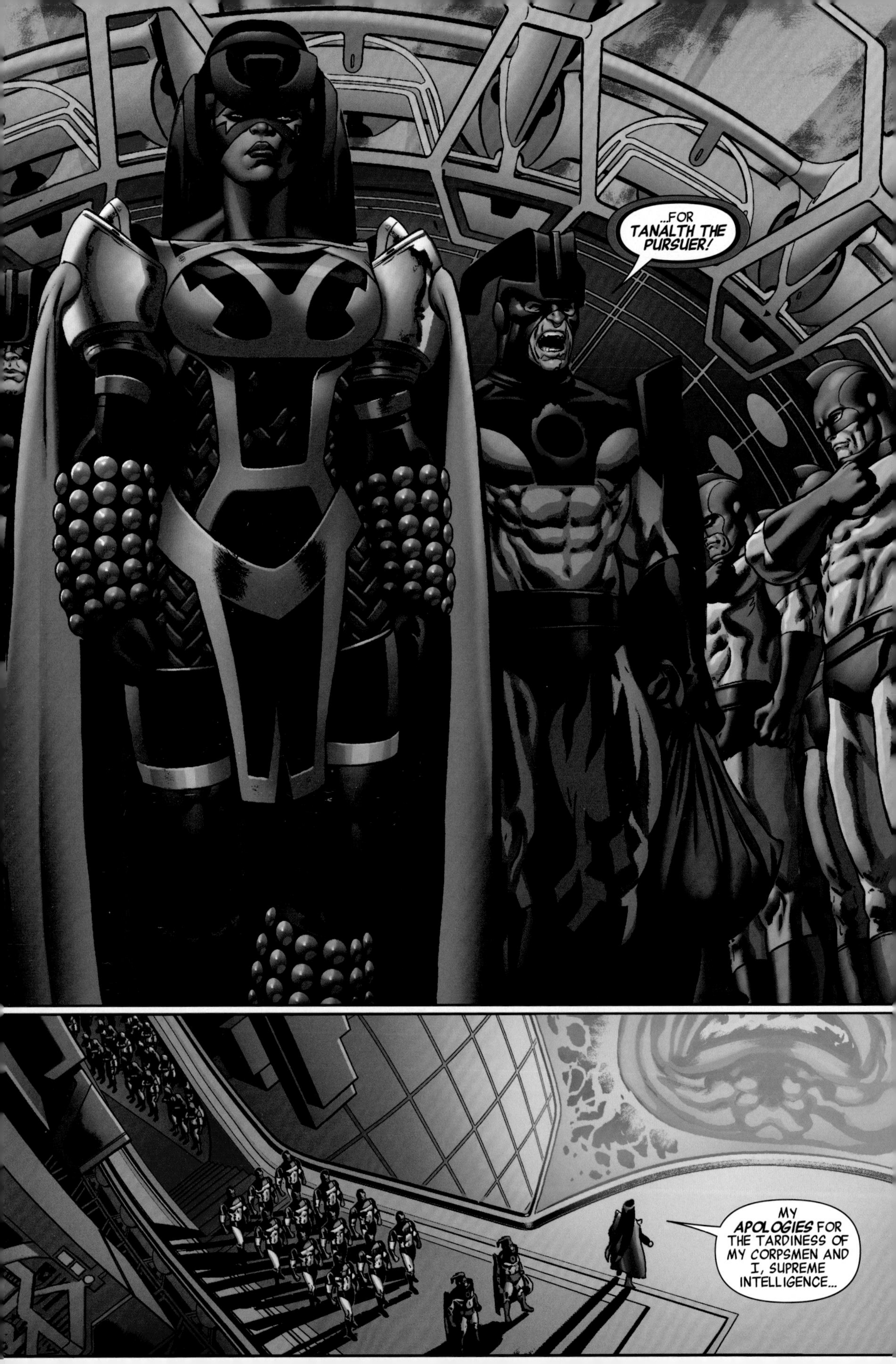
...FOR TANALTH THE PURSUER!
MY APOLOGIES FOR THE TARDINESS OF MY CORPSMEN AND I, SUPREME INTELLIGENCE...

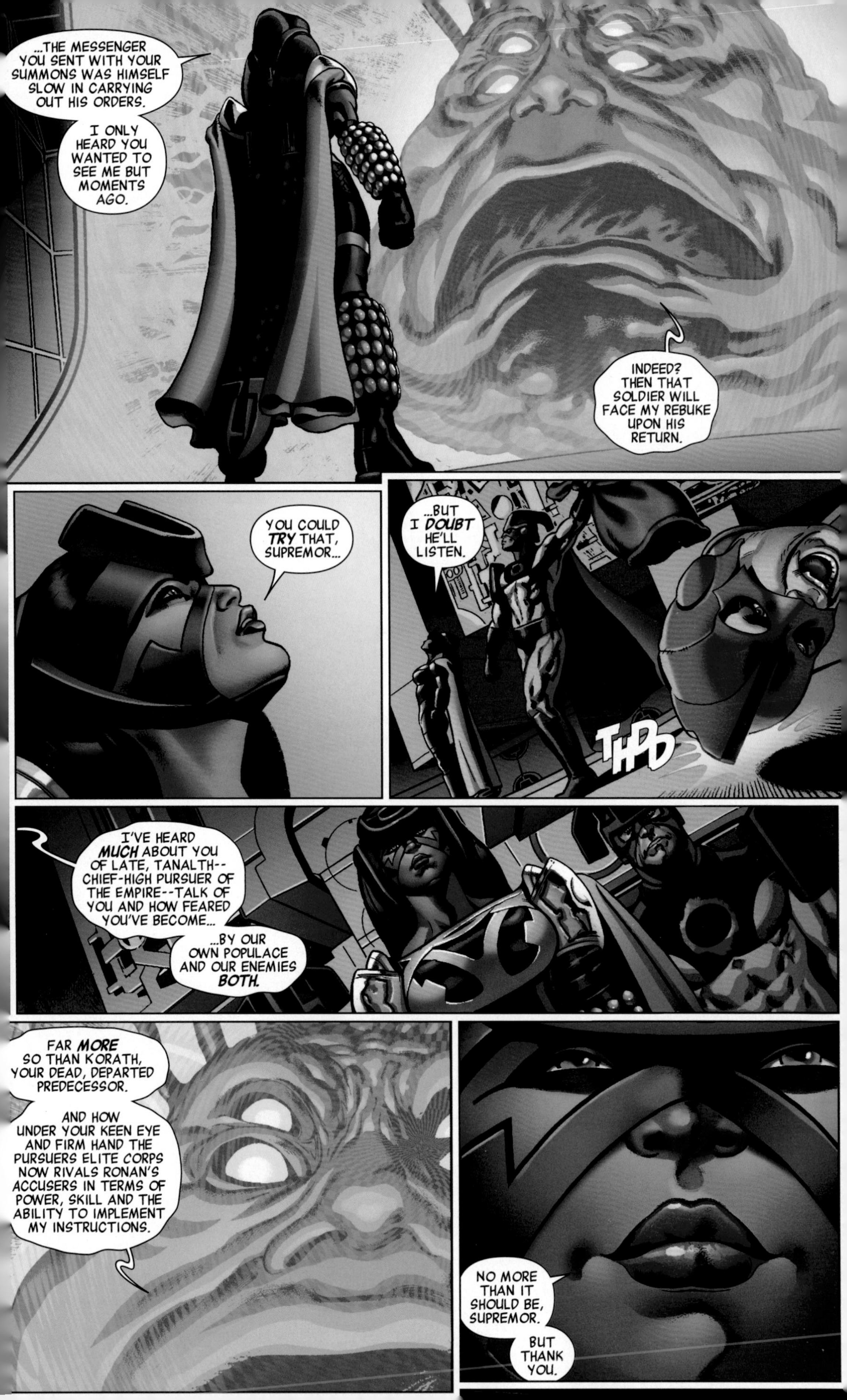
...THE MESSENGER YOU SENT WITH YOUR SUMMONS WAS HIMSELF SLOW IN CARRYING OUT HIS ORDERS.
I ONLY HEARD YOU WANTED TO SEE ME BUT MOMENTS AGO.
INDEED? THEN THAT SOLDIER WILL FACE MY REBUKE UPON HIS RETURN.
YOU COULD TRY THAT, SUPREMOR...
...BUT I DOUBT HE'LL LISTEN.
THDD
I'VE HEARD MUCH ABOUT YOU OF LATE, TANALTH--CHIEF-HIGH PURSUER OF THE EMPIRE--TALK OF YOU AND HOW FEARED YOU'VE BECOME...
...BY OUR OWN POPULACE AND OUR ENEMIES BOTH.
FAR MORE SO THAN KORATH, YOUR DEAD, DEPARTED PREDECESSOR.
AND HOW UNDER YOUR KEEN EYE AND FIRM HAND THE PURSUERS ELITE CORPS NOW RIVALS RONAN'S ACCUSERS IN TERMS OF POWER, SKILL AND THE ABILITY TO IMPLEMENT MY INSTRUCTIONS.
NO MORE THAN IT SHOULD BE, SUPREMOR.
BUT THANK YOU.

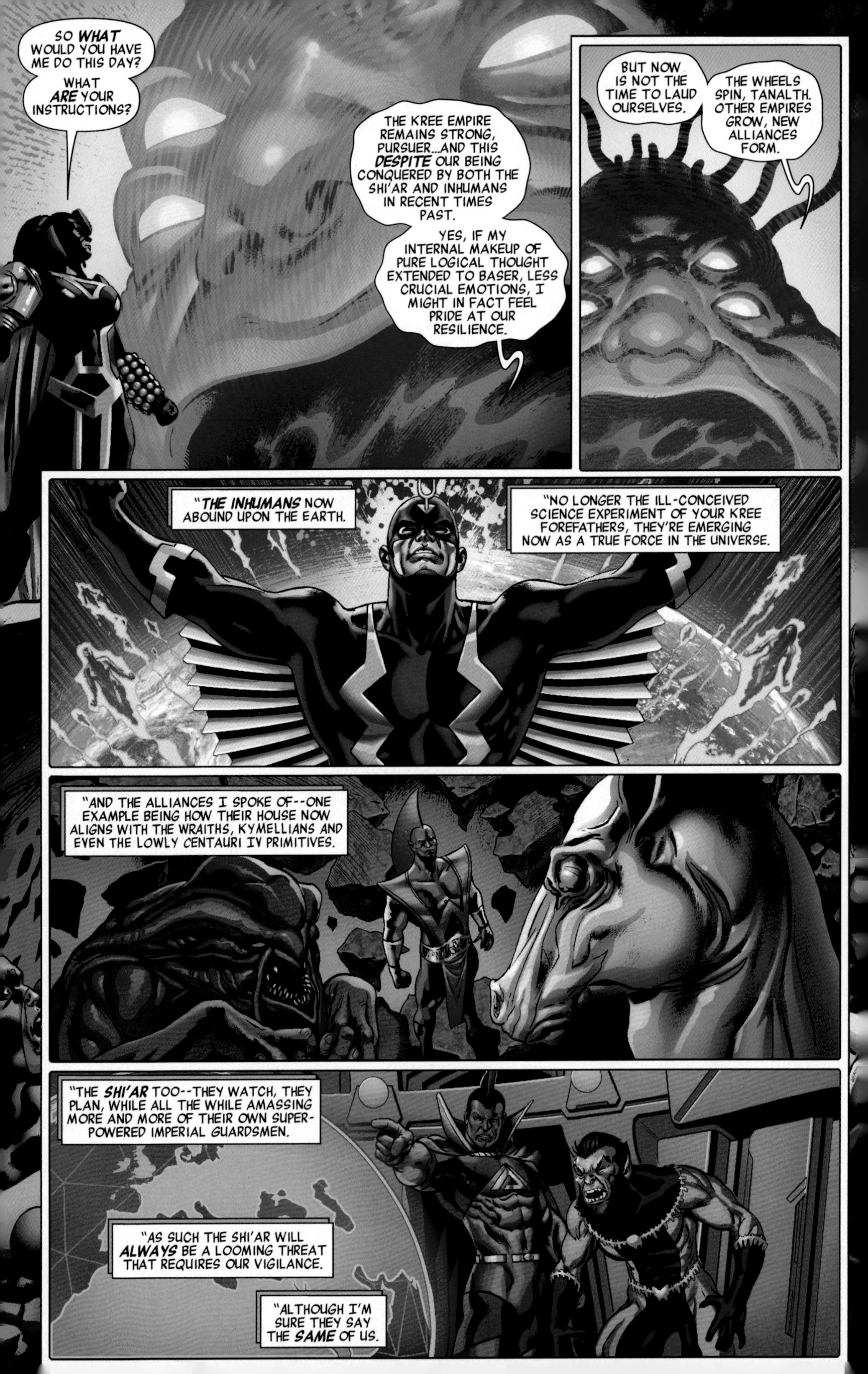
SO WHAT WOULD YOU HAVE ME DO THIS DAY?
WHAT ARE YOUR INSTRUCTIONS?
THE KREE EMPIRE REMAINS STRONG, PURSUER...AND THIS DESPITE OUR BEING CONQUERED BY BOTH THE SHI'AR AND INHUMANS IN RECENT TIMES PAST.
YES, IF MY INTERNAL MAKEUP OF PURE LOGICAL THOUGHT EXTENDED TO BASER, LESS CRUCIAL EMOTIONS, I MIGHT IN FACT FEEL PRIDE AT OUR RESILIENCE.
BUT NOW IS NOT THE TIME TO LAUD OURSELVES.
THE WHEELS SPIN, TANALTH. OTHER EMPIRES GROW, NEW ALLIANCES FORM.
"THE INHUMANS NOW ABOUND UPON THE EARTH.
"NO LONGER THE ILL-CONCEIVED SCIENCE EXPERIMENT OF YOUR KREE FOREFATHERS, THEY'RE EMERGING NOW AS A TRUE FORCE IN THE UNIVERSE.
"AND THE ALLIANCES I SPOKE OF--ONE EXAMPLE BEING HOW THEIR HOUSE NOW ALIGNS WITH THE WRAITHS, KYMELLIANS AND EVEN THE LOWLY CENTAURI IV PRIMITIVES.
"THE SHI'AR TOO--THEY WATCH, THEY PLAN, WHILE ALL THE WHILE AMASSING MORE AND MORE OF THEIR OWN SUPER-POWERED IMPERIAL GUARDSMEN.
"AS SUCH THE SHI'AR WILL ALWAYS BE A LOOMING THREAT THAT REQUIRES OUR VIGILANCE.
"ALTHOUGH I'M SURE THEY SAY THE SAME OF US.

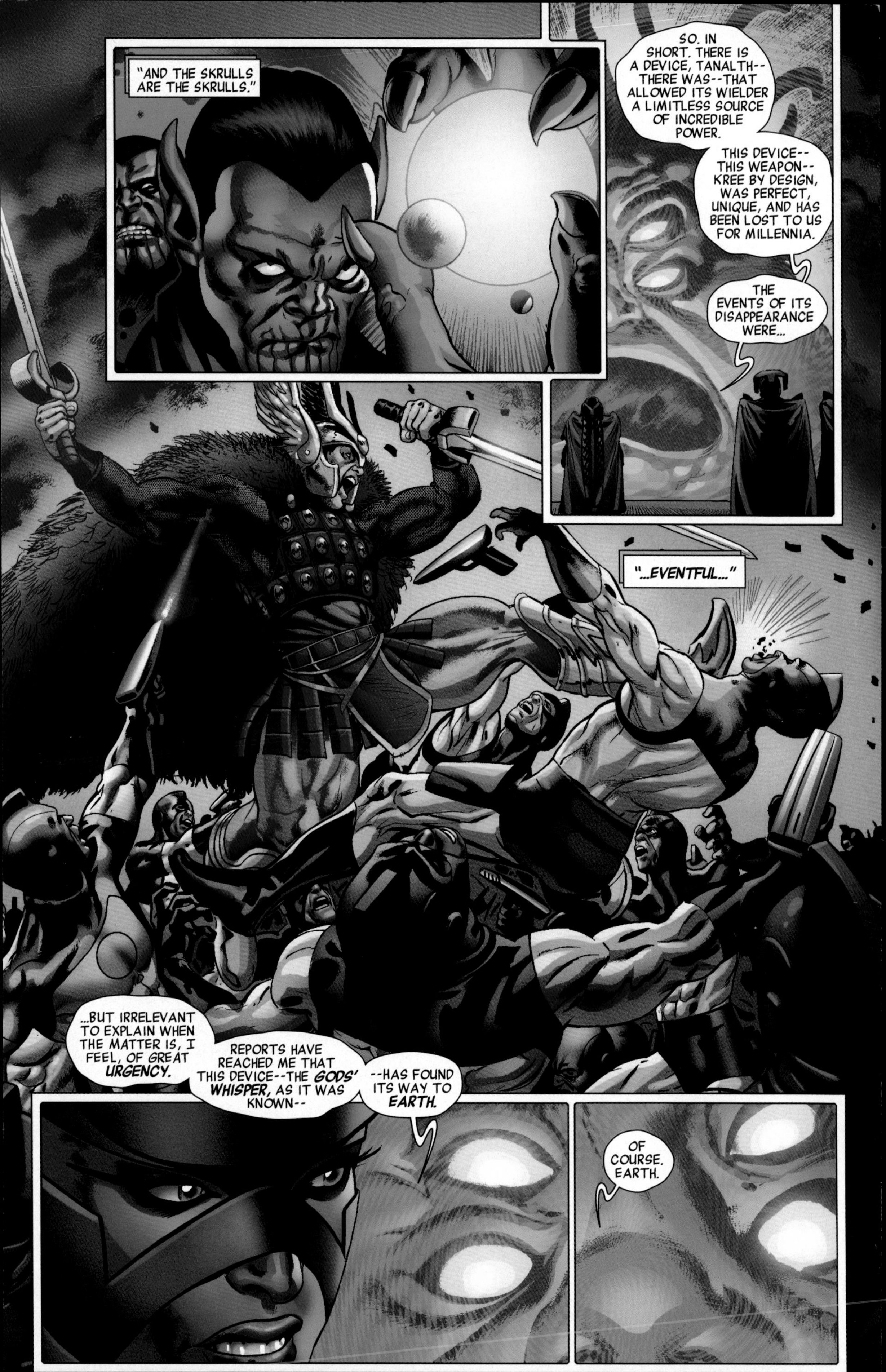
"AND THE SKRULLS ARE THE SKRULLS."
SO. IN SHORT. THERE IS A DEVICE, TANALTH-- THERE WAS--THAT ALLOWED ITS WIELDER A LIMITLESS SOURCE OF INCREDIBLE POWER.
THIS DEVICE-- THIS WEAPON-- KREE BY DESIGN, WAS PERFECT, UNIQUE, AND HAS BEEN LOST TO US FOR MILLENNIA.
THE EVENTS OF ITS DISAPPEARANCE WERE...
"...EVENTFUL..."
...BUT IRRELEVANT TO EXPLAIN WHEN THE MATTER IS, I FEEL, OF GREAT URGENCY.
REPORTS HAVE REACHED ME THAT THIS DEVICE--THE GODS' WHISPER, AS IT WAS KNOWN--
--HAS FOUND ITS WAY TO EARTH.
OF COURSE. EARTH.

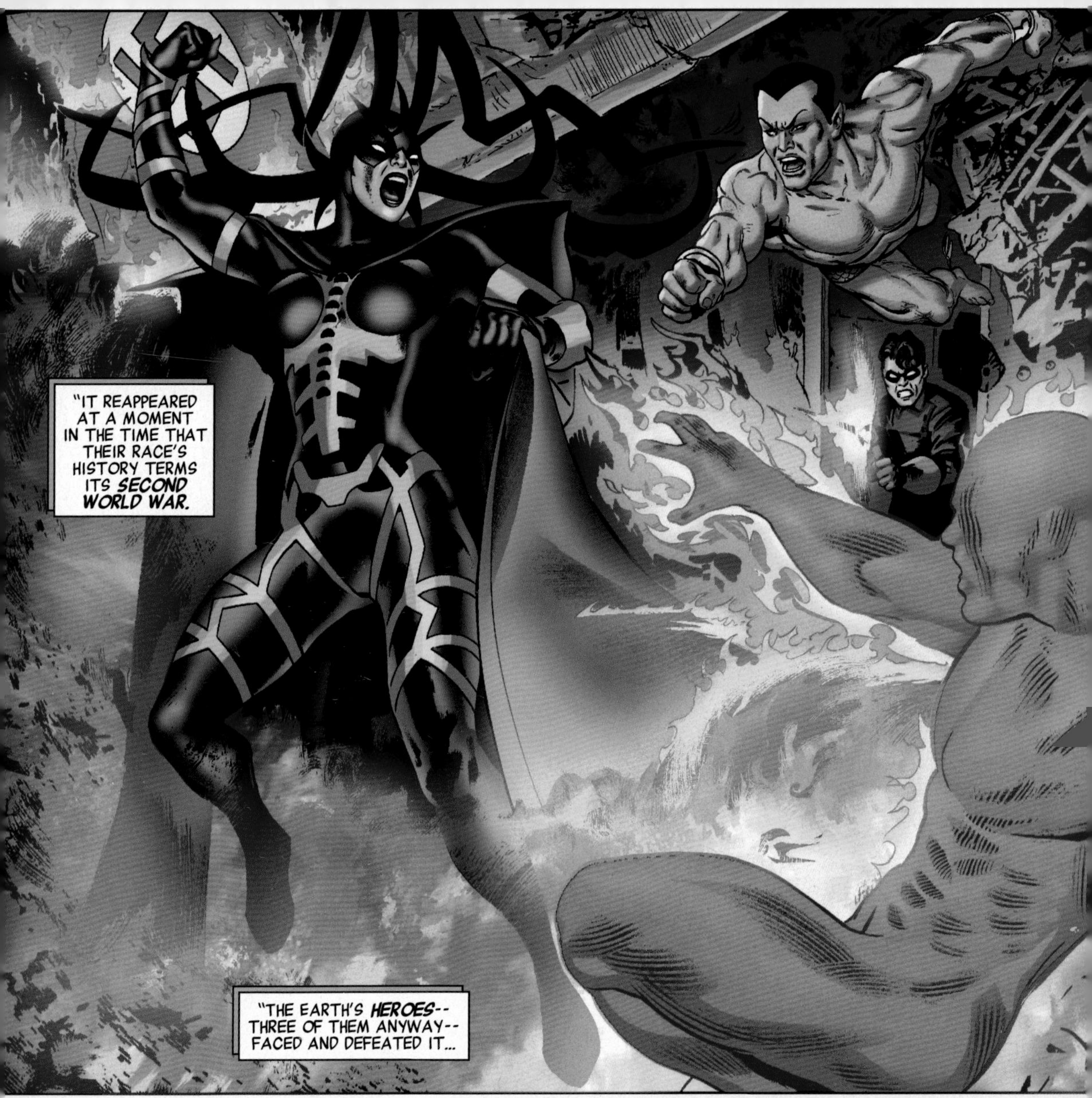
"IT REAPPEARED AT A MOMENT IN THE TIME THAT THEIR RACE'S HISTORY TERMS ITS SECOND WORLD WAR.
"THE EARTH'S HEROES--THREE OF THEM ANYWAY--FACED AND DEFEATED IT...

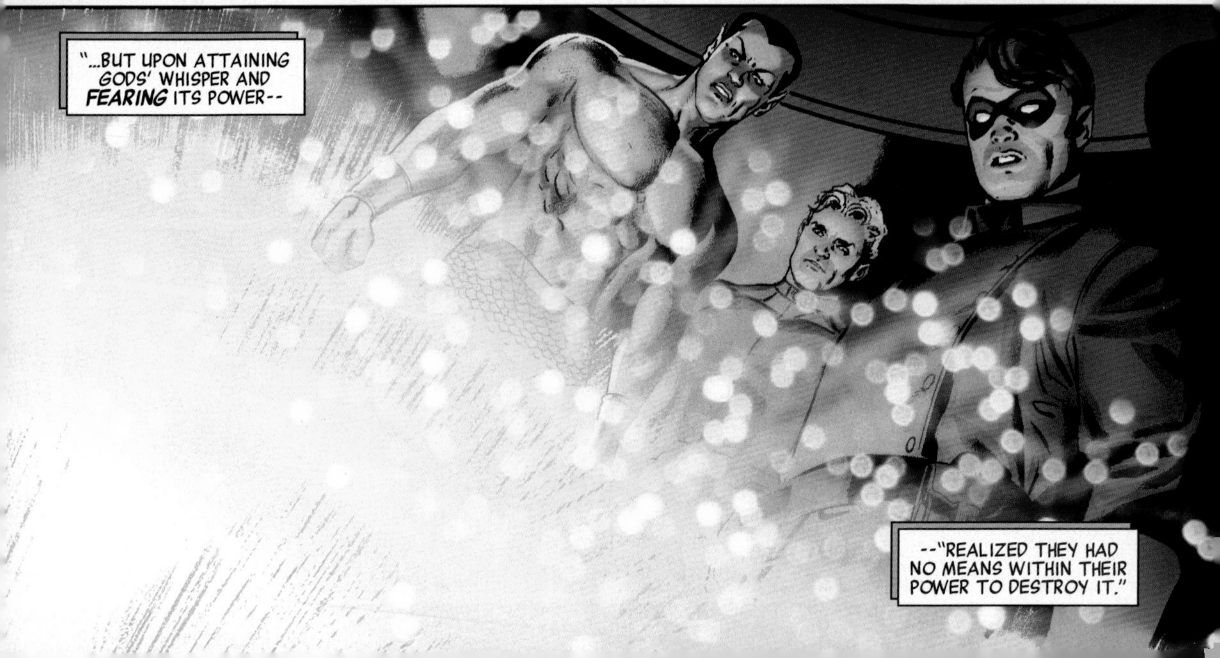
"...BUT UPON ATTAINING GODS' WHISPER AND FEARING ITS POWER--
--"REALIZED THEY HAD NO MEANS WITHIN THEIR POWER TO DESTROY IT."

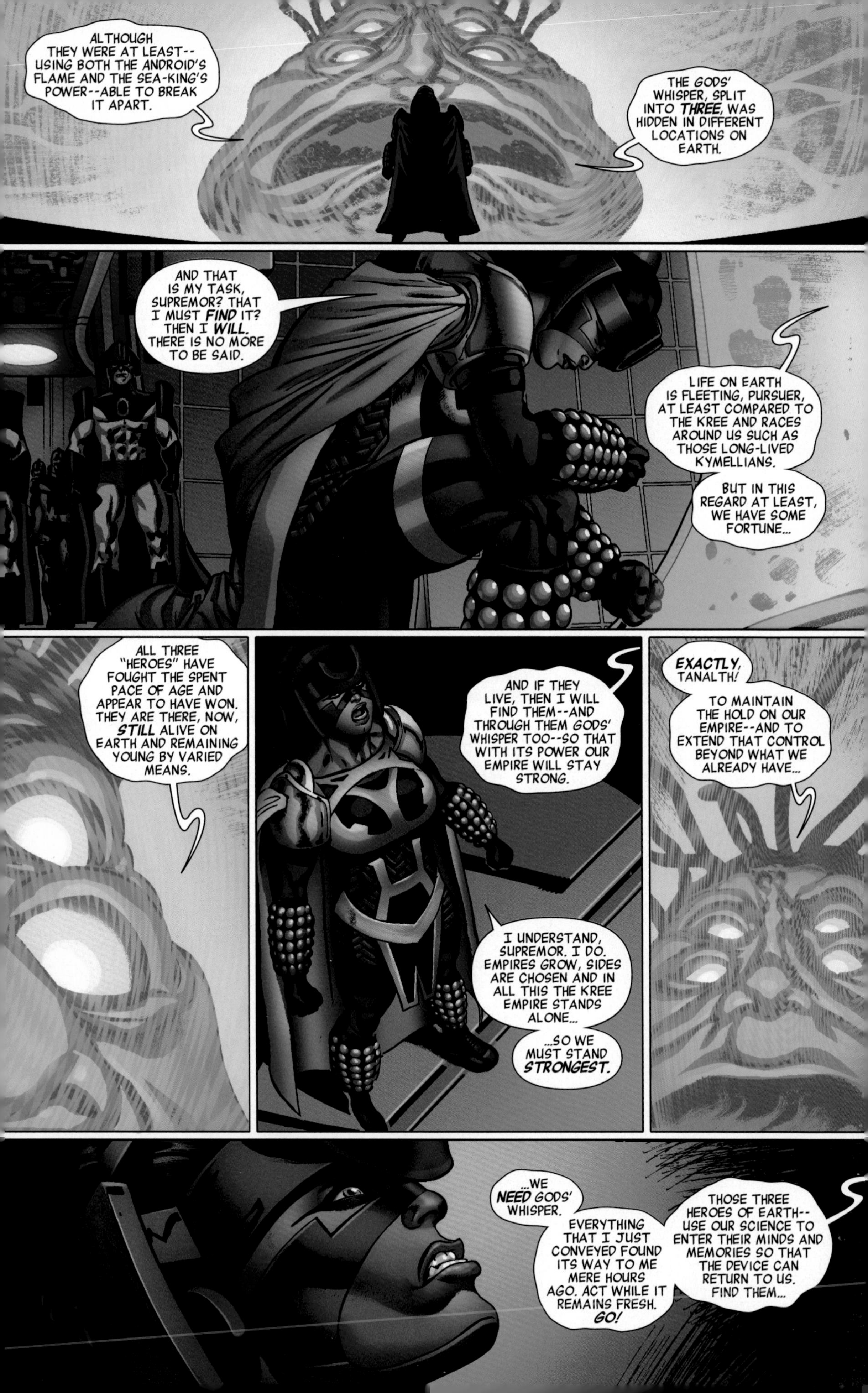
ALTHOUGH THEY WERE AT LEAST--USING BOTH THE ANDROID'S FLAME AND THE SEA-KING'S POWER--ABLE TO BREAK IT APART.
THE GODS' WHISPER, SPLIT INTO THREE, WAS HIDDEN IN DIFFERENT LOCATIONS ON EARTH.
AND THAT IS MY TASK, SUPREMOR? THAT I MUST FIND IT? THEN I WILL. THERE IS NO MORE TO BE SAID.
LIFE ON EARTH IS FLEETING, PURSUER, AT LEAST COMPARED TO THE KREE AND RACES AROUND US SUCH AS THOSE LONG-LIVED KYMELLIANS.
BUT IN THIS REGARD AT LEAST, WE HAVE SOME FORTUNE...
ALL THREE "HEROES" HAVE FOUGHT THE SPENT PACE OF AGE AND APPEAR TO HAVE WON. THEY ARE THERE, NOW, STILL ALIVE ON EARTH AND REMAINING YOUNG BY VARIED MEANS.
AND IF THEY LIVE, THEN I WILL FIND THEM--AND THROUGH THEM GODS' WHISPER TOO--SO THAT WITH ITS POWER OUR EMPIRE WILL STAY STRONG.
EXACTLY, TANALTH!
TO MAINTAIN THE HOLD ON OUR EMPIRE--AND TO EXTEND THAT CONTROL BEYOND WHAT WE ALREADY HAVE...
I UNDERSTAND, SUPREMOR. I DO. EMPIRES GROW, SIDES ARE CHOSEN AND IN ALL THIS THE KREE EMPIRE STANDS ALONE...
...SO WE MUST STAND STRONGEST.
...WE NEED GODS' WHISPER.
THOSE THREE HEROES OF EARTH--USE OUR SCIENCE TO ENTER THEIR MINDS AND MEMORIES SO THAT THE DEVICE CAN RETURN TO US. FIND THEM...
EVERYTHING THAT I JUST CONVEYED FOUND ITS WAY TO ME MERE HOURS AGO. ACT WHILE IT REMAINS FRESH. GO!

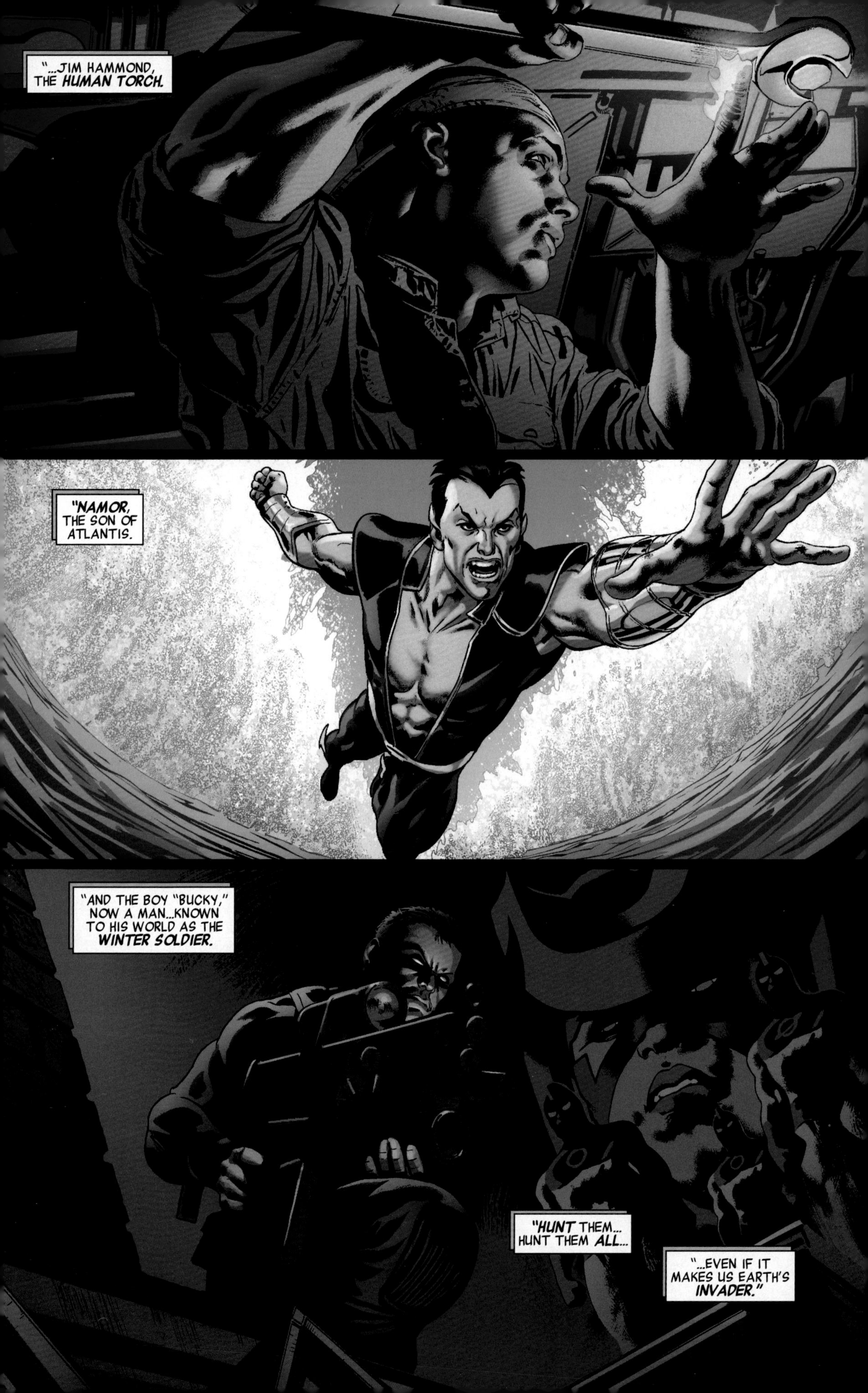
"...JIM HAMMOND, THE HUMAN TORCH.
"NAMOR, THE SON OF ATLANTIS.
"AND THE BOY "BUCKY," NOW A MAN...KNOWN TO HIS WORLD AS THE WINTER SOLDIER.
"HUNT THEM... HUNT THEM ALL...
"...EVEN IF IT MAKES US EARTH'S INVADER."

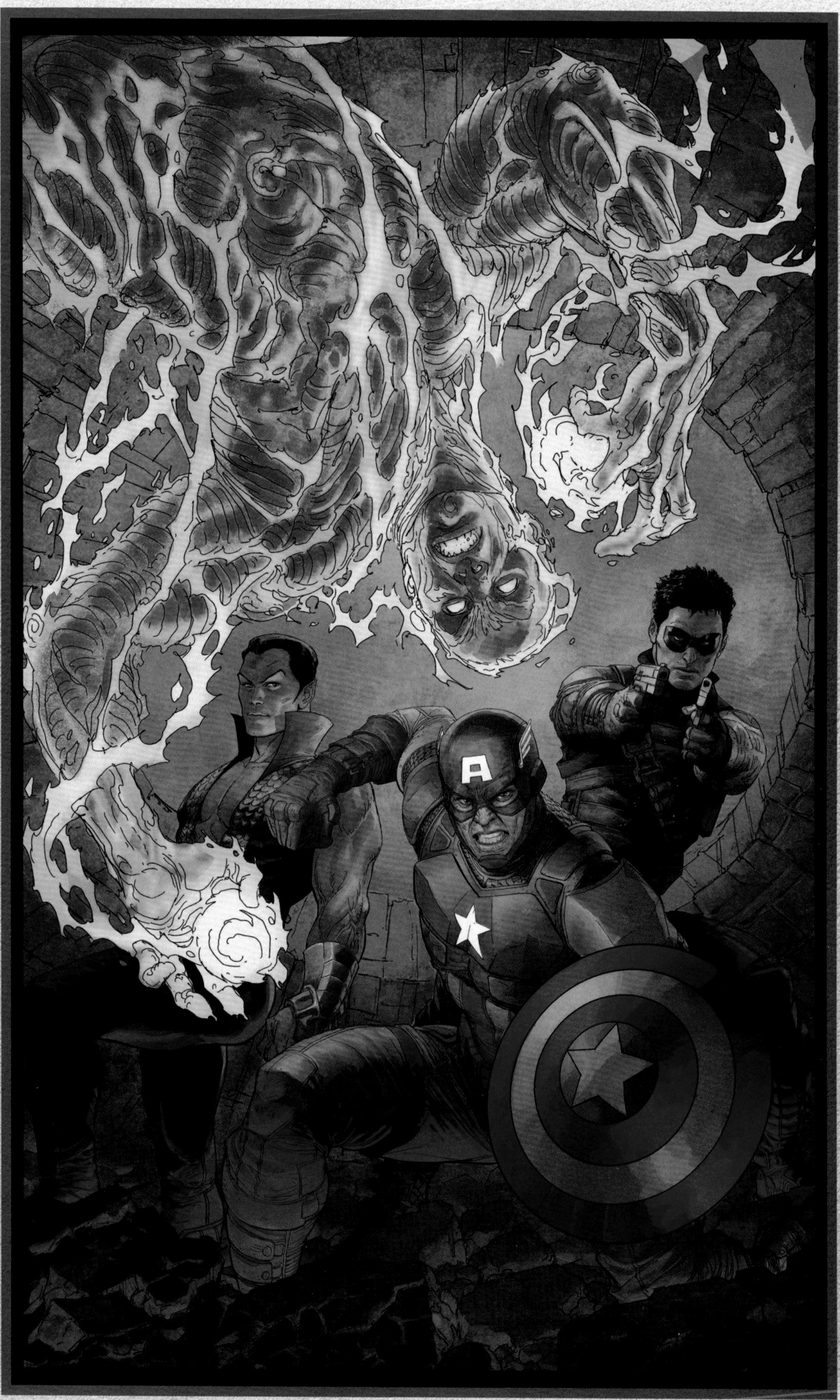

#1

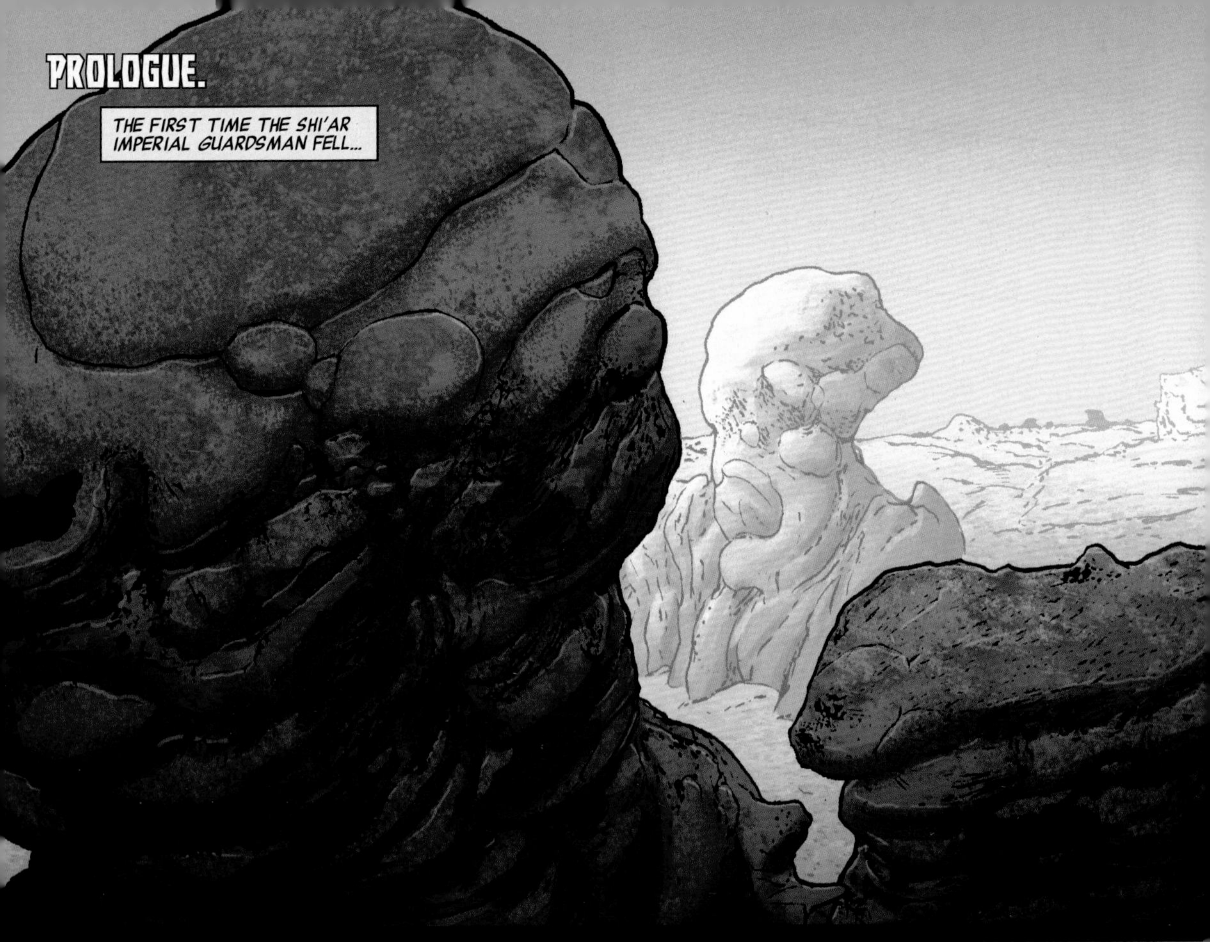
PROLOGUE.
THE FIRST TIME THE SHI'AR IMPERIAL GUARDSMAN FELL...

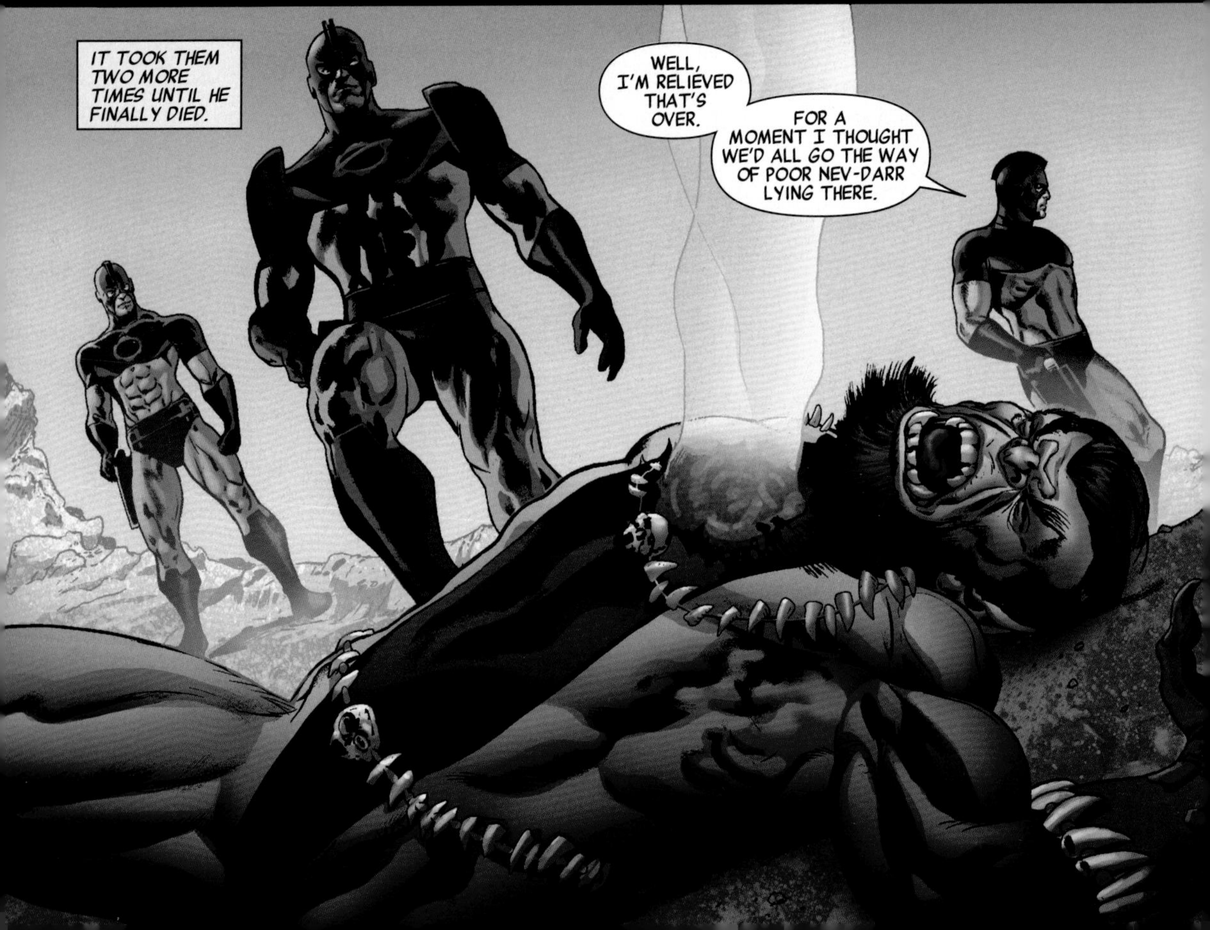
IT TOOK THEM TWO MORE TIMES UNTIL HE FINALLY DIED.
WELL, I'M RELIEVED THAT'S OVER.
FOR A MOMENT I THOUGHT WE'D ALL GO THE WAY OF POOR NEV-DARR LYING THERE.

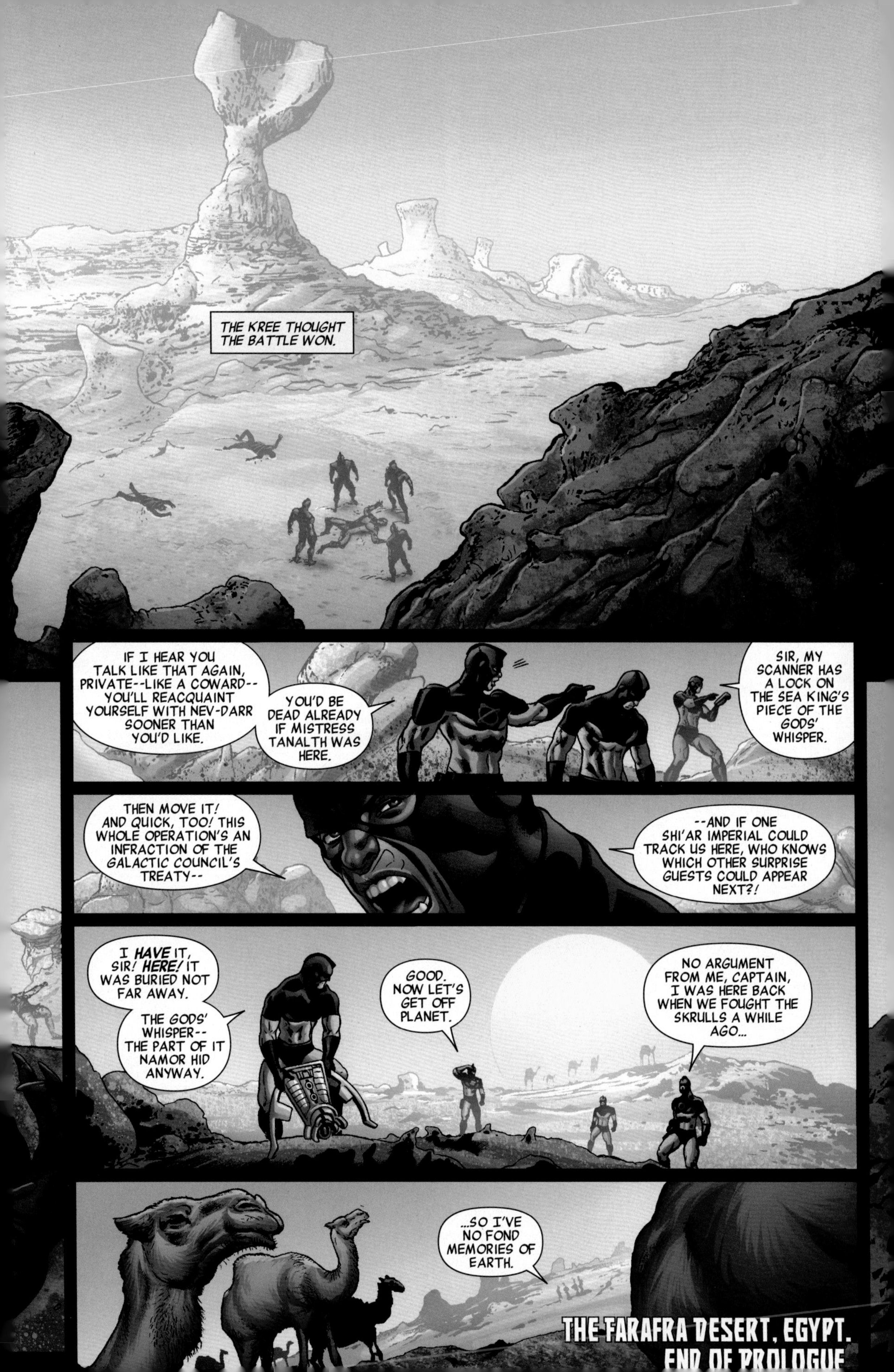
THE KREE THOUGHT THE BATTLE WON.
IF I HEAR YOU TALK LIKE THAT AGAIN, PRIVATE--LIKE A COWARD--YOU'LL REACQUAINT YOURSELF WITH NEV-DARR SOONER THAN YOU'D LIKE.
YOU'D BE DEAD ALREADY IF MISTRESS TANALTH WAS HERE.
SIR, MY SCANNER HAS A LOCK ON THE SEA KING'S PIECE OF THE GODS' WHISPER.
THEN MOVE IT! AND QUICK, TOO! THIS WHOLE OPERATION'S AN INFRACTION OF THE GALACTIC COUNCIL'S TREATY--
--AND IF ONE SHI'AR IMPERIAL COULD TRACK US HERE, WHO KNOWS WHICH OTHER SURPRISE GUESTS COULD APPEAR NEXT?!
I **HAVE** IT, SIR! **HERE!** IT WAS BURIED NOT FAR AWAY.
THE GODS' WHISPER-- THE PART OF IT NAMOR HID ANYWAY.
GOOD. NOW LET'S GET OFF PLANET.
NO ARGUMENT FROM ME, CAPTAIN, I WAS HERE BACK WHEN WE FOUGHT THE SKRULLS A WHILE AGO...
...SO I'VE NO FOND MEMORIES OF EARTH.
THE FARAFRA DESERT, EGYPT.
END OF PROLOGUE

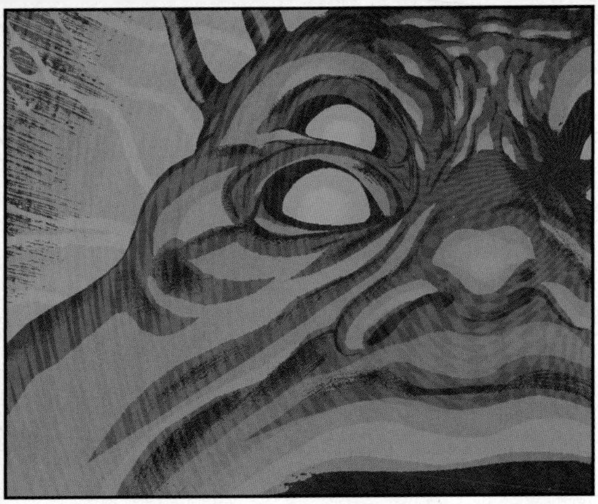
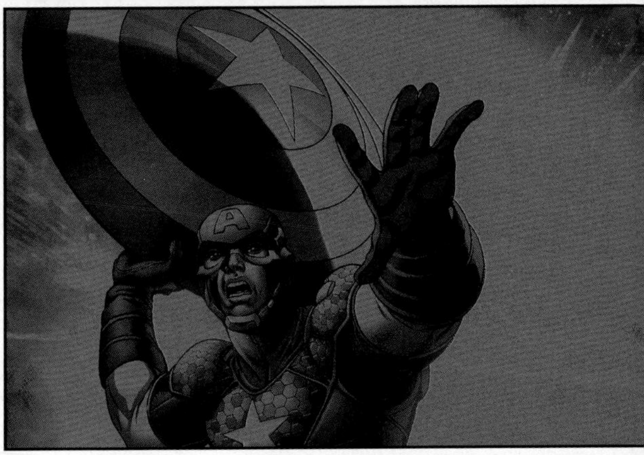

GODS

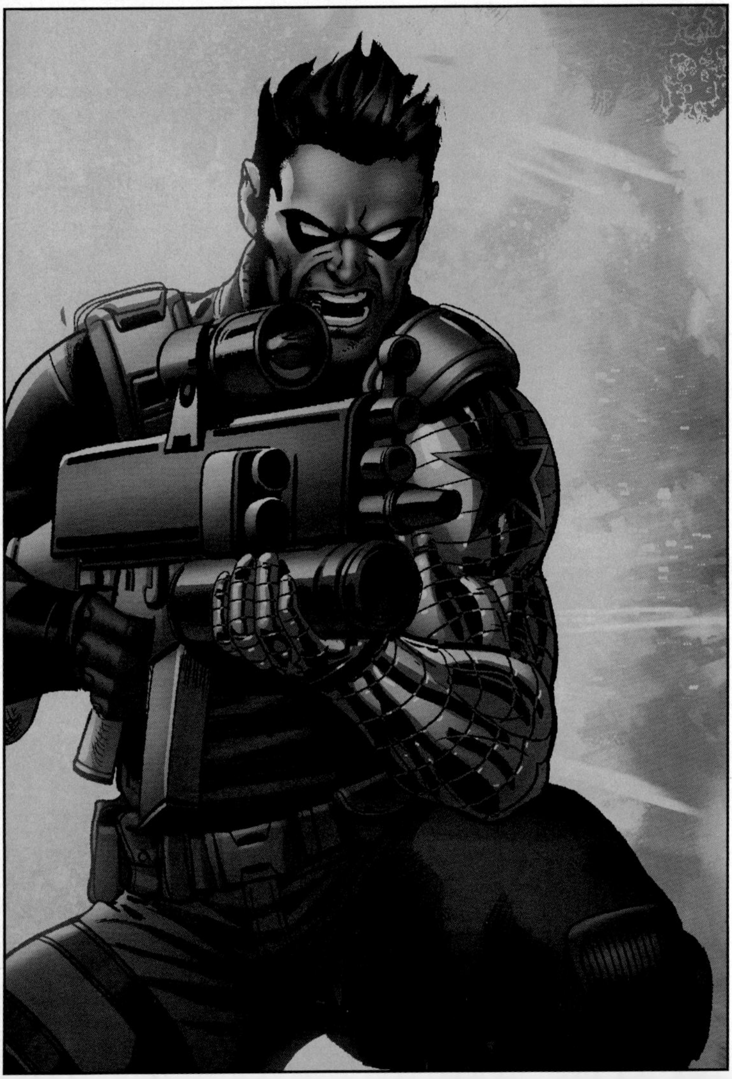
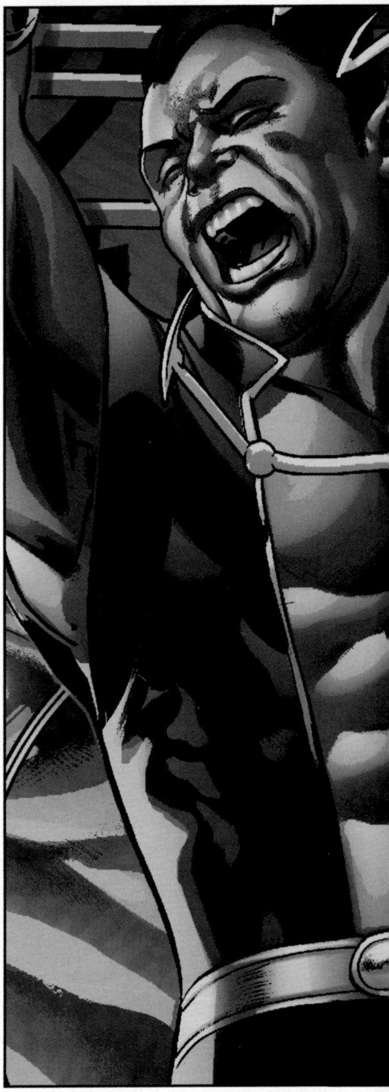

AND

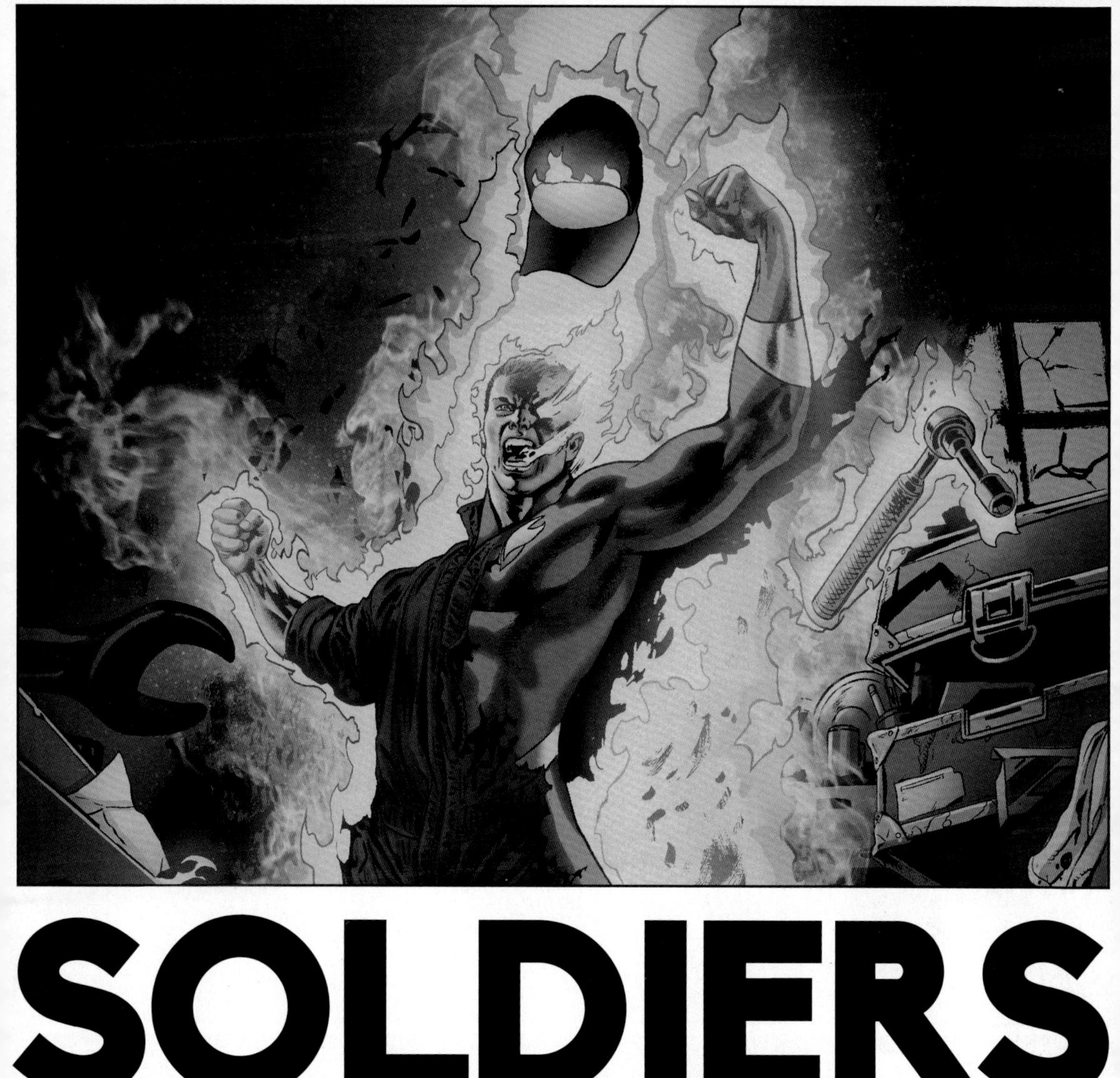

SOLDIERS

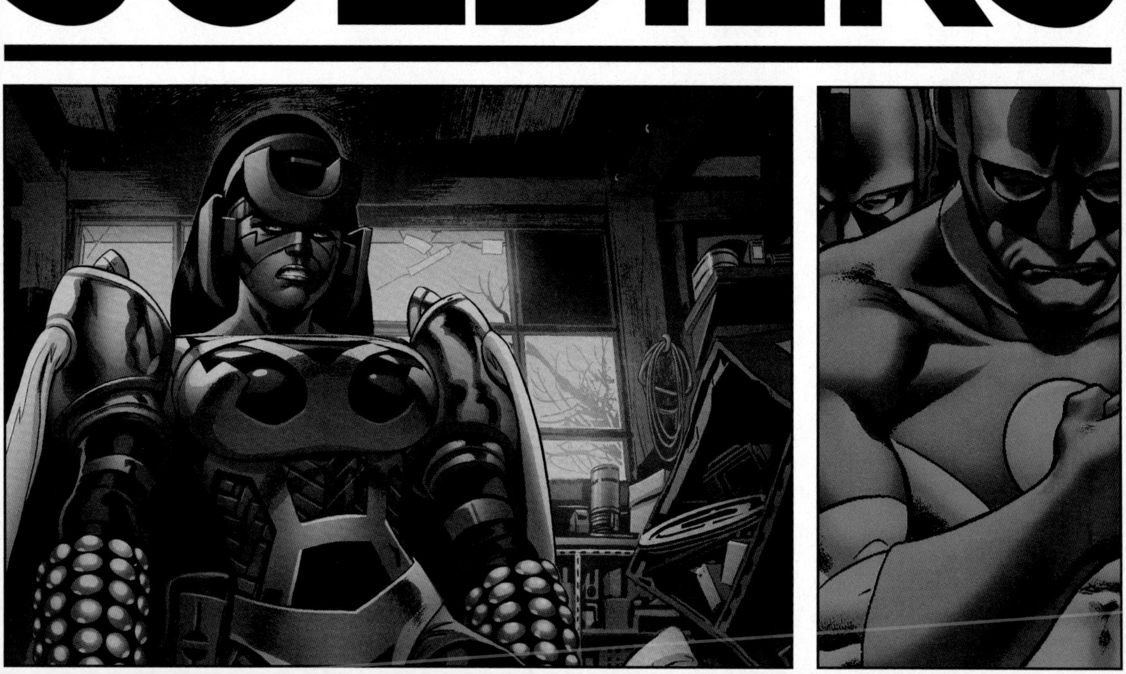

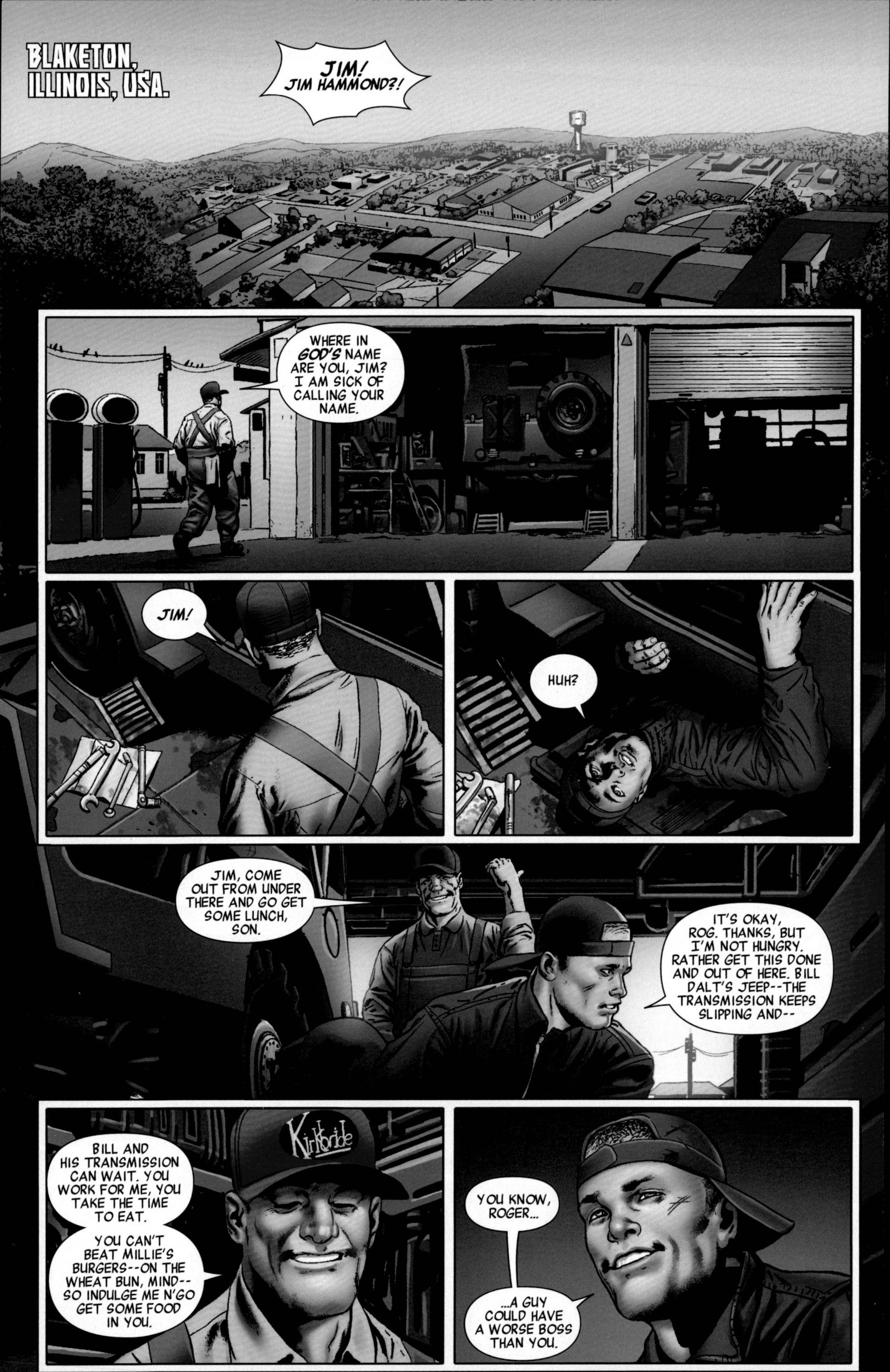
BLAKETON, ILLINOIS, USA.
JIM! JIM HAMMOND?!
WHERE IN GOD'S NAME ARE YOU, JIM? I AM SICK OF CALLING YOUR NAME.
JIM!
HUH?
JIM, COME OUT FROM UNDER THERE AND GO GET SOME LUNCH, SON.
IT'S OKAY, ROG. THANKS, BUT I'M NOT HUNGRY. RATHER GET THIS DONE AND OUT OF HERE. BILL DALT'S JEEP--THE TRANSMISSION KEEPS SLIPPING AND--
Kirkbride
BILL AND HIS TRANSMISSION CAN WAIT. YOU WORK FOR ME, YOU TAKE THE TIME TO EAT.
YOU CAN'T BEAT MILLIE'S BURGERS--ON THE WHEAT BUN, MIND--SO INDULGE ME N'GO GET SOME FOOD IN YOU.
YOU KNOW, ROGER...
...A GUY COULD HAVE A WORSE BOSS THAN YOU.

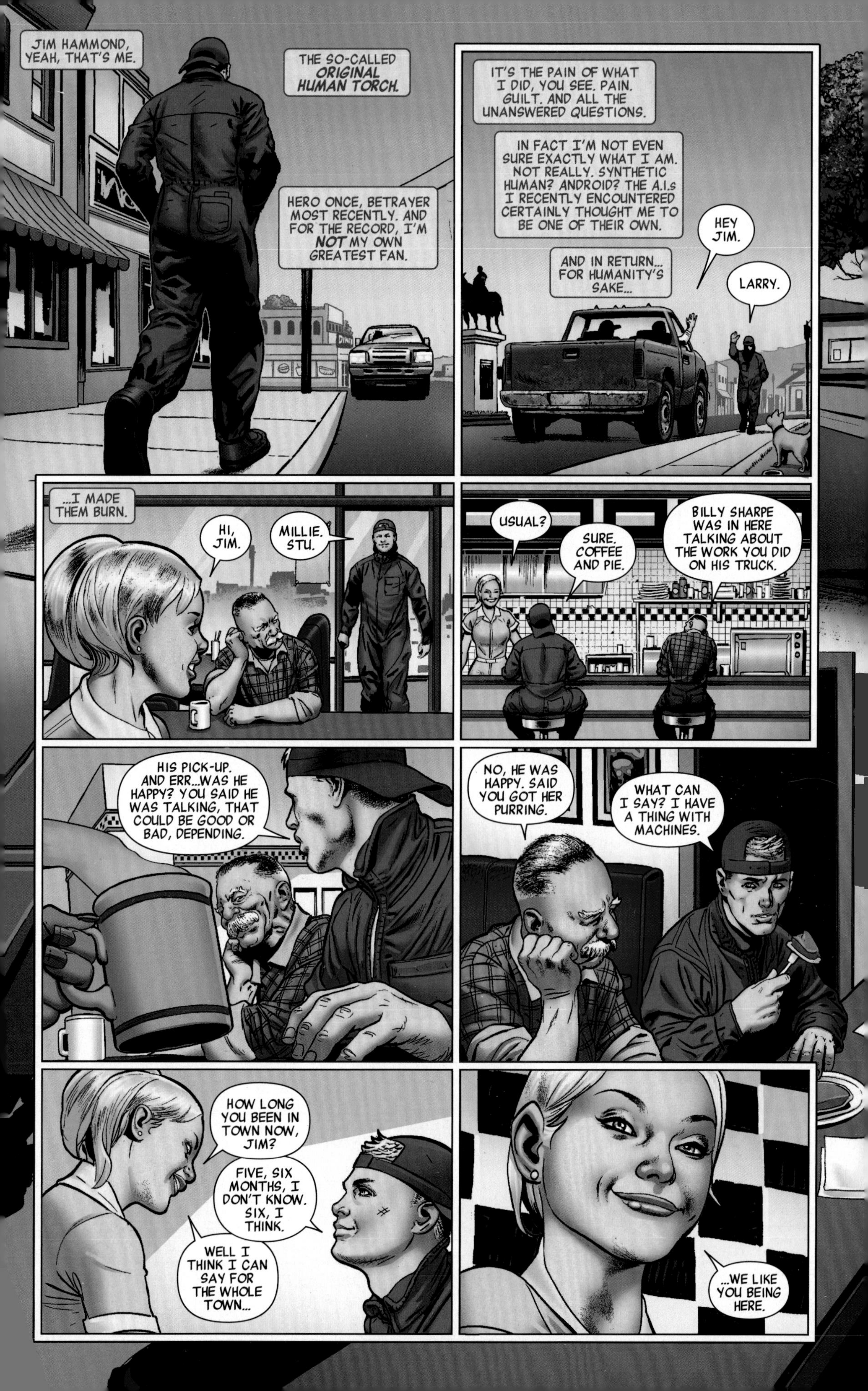
JIM HAMMOND, YEAH, THAT'S ME.
THE SO-CALLED ORIGINAL HUMAN TORCH.
HERO ONCE, BETRAYER MOST RECENTLY. AND FOR THE RECORD, I'M NOT MY OWN GREATEST FAN.
DINER
IT'S THE PAIN OF WHAT I DID, YOU SEE. PAIN. GUILT. AND ALL THE UNANSWERED QUESTIONS.
IN FACT I'M NOT EVEN SURE EXACTLY WHAT I AM. NOT REALLY. SYNTHETIC HUMAN? ANDROID? THE A.I.s I RECENTLY ENCOUNTERED CERTAINLY THOUGHT ME TO BE ONE OF THEIR OWN.
AND IN RETURN... FOR HUMANITY'S SAKE...
HEY JIM.
LARRY.
...I MADE THEM BURN.
HI, JIM.
MILLIE. STU.
USUAL?
SURE. COFFEE AND PIE.
BILLY SHARPE WAS IN HERE TALKING ABOUT THE WORK YOU DID ON HIS TRUCK.
HIS PICK-UP. AND ERR...WAS HE HAPPY? YOU SAID HE WAS TALKING, THAT COULD BE GOOD OR BAD, DEPENDING.
NO, HE WAS HAPPY. SAID YOU GOT HER PURRING.
WHAT CAN I SAY? I HAVE A THING WITH MACHINES.
HOW LONG YOU BEEN IN TOWN NOW, JIM?
FIVE, SIX MONTHS, I DON'T KNOW. SIX, I THINK.
WELL I THINK I CAN SAY FOR THE WHOLE TOWN...
...WE LIKE YOU BEING HERE.

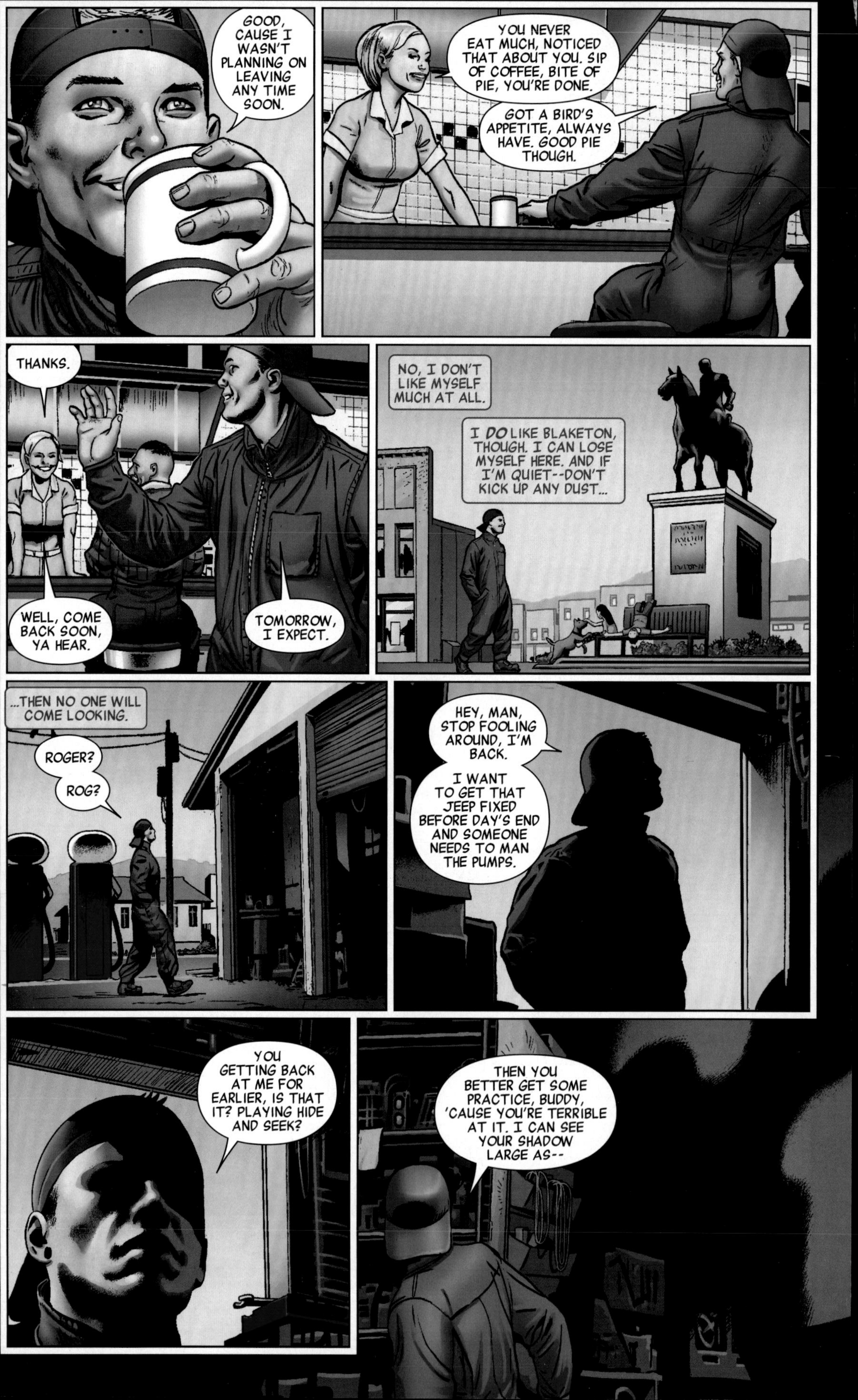
GOOD, CAUSE I WASN'T PLANNING ON LEAVING ANY TIME SOON.
YOU NEVER EAT MUCH, NOTICED THAT ABOUT YOU. SIP OF COFFEE, BITE OF PIE, YOU'RE DONE.
GOT A BIRD'S APPETITE, ALWAYS HAVE. GOOD PIE THOUGH.
THANKS.
WELL, COME BACK SOON, YA HEAR.
TOMORROW, I EXPECT.
NO, I DON'T LIKE MYSELF MUCH AT ALL.
I DO LIKE BLAKETON, THOUGH. I CAN LOSE MYSELF HERE. AND IF I'M QUIET--DON'T KICK UP ANY DUST...
...THEN NO ONE WILL COME LOOKING.
ROGER?
ROG?
HEY, MAN, STOP FOOLING AROUND, I'M BACK.
I WANT TO GET THAT JEEP FIXED BEFORE DAY'S END AND SOMEONE NEEDS TO MAN THE PUMPS.
YOU GETTING BACK AT ME FOR EARLIER, IS THAT IT? PLAYING HIDE AND SEEK?
THEN YOU BETTER GET SOME PRACTICE, BUDDY, 'CAUSE YOU'RE TERRIBLE AT IT. I CAN SEE YOUR SHADOW LARGE AS--

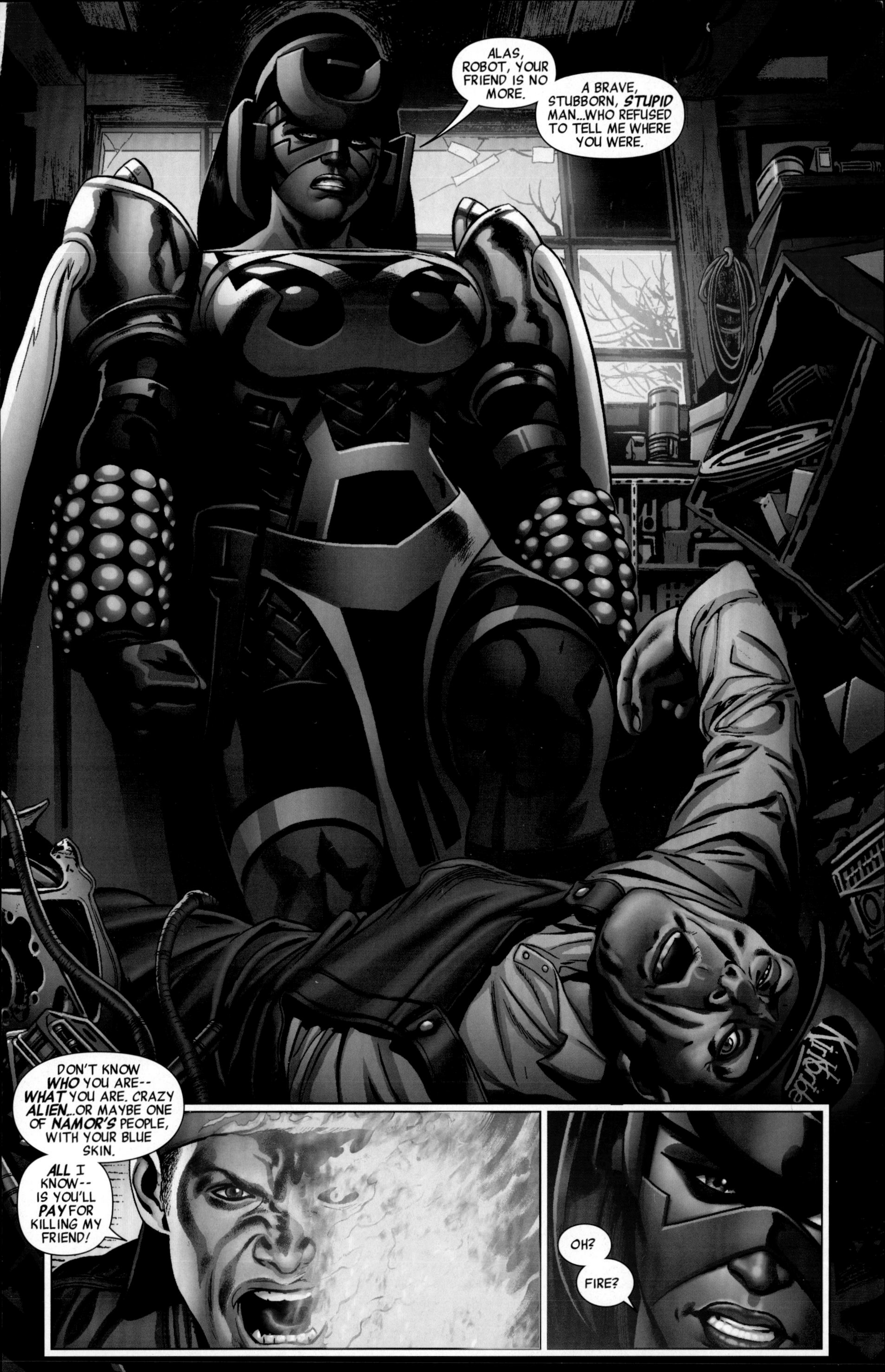
ALAS, ROBOT, YOUR FRIEND IS NO MORE.
A BRAVE, STUBBORN, STUPID MAN...WHO REFUSED TO TELL ME WHERE YOU WERE.
DON'T KNOW WHO YOU ARE-- WHAT YOU ARE. CRAZY ALIEN...OR MAYBE ONE OF NAMOR'S PEOPLE, WITH YOUR BLUE SKIN.
ALL I KNOW-- IS YOU'LL PAY FOR KILLING MY FRIEND!
OH?
FIRE?

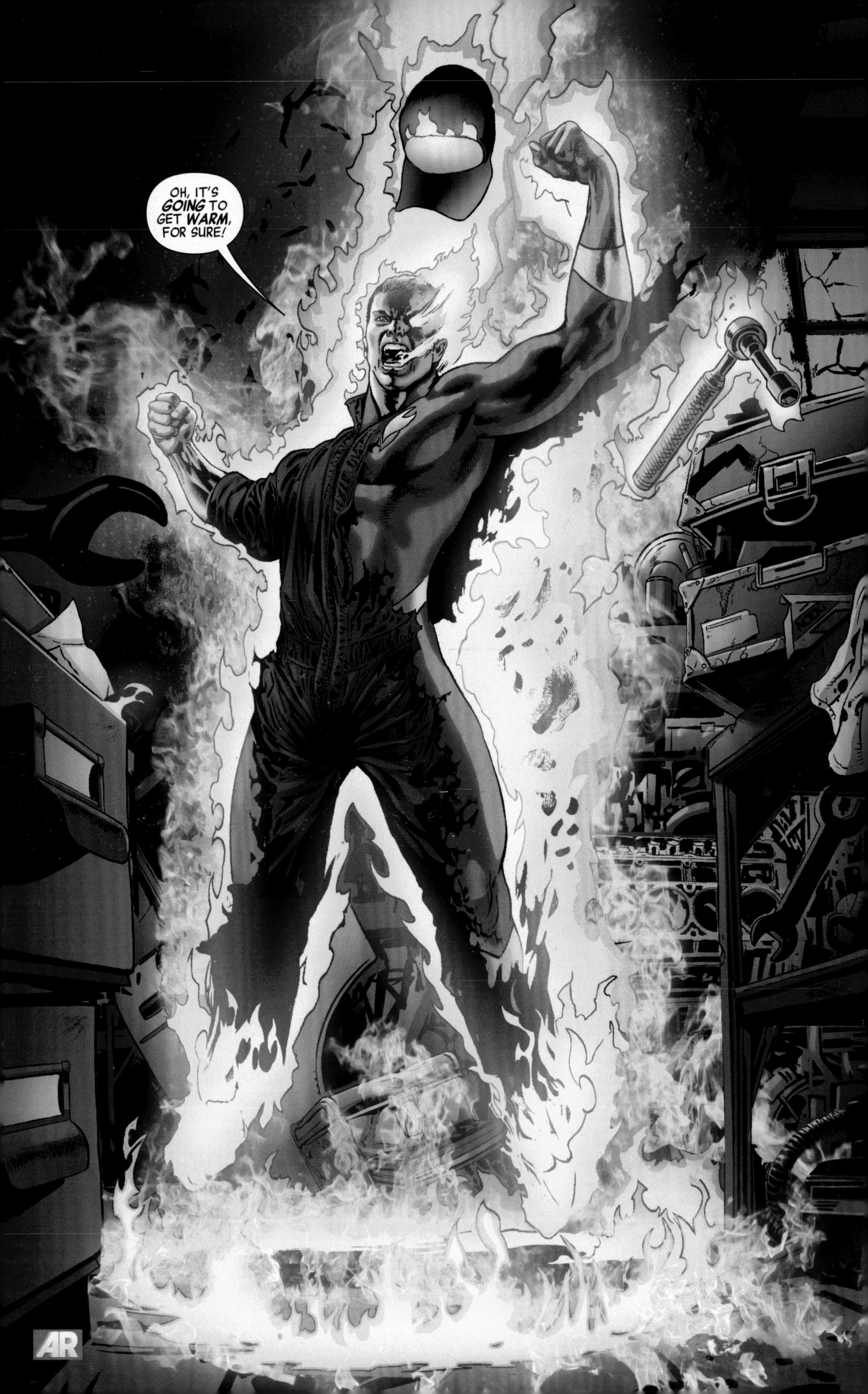
OH, IT'S GOING TO GET WARM, FOR SURE!

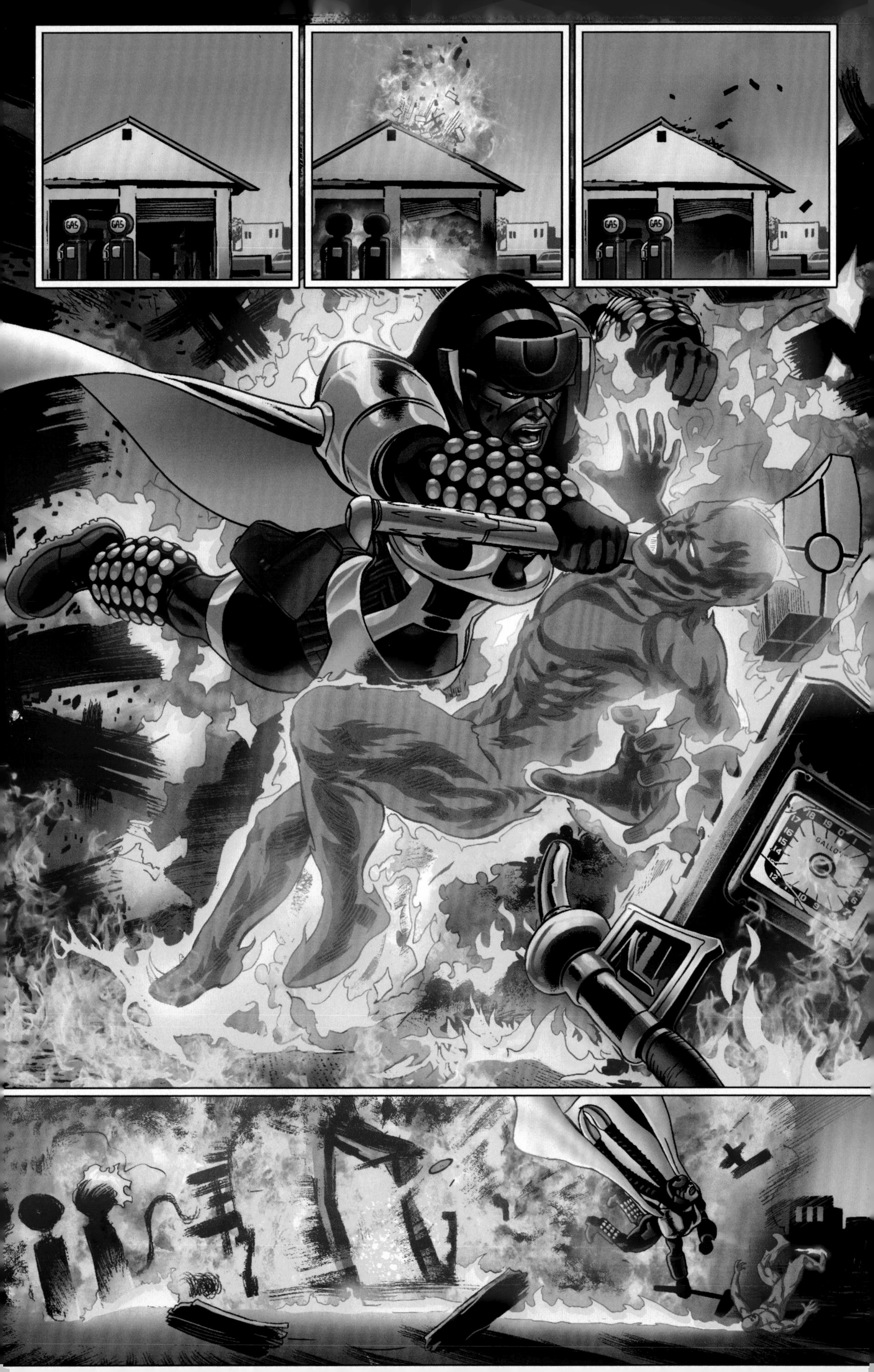
GAS
GAS
GAS
GAS

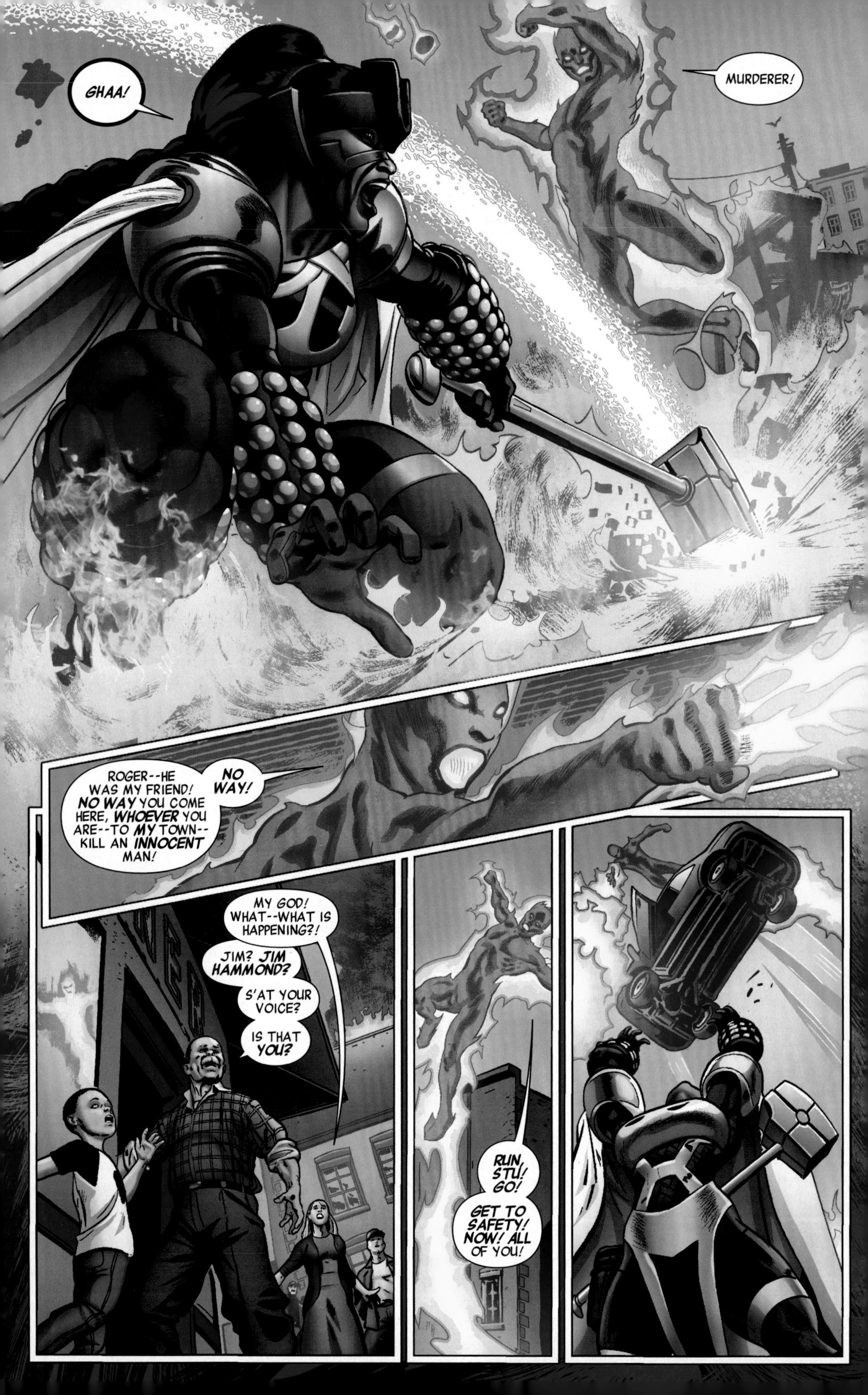
GHAA!
MURDERER!
ROGER--HE WAS MY FRIEND! NO WAY YOU COME HERE, WHOEVER YOU ARE--TO MY TOWN--KILL AN INNOCENT MAN!
NO WAY!
MY GOD! WHAT--WHAT IS HAPPENING?!
JIM? JIM HAMMOND?
S'AT YOUR VOICE?
IS THAT YOU?
RUN, STU! GO!
GET TO SAFETY! NOW! ALL OF YOU!

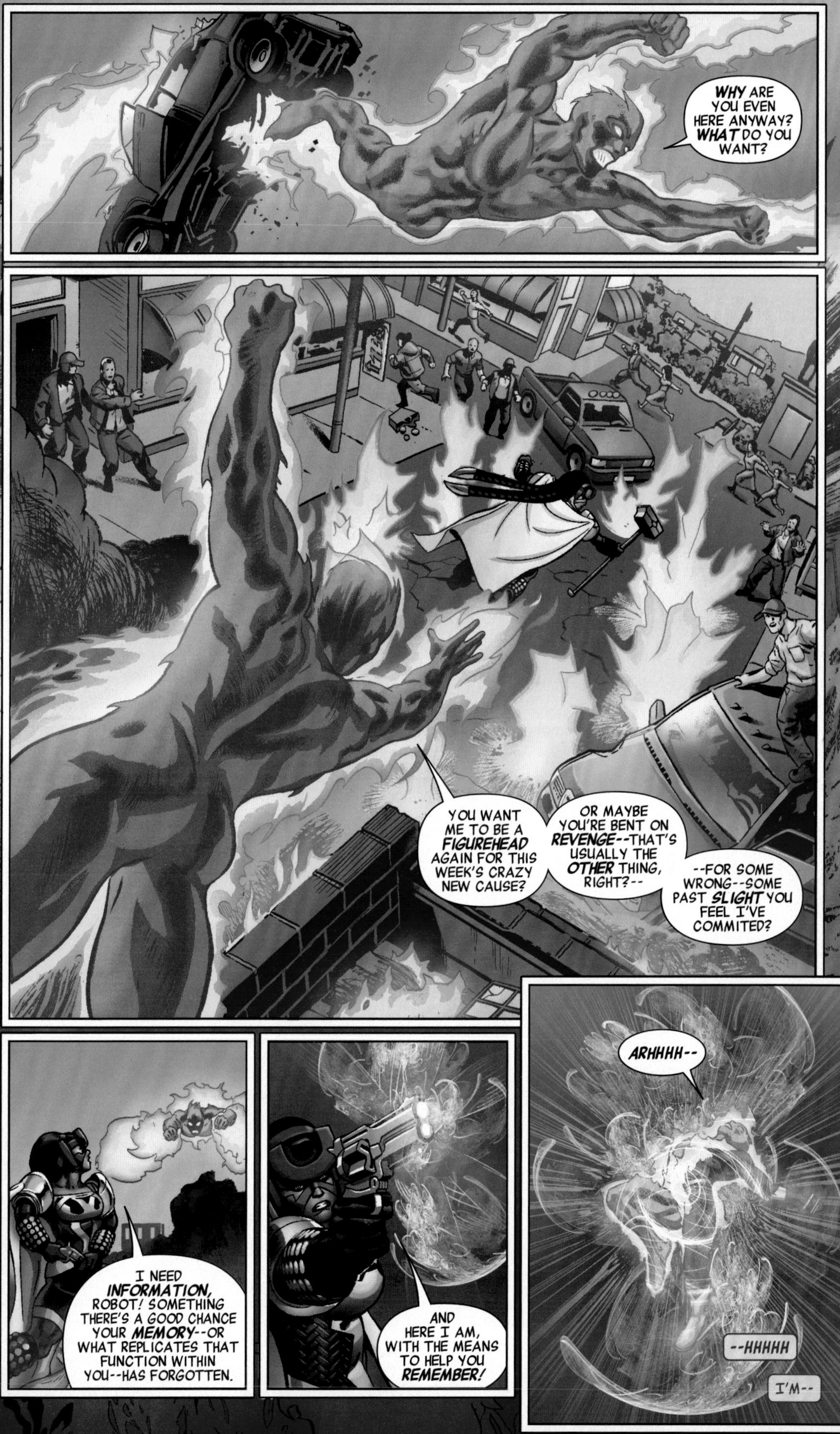
WHY ARE YOU EVEN HERE ANYWAY? WHAT DO YOU WANT?
YOU WANT ME TO BE A FIGUREHEAD AGAIN FOR THIS WEEK'S CRAZY NEW CAUSE?
OR MAYBE YOU'RE BENT ON REVENGE--THAT'S USUALLY THE OTHER THING, RIGHT?--
--FOR SOME WRONG--SOME PAST SLIGHT YOU FEEL I'VE COMMITED?
I NEED INFORMATION, ROBOT! SOMETHING THERE'S A GOOD CHANCE YOUR MEMORY--OR WHAT REPLICATES THAT FUNCTION WITHIN YOU--HAS FORGOTTEN.
AND HERE I AM, WITH THE MEANS TO HELP YOU REMEMBER!
ARHHHH--
--HHHHH
I'M--

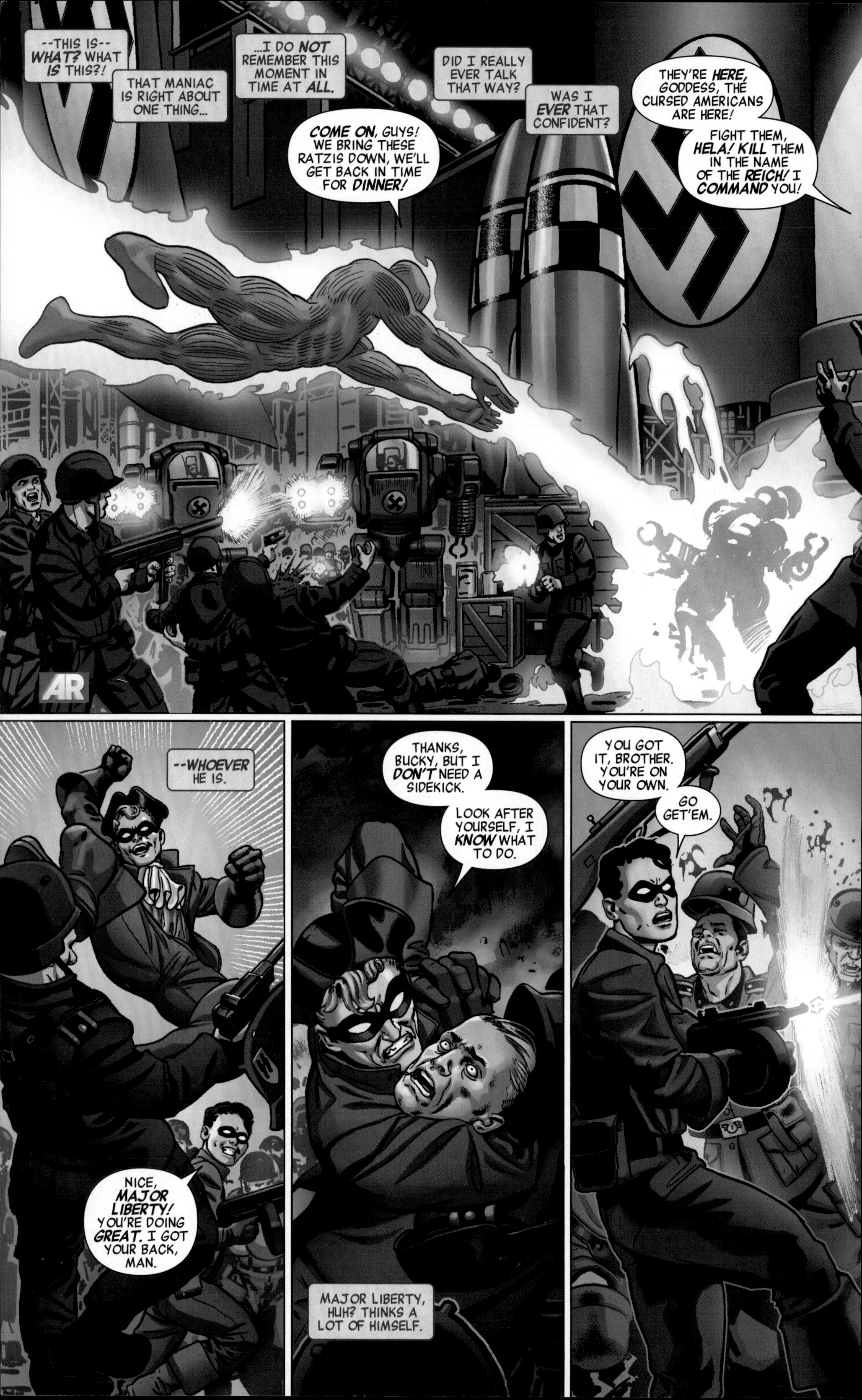
--THIS IS-- WHAT? WHAT IS THIS?!
THAT MANIAC IS RIGHT ABOUT ONE THING...
...I DO NOT REMEMBER THIS MOMENT IN TIME AT ALL.
DID I REALLY EVER TALK THAT WAY?
WAS I EVER THAT CONFIDENT?
COME ON, GUYS! WE BRING THESE RATZIS DOWN, WE'LL GET BACK IN TIME FOR DINNER!
THEY'RE HERE, GODDESS, THE CURSED AMERICANS ARE HERE!
FIGHT THEM, HELA! KILL THEM IN THE NAME OF THE REICH! I COMMAND YOU!
AR
--WHOEVER HE IS.
NICE, MAJOR LIBERTY! YOU'RE DOING GREAT. I GOT YOUR BACK, MAN.
THANKS, BUCKY, BUT I DON'T NEED A SIDEKICK.
LOOK AFTER YOURSELF, I KNOW WHAT TO DO.
MAJOR LIBERTY, HUH? THINKS A LOT OF HIMSELF.
YOU GOT IT, BROTHER. YOU'RE ON YOUR OWN.
GO GET'EM.

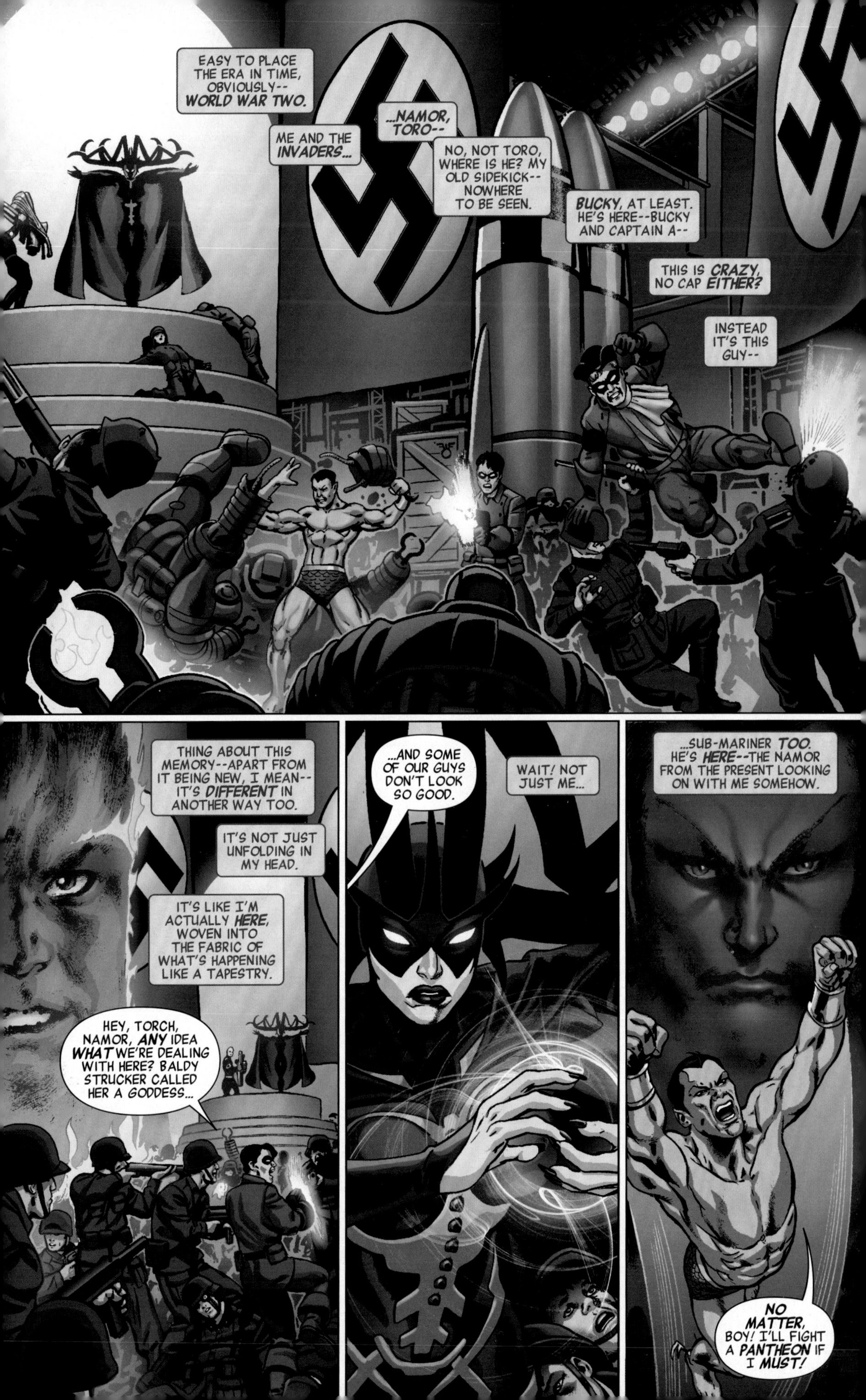
EASY TO PLACE THE ERA IN TIME, OBVIOUSLY-- WORLD WAR TWO.
ME AND THE INVADERS...
...NAMOR, TORO--
NO, NOT TORO, WHERE IS HE? MY OLD SIDEKICK-- NOWHERE TO BE SEEN.
BUCKY, AT LEAST. HE'S HERE--BUCKY AND CAPTAIN A--
THIS IS CRAZY, NO CAP EITHER?
INSTEAD IT'S THIS GUY--
THING ABOUT THIS MEMORY--APART FROM IT BEING NEW, I MEAN-- IT'S DIFFERENT IN ANOTHER WAY TOO.
IT'S NOT JUST UNFOLDING IN MY HEAD.
IT'S LIKE I'M ACTUALLY HERE, WOVEN INTO THE FABRIC OF WHAT'S HAPPENING LIKE A TAPESTRY.
HEY, TORCH, NAMOR, ANY IDEA WHAT WE'RE DEALING WITH HERE? BALDY STRUCKER CALLED HER A GODDESS...
...AND SOME OF OUR GUYS DON'T LOOK SO GOOD.
WAIT! NOT JUST ME...
...SUB-MARINER TOO. HE'S HERE--THE NAMOR FROM THE PRESENT LOOKING ON WITH ME SOMEHOW.
NO MATTER, BOY! I'LL FIGHT A PANTHEON IF I MUST!

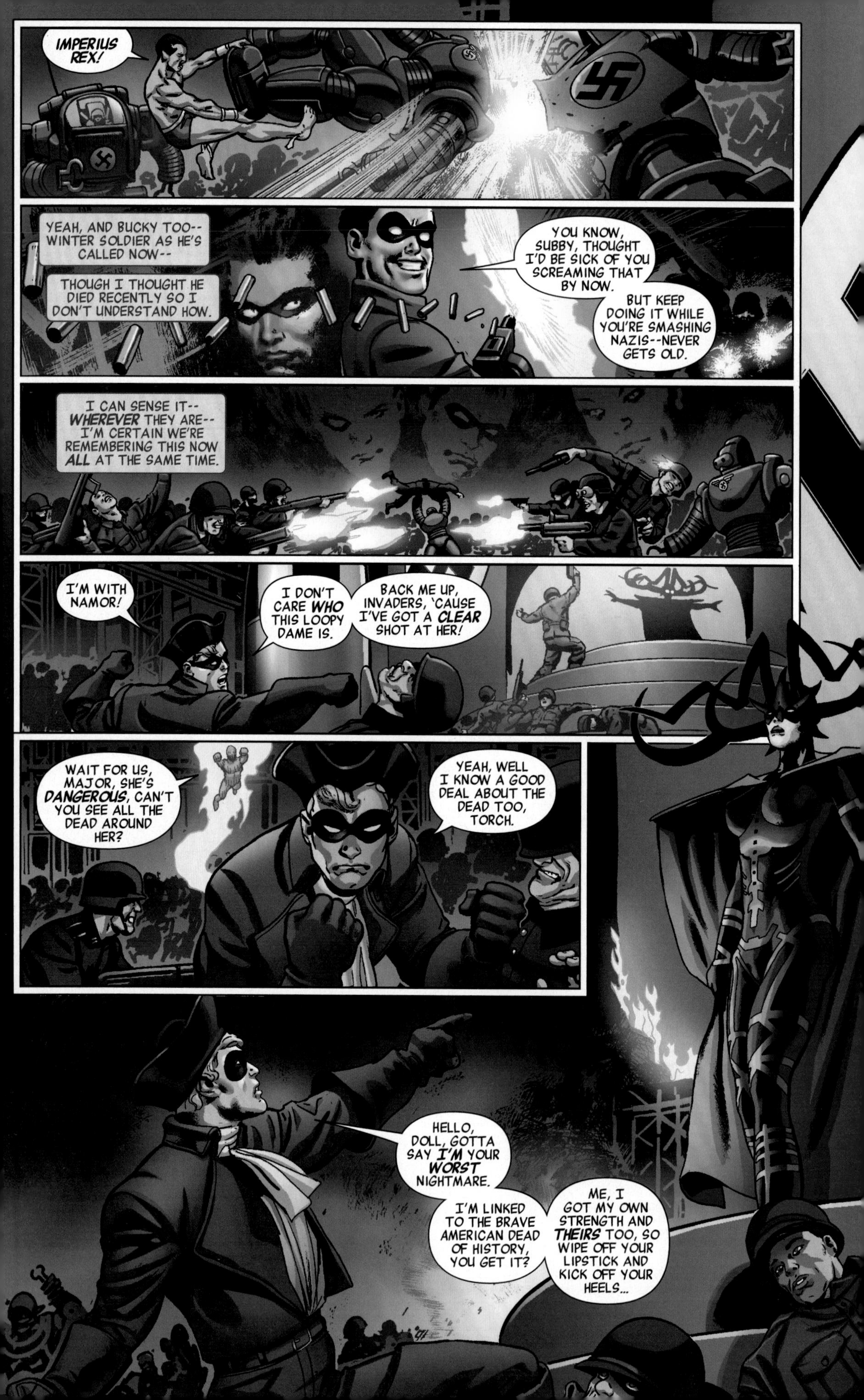
IMPERIUS REX!
YEAH, AND BUCKY TOO--WINTER SOLDIER AS HE'S CALLED NOW--
THOUGH I THOUGHT HE DIED RECENTLY SO I DON'T UNDERSTAND HOW.
YOU KNOW, SUBBY, THOUGHT I'D BE SICK OF YOU SCREAMING THAT BY NOW.
BUT KEEP DOING IT WHILE YOU'RE SMASHING NAZIS--NEVER GETS OLD.
I CAN SENSE IT--WHEREVER THEY ARE--I'M CERTAIN WE'RE REMEMBERING THIS NOW ALL AT THE SAME TIME.
I'M WITH NAMOR!
I DON'T CARE WHO THIS LOOPY DAME IS.
BACK ME UP, INVADERS, 'CAUSE I'VE GOT A CLEAR SHOT AT HER!
WAIT FOR US, MAJOR, SHE'S DANGEROUS, CAN'T YOU SEE ALL THE DEAD AROUND HER?
YEAH, WELL I KNOW A GOOD DEAL ABOUT THE DEAD TOO, TORCH.
HELLO, DOLL, GOTTA SAY I'M YOUR WORST NIGHTMARE.
I'M LINKED TO THE BRAVE AMERICAN DEAD OF HISTORY, YOU GET IT?
ME, I GOT MY OWN STRENGTH AND THEIRS TOO, SO WIPE OFF YOUR LIPSTICK AND KICK OFF YOUR HEELS...

...TIME TO CALL IT A NIGHT!

SILLY CREATURE, YOU MAY KNOW THE DEAD...IN FACT I CAN TELL LOOKING AT YOU THAT YOU *DO.*

BUT I *AM* DEATH.

YES, THE GHOSTS OF YOUR COUNTRY'S PAST ARE ALL AROUND YOU...

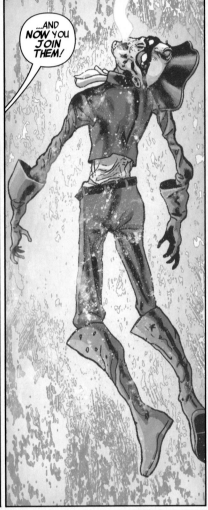

...AND *NOW* YOU *JOIN* THEM!

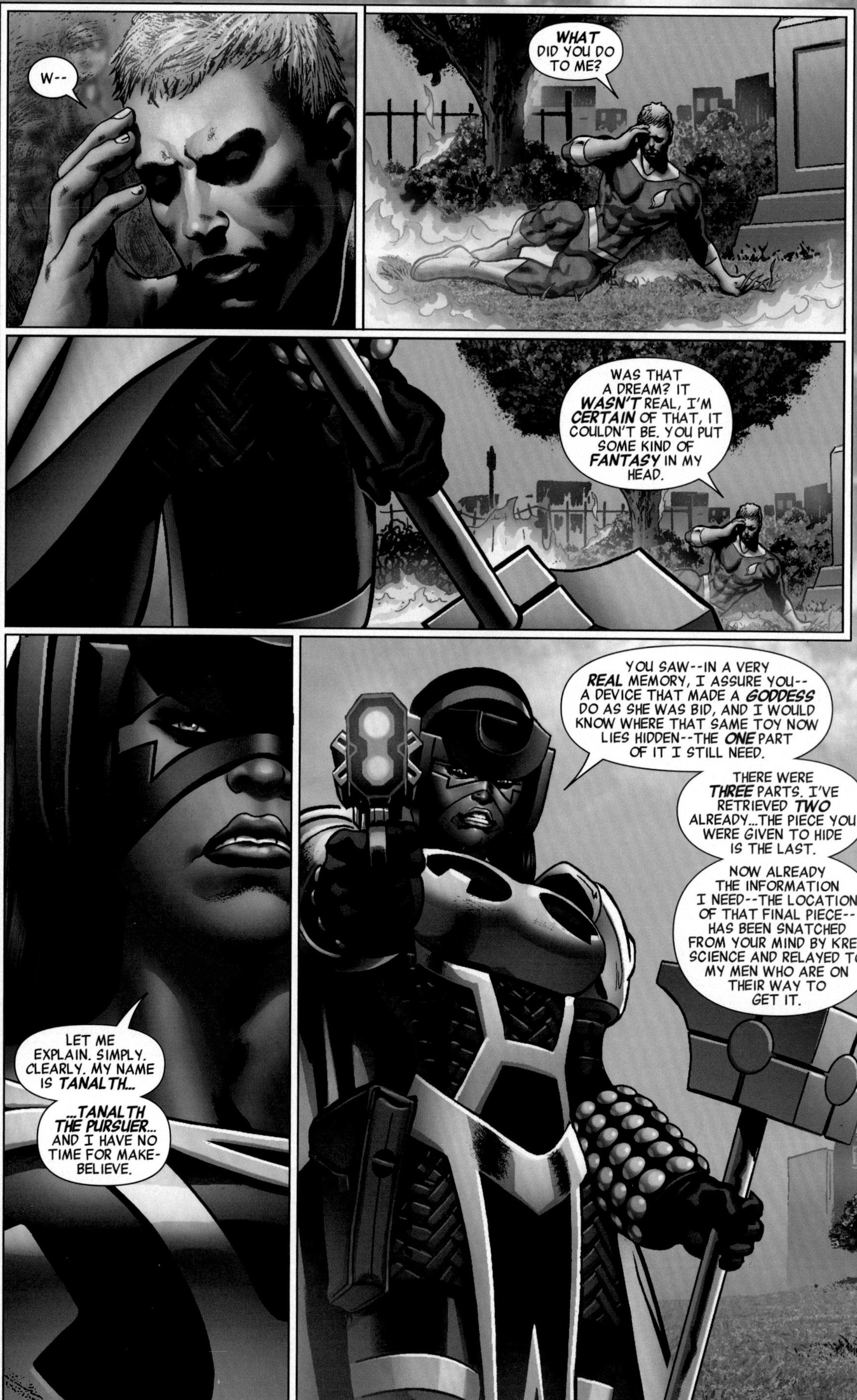
W--
WHAT DID YOU DO TO ME?
WAS THAT A DREAM? IT WASN'T REAL, I'M CERTAIN OF THAT, IT COULDN'T BE. YOU PUT SOME KIND OF FANTASY IN MY HEAD.
LET ME EXPLAIN. SIMPLY. CLEARLY. MY NAME IS TANALTH...
...TANALTH THE PURSUER... AND I HAVE NO TIME FOR MAKE-BELIEVE.
YOU SAW--IN A VERY REAL MEMORY, I ASSURE YOU--A DEVICE THAT MADE A GODDESS DO AS SHE WAS BID, AND I WOULD KNOW WHERE THAT SAME TOY NOW LIES HIDDEN--THE ONE PART OF IT I STILL NEED.
THERE WERE THREE PARTS. I'VE RETRIEVED TWO ALREADY...THE PIECE YOU WERE GIVEN TO HIDE IS THE LAST.
NOW ALREADY THE INFORMATION I NEED--THE LOCATION OF THAT FINAL PIECE--HAS BEEN SNATCHED FROM YOUR MIND BY KREE SCIENCE AND RELAYED TO MY MEN WHO ARE ON THEIR WAY TO GET IT.

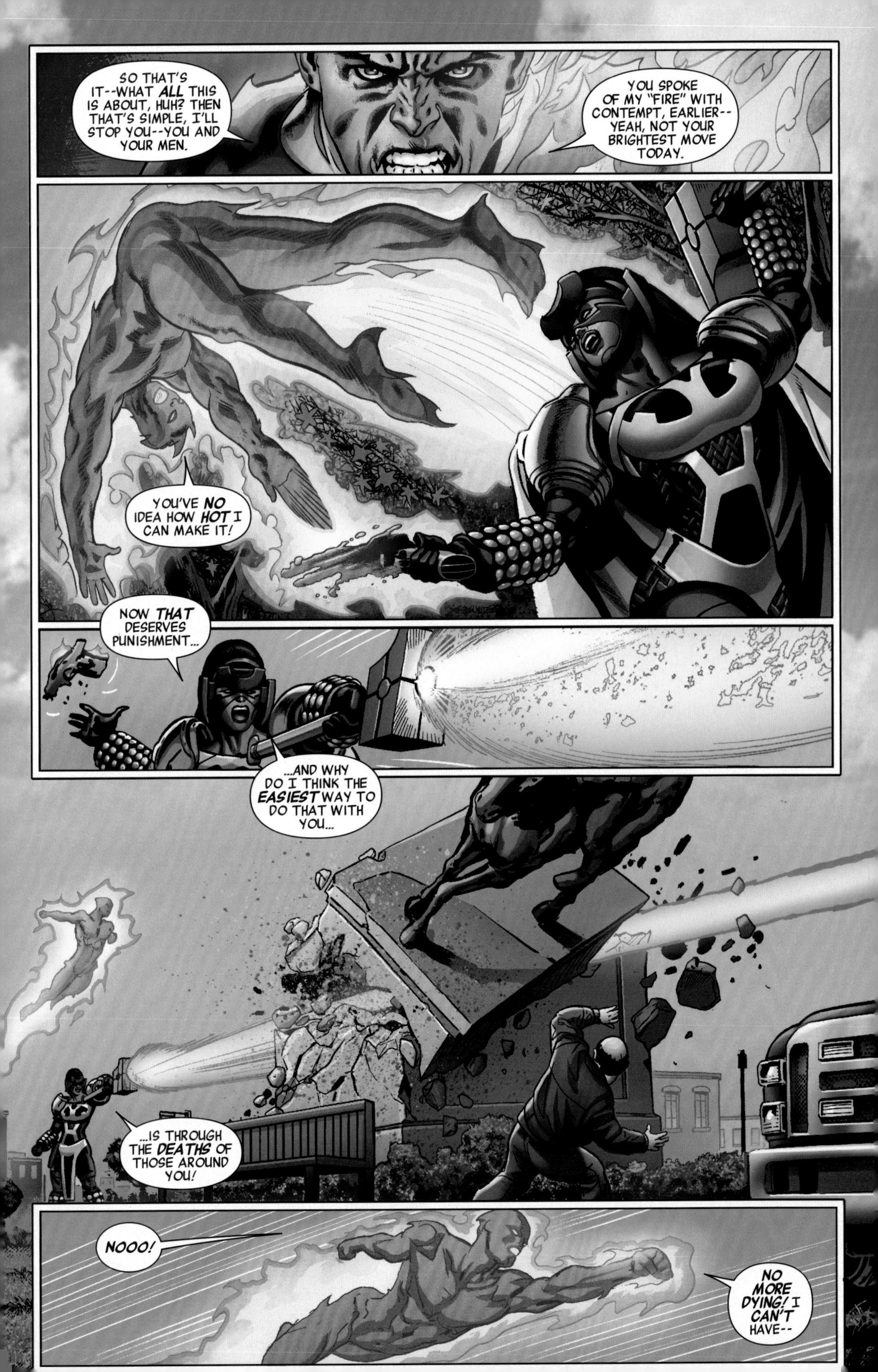
SO THAT'S IT--WHAT ALL THIS IS ABOUT, HUH? THEN THAT'S SIMPLE, I'LL STOP YOU--YOU AND YOUR MEN.
YOU SPOKE OF MY "FIRE" WITH CONTEMPT, EARLIER--YEAH, NOT YOUR BRIGHTEST MOVE TODAY.
YOU'VE NO IDEA HOW HOT I CAN MAKE IT!
NOW THAT DESERVES PUNISHMENT...
...AND WHY DO I THINK THE EASIEST WAY TO DO THAT WITH YOU...
...IS THROUGH THE DEATHS OF THOSE AROUND YOU!
NOOO!
NO MORE DYING! I CAN'T HAVE--

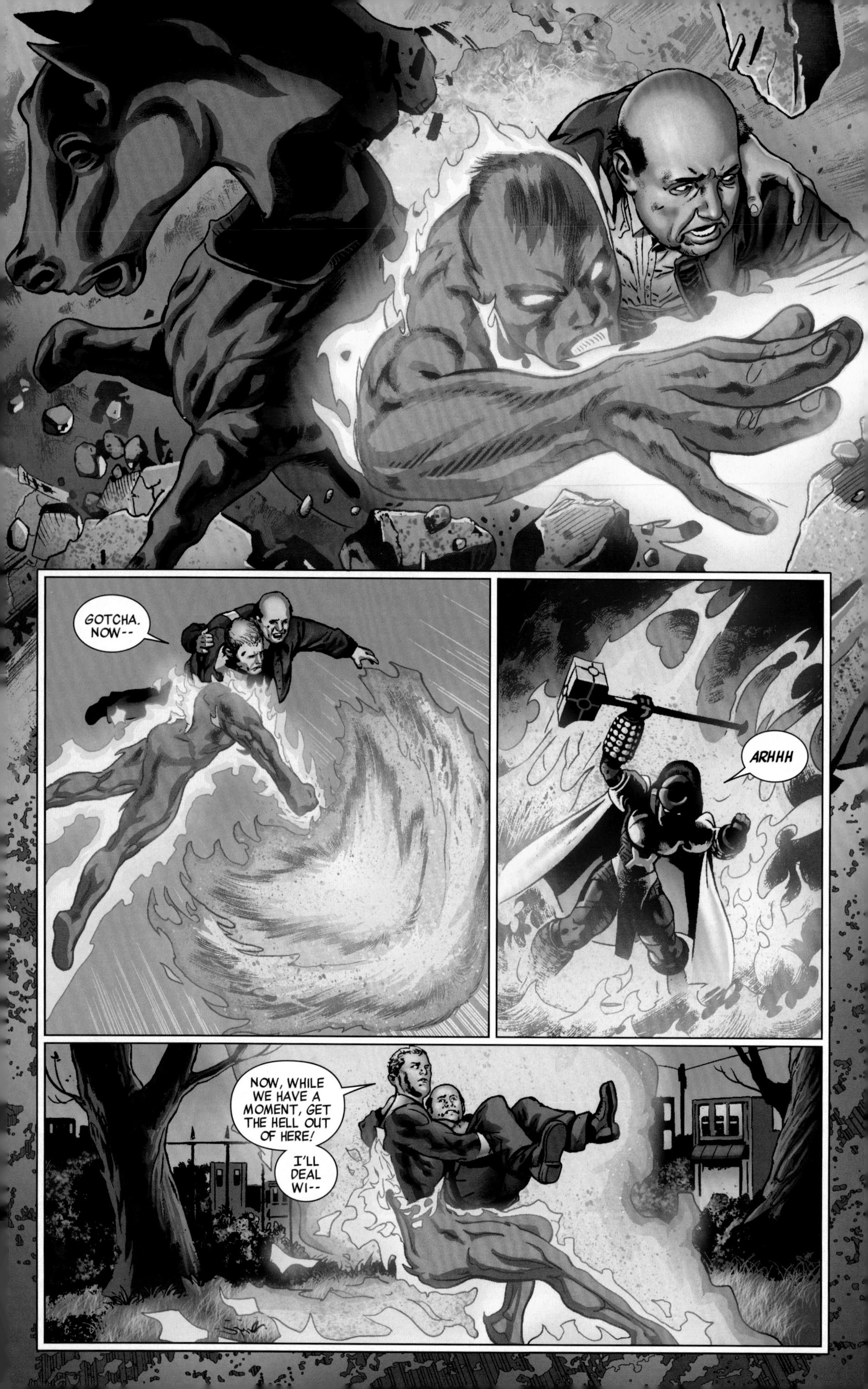
GOTCHA. NOW--
ARHHH
NOW, WHILE WE HAVE A MOMENT, GET THE HELL OUT OF HERE!
I'LL DEAL WI--

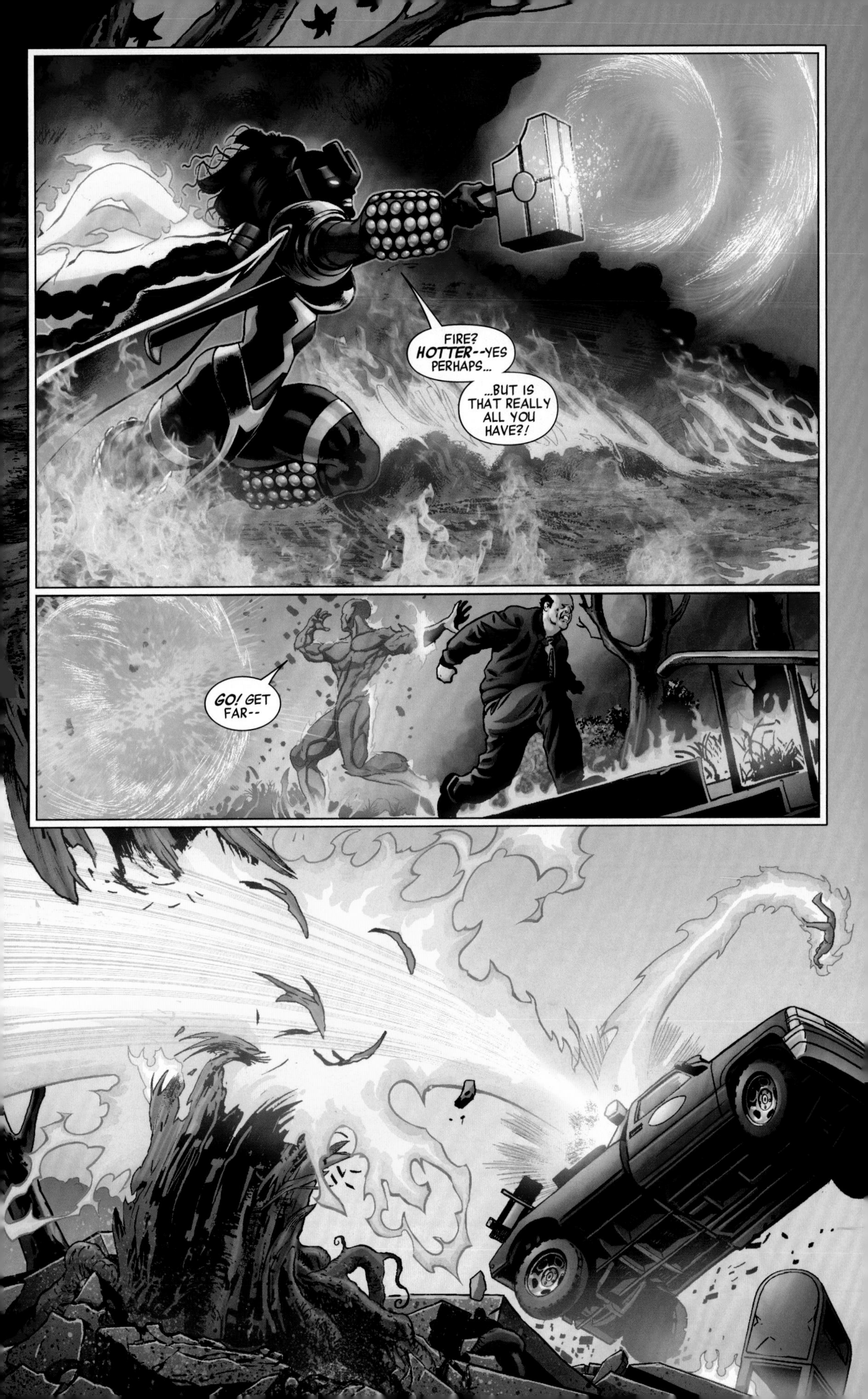
FIRE? HOTTER--YES PERHAPS...
...BUT IS THAT REALLY ALL YOU HAVE?!
GO! GET FAR--

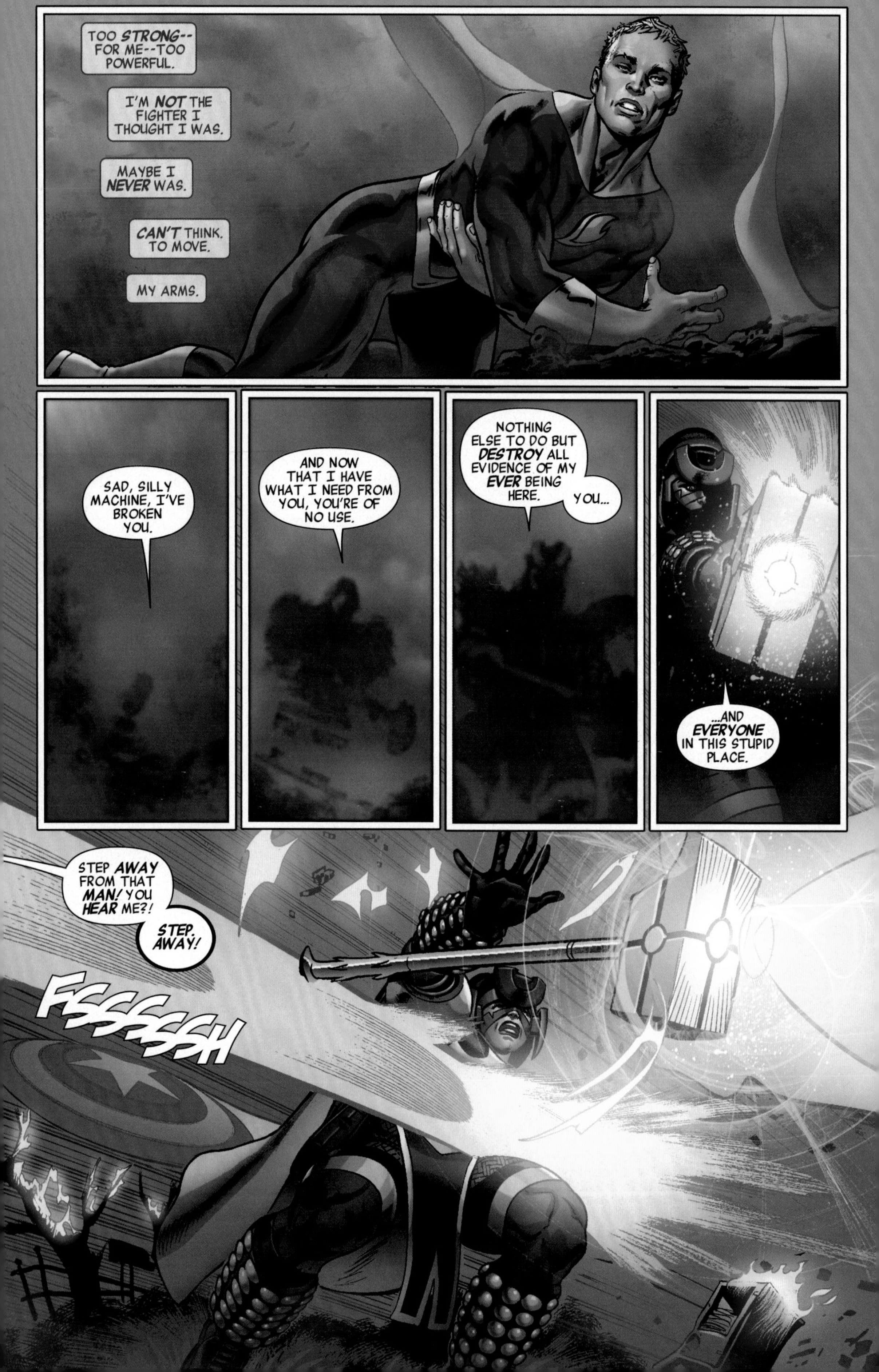
TOO STRONG--
FOR ME--TOO
POWERFUL.
I'M NOT THE
FIGHTER I
THOUGHT I WAS.
MAYBE I
NEVER WAS.
CAN'T THINK.
TO MOVE.
MY ARMS.
SAD, SILLY
MACHINE, I'VE
BROKEN
YOU.
AND NOW
THAT I HAVE
WHAT I NEED FROM
YOU, YOU'RE OF
NO USE.
NOTHING
ELSE TO DO BUT
DESTROY ALL
EVIDENCE OF MY
EVER BEING
HERE.
YOU...
...AND
EVERYONE
IN THIS STUPID
PLACE.
STEP AWAY
FROM THAT
MAN! YOU
HEAR ME?!
STEP.
AWAY!
FSSSSSH

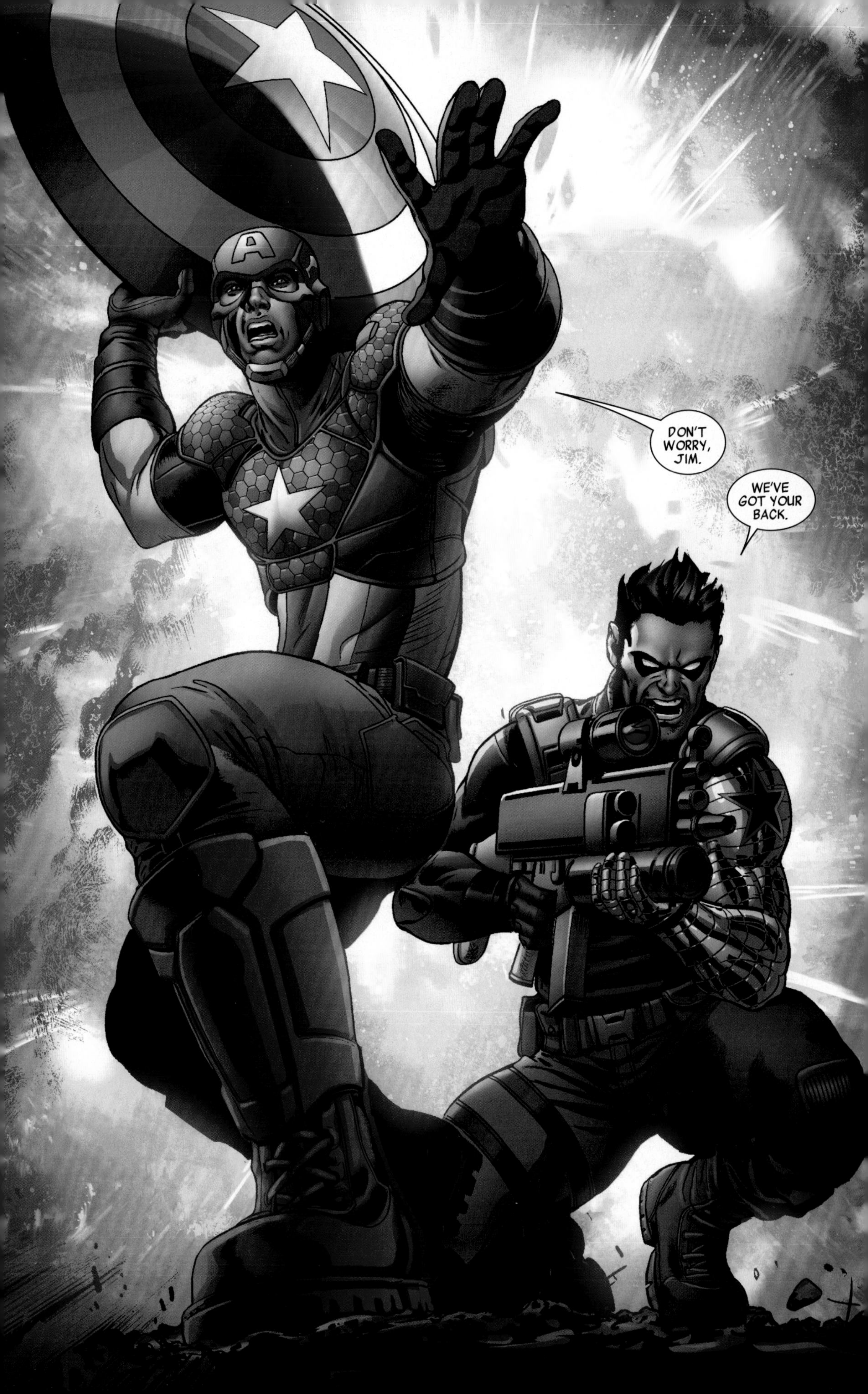
DON'T WORRY, JIM.
WE'VE GOT YOUR BACK.

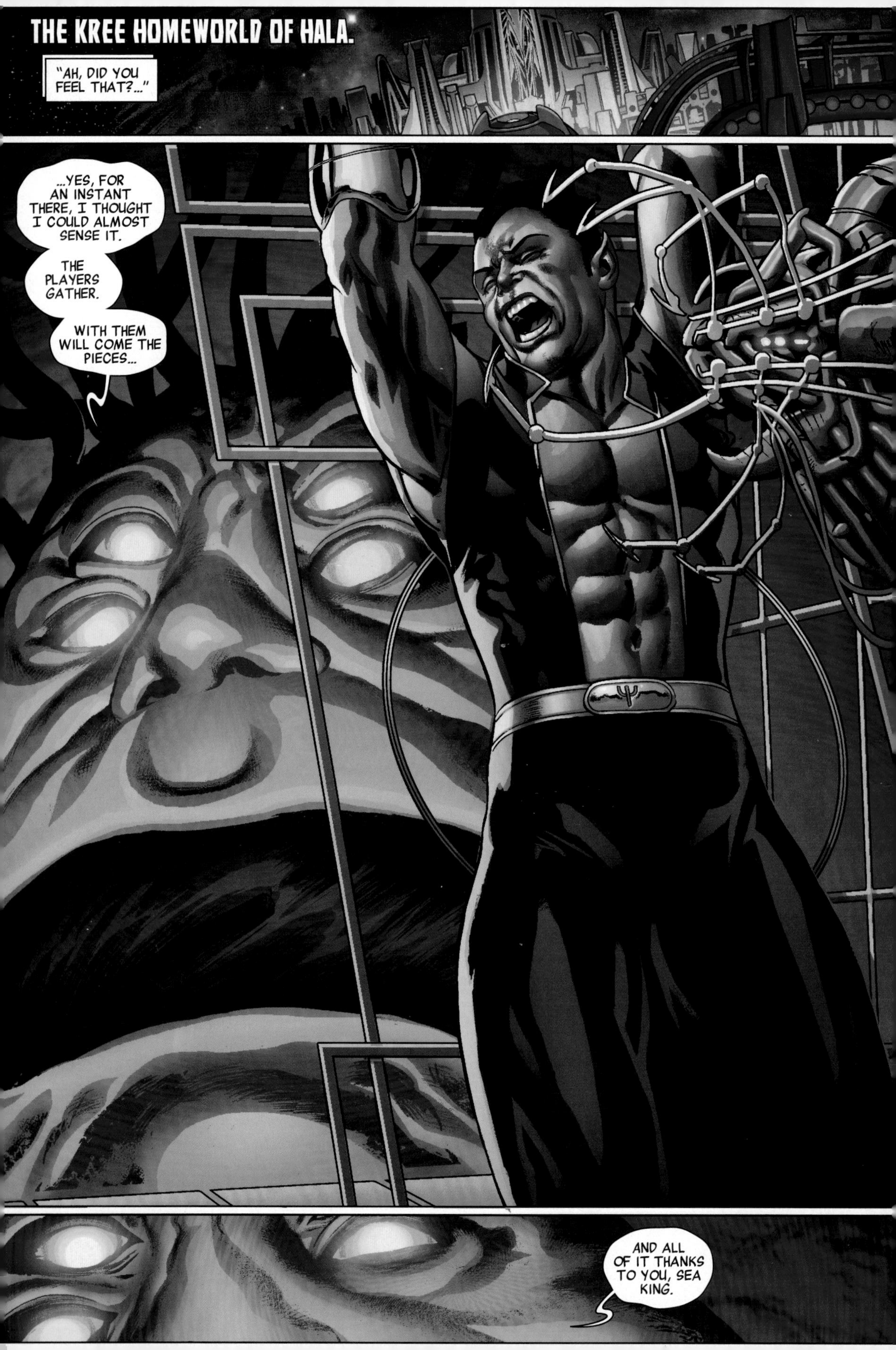
THE KREE HOMEWORLD OF HALA.
"AH, DID YOU FEEL THAT?..."
...YES, FOR AN INSTANT THERE, I THOUGHT I COULD ALMOST SENSE IT.
THE PLAYERS GATHER.
WITH THEM WILL COME THE PIECES...
AND ALL OF IT THANKS TO YOU, SEA KING.

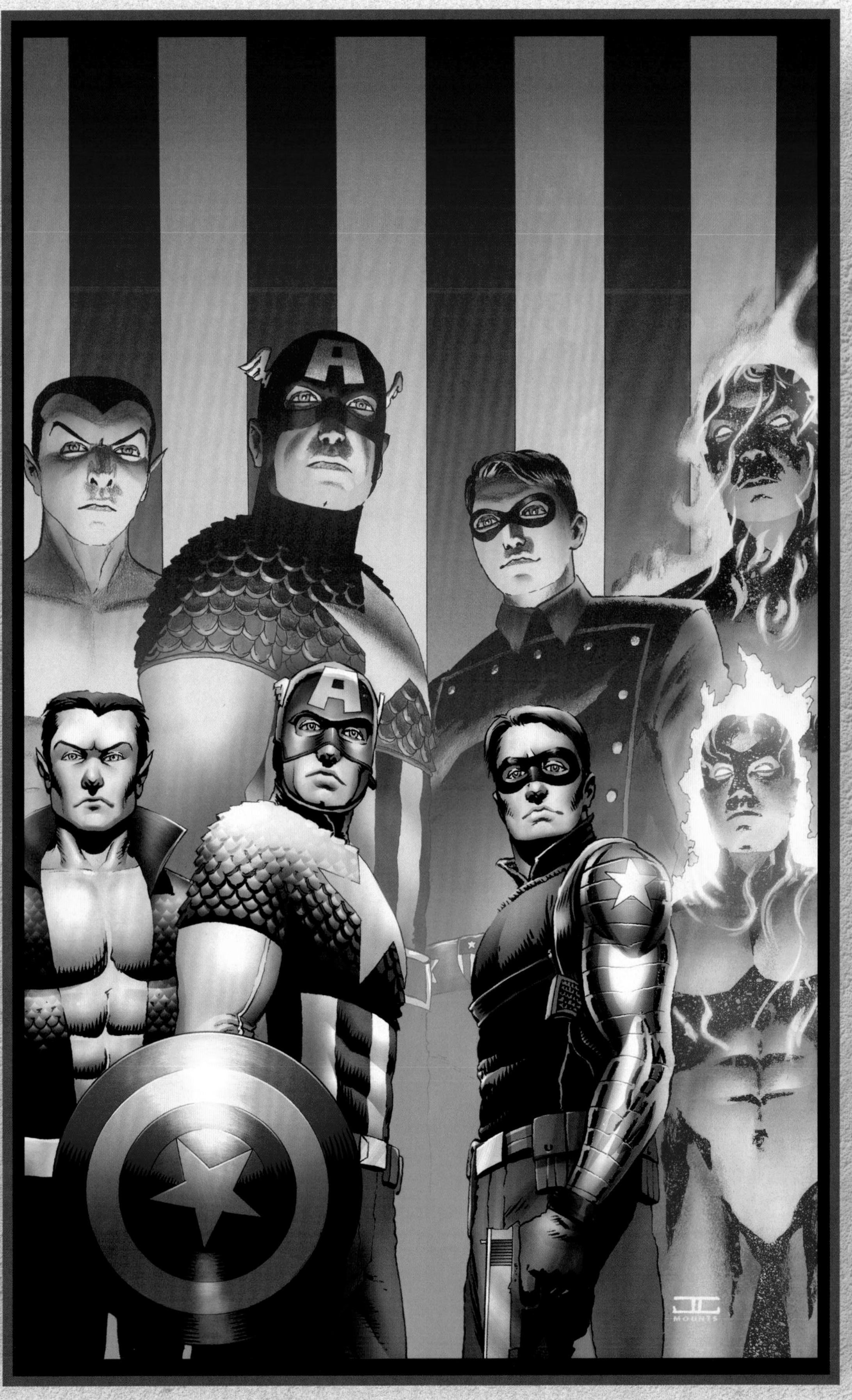

#1 Variant by John Cassaday & Paul Mounts

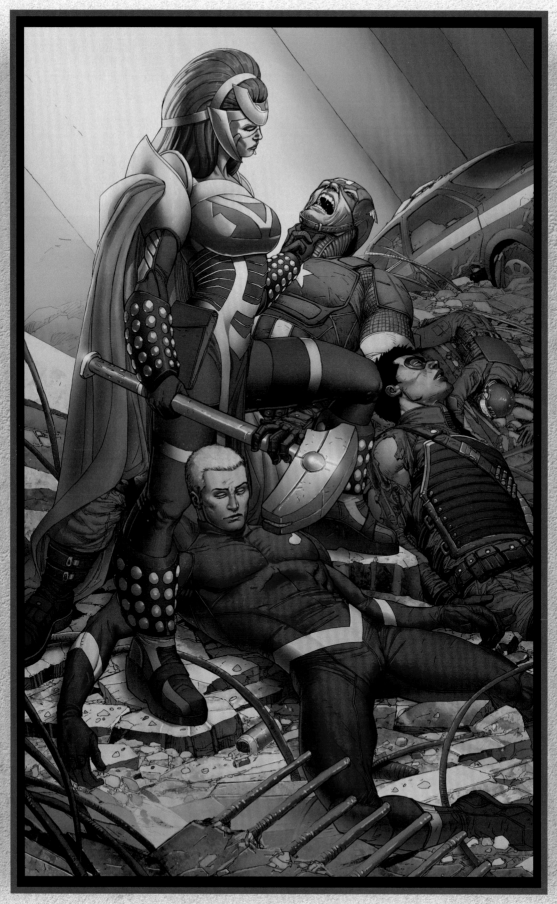

#2

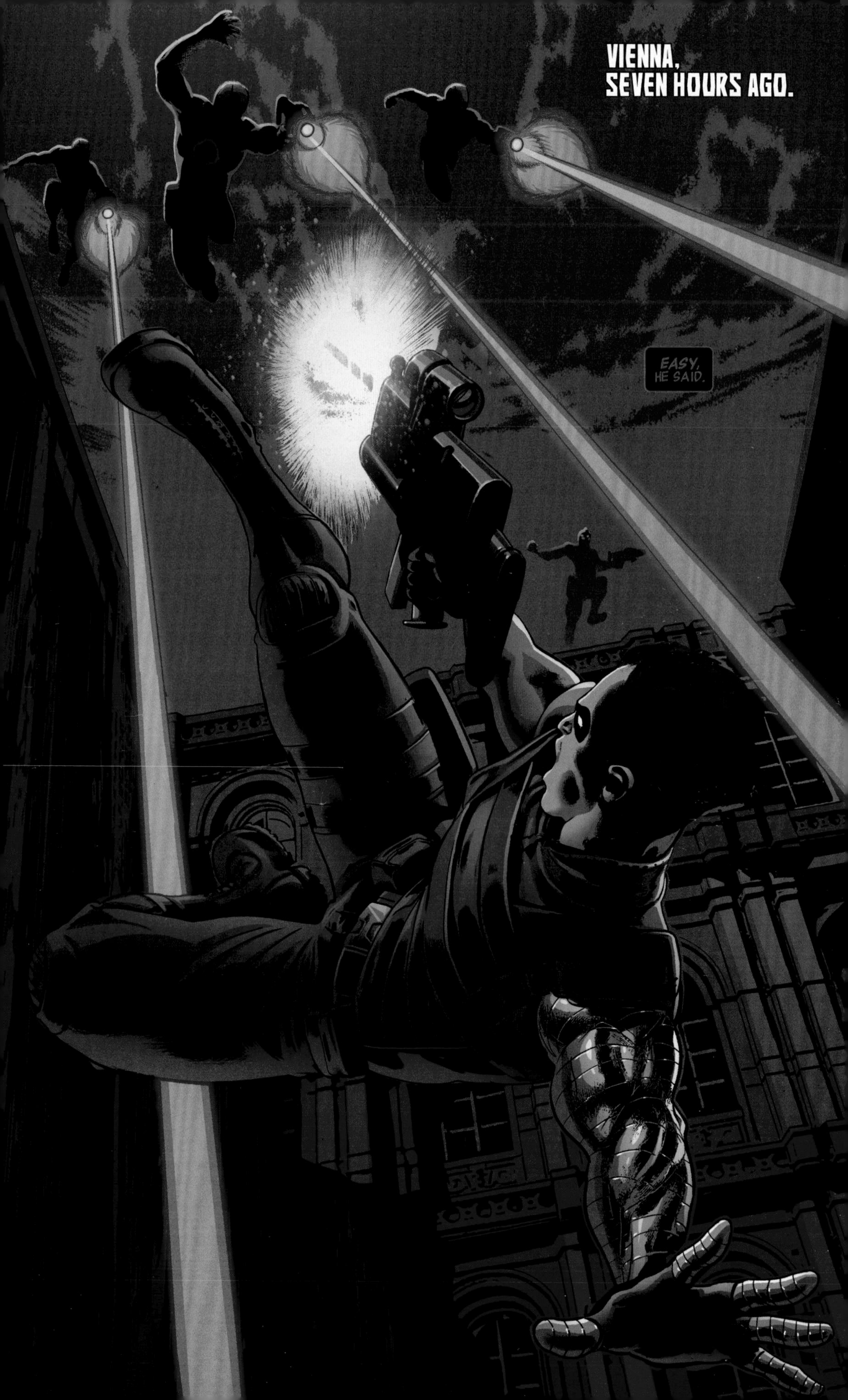
VIENNA,
SEVEN HOURS AGO.
EASY, HE SAID.

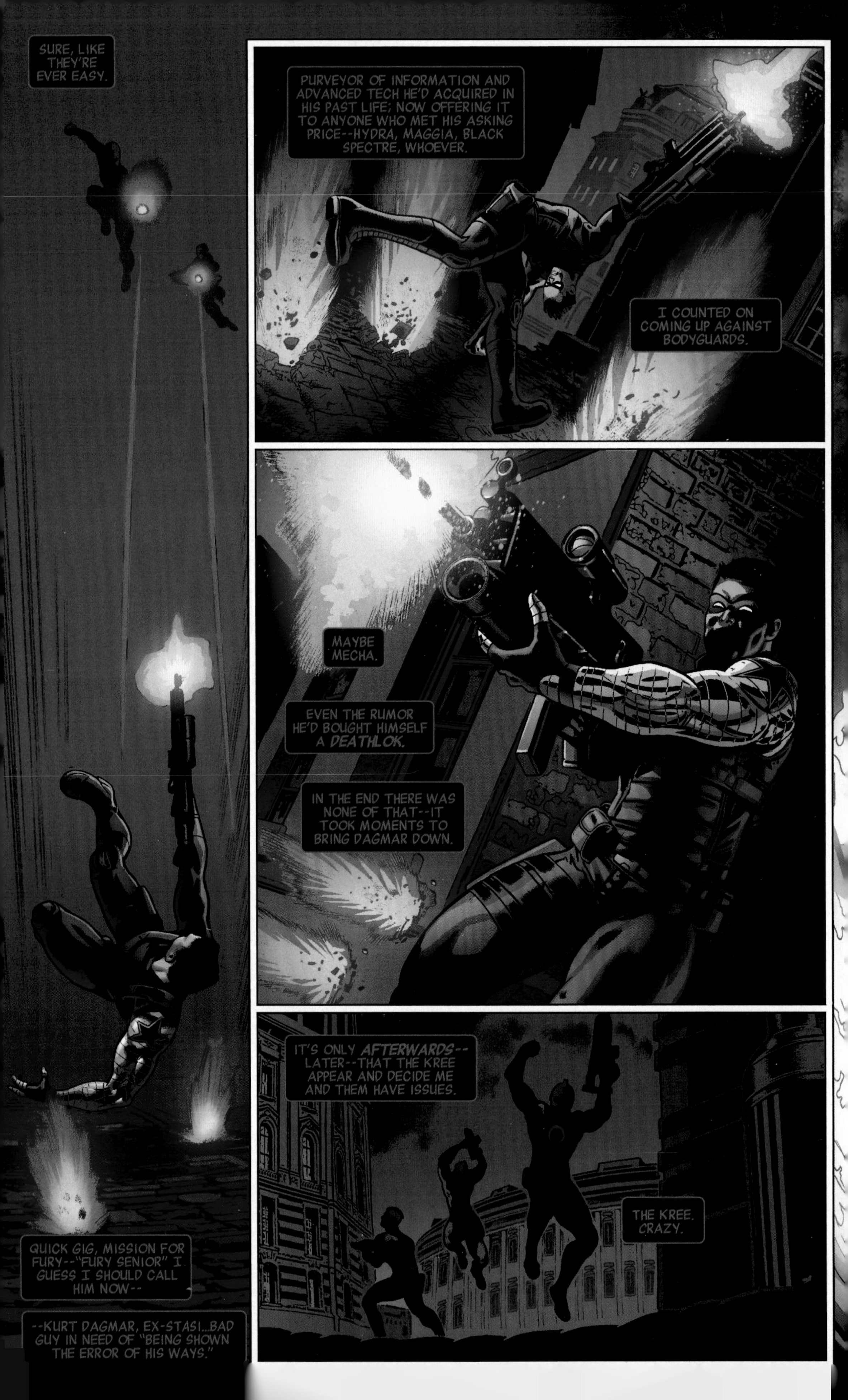
SURE, LIKE THEY'RE EVER EASY.
QUICK GIG, MISSION FOR FURY--"FURY SENIOR" I GUESS I SHOULD CALL HIM NOW--
--KURT DAGMAR, EX-STASI...BAD GUY IN NEED OF "BEING SHOWN THE ERROR OF HIS WAYS."
PURVEYOR OF INFORMATION AND ADVANCED TECH HE'D ACQUIRED IN HIS PAST LIFE; NOW OFFERING IT TO ANYONE WHO MET HIS ASKING PRICE--HYDRA, MAGGIA, BLACK SPECTRE, WHOEVER.
I COUNTED ON COMING UP AGAINST BODYGUARDS.
MAYBE MECHA.
EVEN THE RUMOR HE'D BOUGHT HIMSELF A DEATHLOK.
IN THE END THERE WAS NONE OF THAT--IT TOOK MOMENTS TO BRING DAGMAR DOWN.
IT'S ONLY AFTERWARDS--LATER--THAT THE KREE APPEAR AND DECIDE ME AND THEM HAVE ISSUES.
THE KREE. CRAZY.

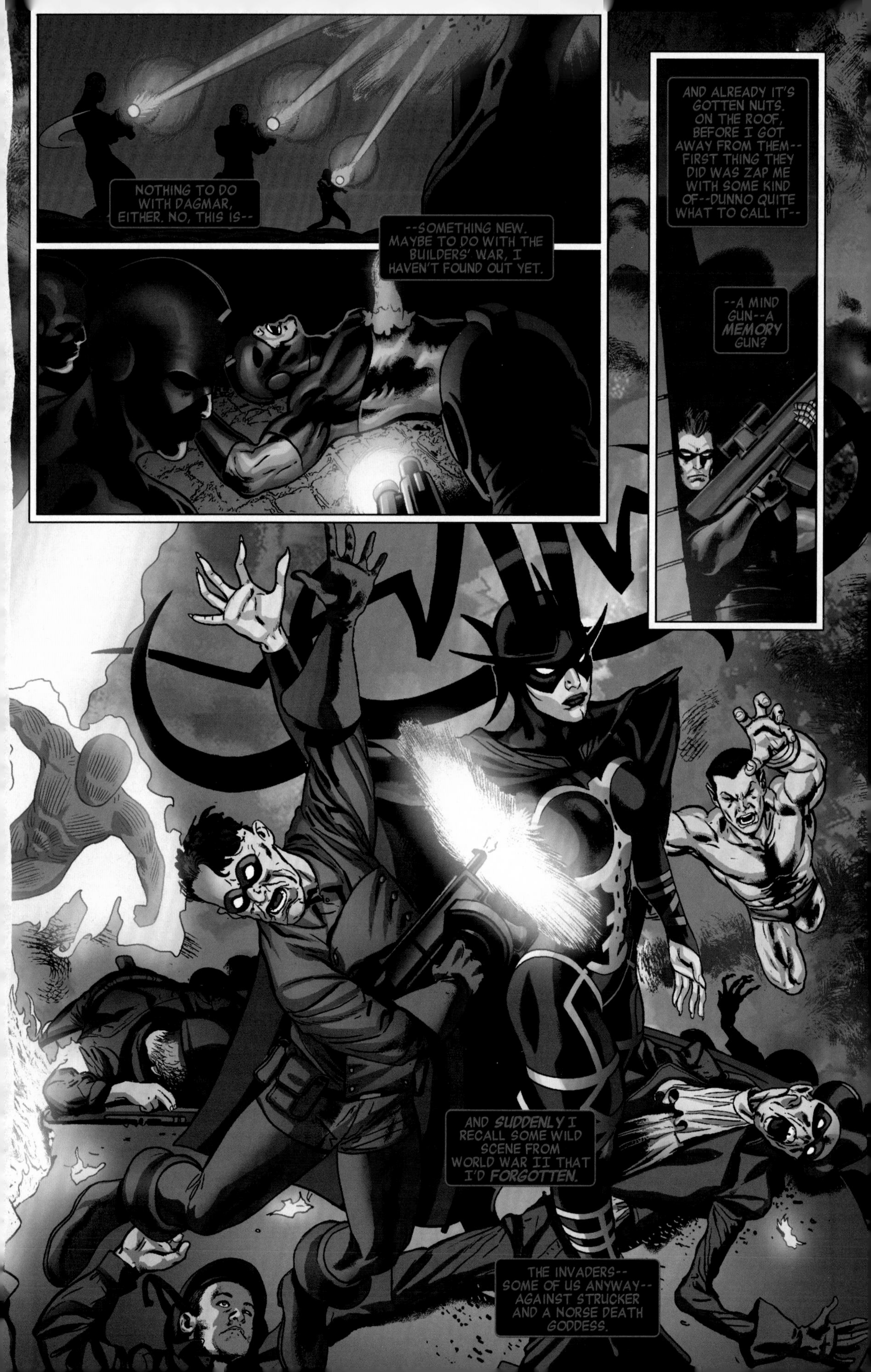
NOTHING TO DO WITH DAGMAR, EITHER. NO, THIS IS--
--SOMETHING NEW. MAYBE TO DO WITH THE BUILDERS' WAR, I HAVEN'T FOUND OUT YET.
AND ALREADY IT'S GOTTEN NUTS. ON THE ROOF, BEFORE I GOT AWAY FROM THEM-- FIRST THING THEY DID WAS ZAP ME WITH SOME KIND OF--DUNNO QUITE WHAT TO CALL IT--
--A MIND GUN--A MEMORY GUN?
AND SUDDENLY I RECALL SOME WILD SCENE FROM WORLD WAR II THAT I'D FORGOTTEN.
THE INVADERS-- SOME OF US ANYWAY-- AGAINST STRUCKER AND A NORSE DEATH GODDESS.

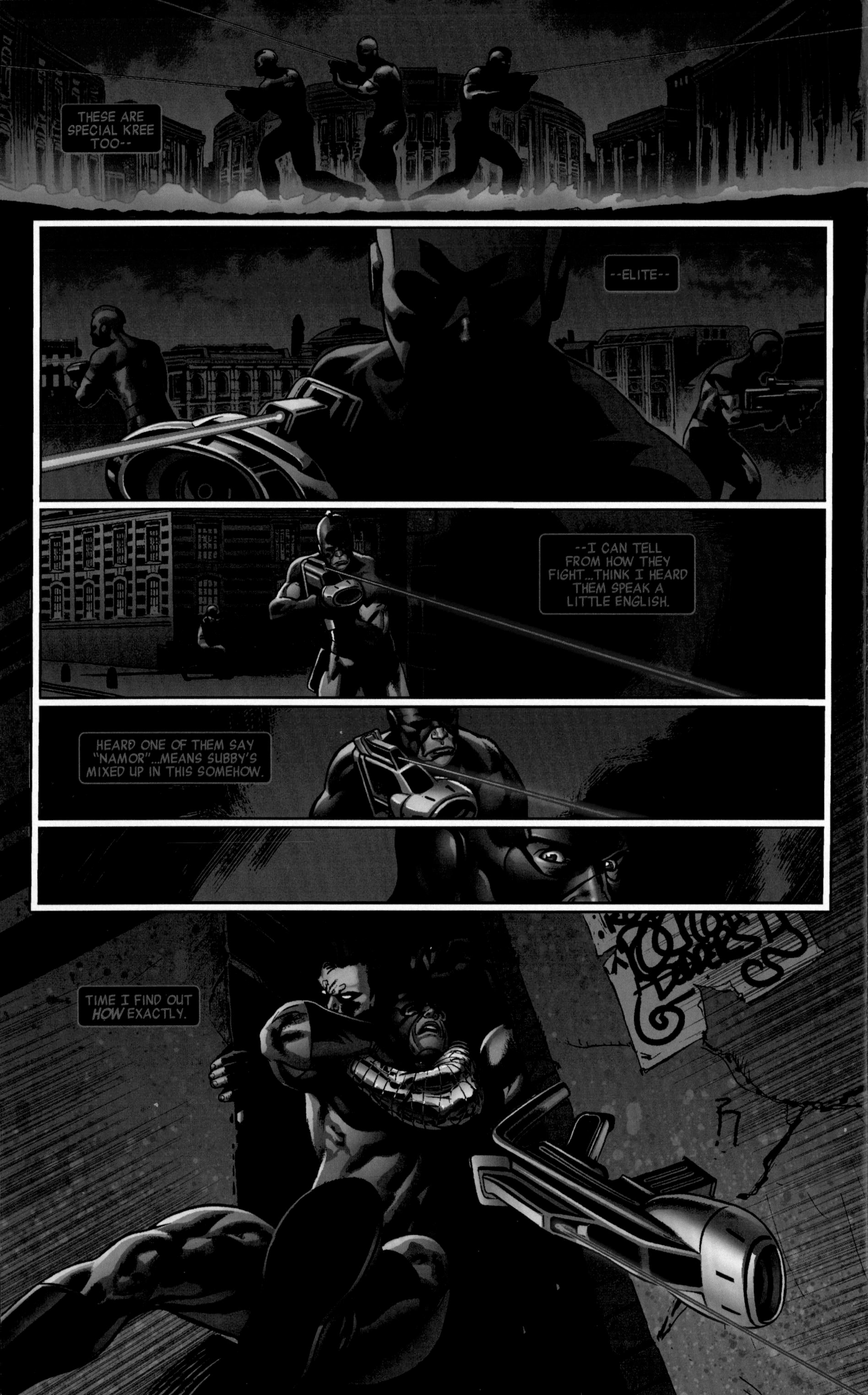
THESE ARE SPECIAL KREE TOO--
--ELITE--
--I CAN TELL FROM HOW THEY FIGHT...THINK I HEARD THEM SPEAK A LITTLE ENGLISH.
HEARD ONE OF THEM SAY "NAMOR"...MEANS SUBBY'S MIXED UP IN THIS SOMEHOW.
TIME I FIND OUT *HOW* EXACTLY.

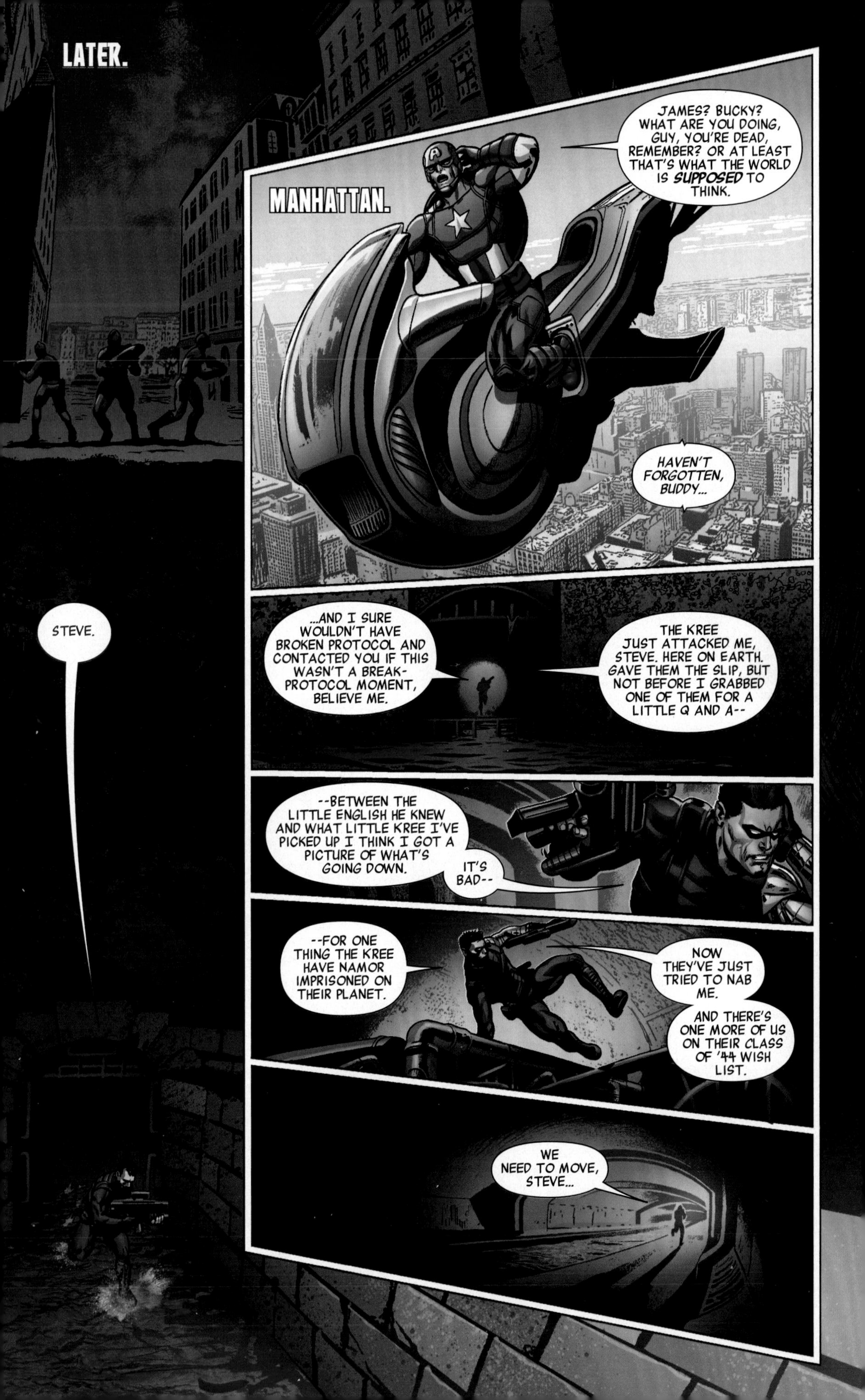
LATER.
MANHATTAN.
JAMES? BUCKY? WHAT ARE YOU DOING, GUY, YOU'RE DEAD, REMEMBER? OR AT LEAST THAT'S WHAT THE WORLD IS SUPPOSED TO THINK.
HAVEN'T FORGOTTEN, BUDDY...
STEVE.
...AND I SURE WOULDN'T HAVE BROKEN PROTOCOL AND CONTACTED YOU IF THIS WASN'T A BREAK-PROTOCOL MOMENT, BELIEVE ME.
THE KREE JUST ATTACKED ME, STEVE. HERE ON EARTH. GAVE THEM THE SLIP, BUT NOT BEFORE I GRABBED ONE OF THEM FOR A LITTLE Q AND A--
--BETWEEN THE LITTLE ENGLISH HE KNEW AND WHAT LITTLE KREE I'VE PICKED UP I THINK I GOT A PICTURE OF WHAT'S GOING DOWN.
IT'S BAD--
--FOR ONE THING THE KREE HAVE NAMOR IMPRISONED ON THEIR PLANET.
NOW THEY'VE JUST TRIED TO NAB ME.
AND THERE'S ONE MORE OF US ON THEIR CLASS OF '44 WISH LIST.
WE NEED TO MOVE, STEVE...

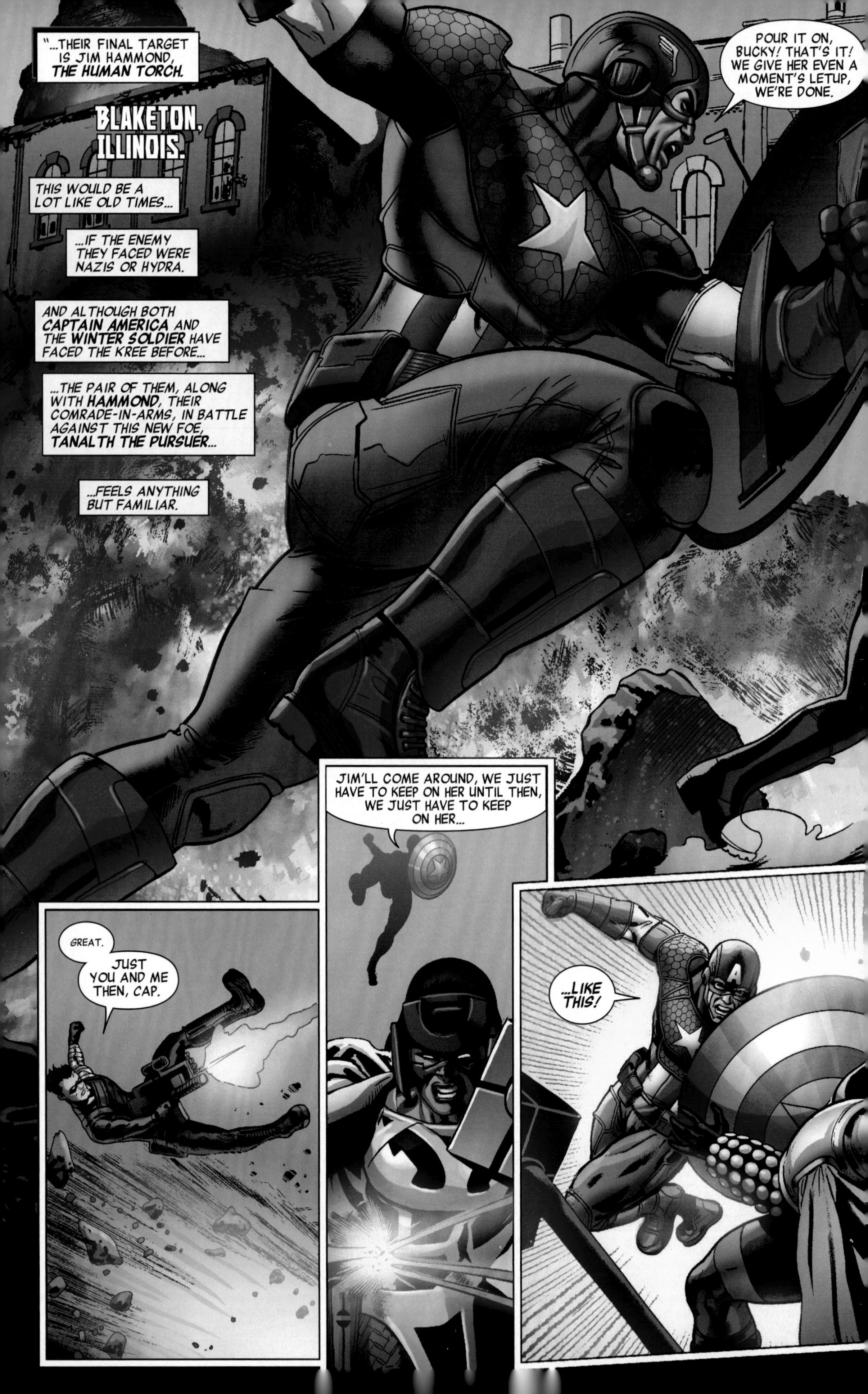
"...THEIR FINAL TARGET IS JIM HAMMOND, THE HUMAN TORCH.
BLAKETON, ILLINOIS.
POUR IT ON, BUCKY! THAT'S IT! WE GIVE HER EVEN A MOMENT'S LETUP, WE'RE DONE.
THIS WOULD BE A LOT LIKE OLD TIMES...
...IF THE ENEMY THEY FACED WERE NAZIS OR HYDRA.
AND ALTHOUGH BOTH CAPTAIN AMERICA AND THE WINTER SOLDIER HAVE FACED THE KREE BEFORE...
...THE PAIR OF THEM, ALONG WITH HAMMOND, THEIR COMRADE-IN-ARMS, IN BATTLE AGAINST THIS NEW FOE, TANALTH THE PURSUER...
...FEELS ANYTHING BUT FAMILIAR.
GREAT.
JUST YOU AND ME THEN, CAP.
JIM'LL COME AROUND, WE JUST HAVE TO KEEP ON HER UNTIL THEN, WE JUST HAVE TO KEEP ON HER...
...LIKE THIS!

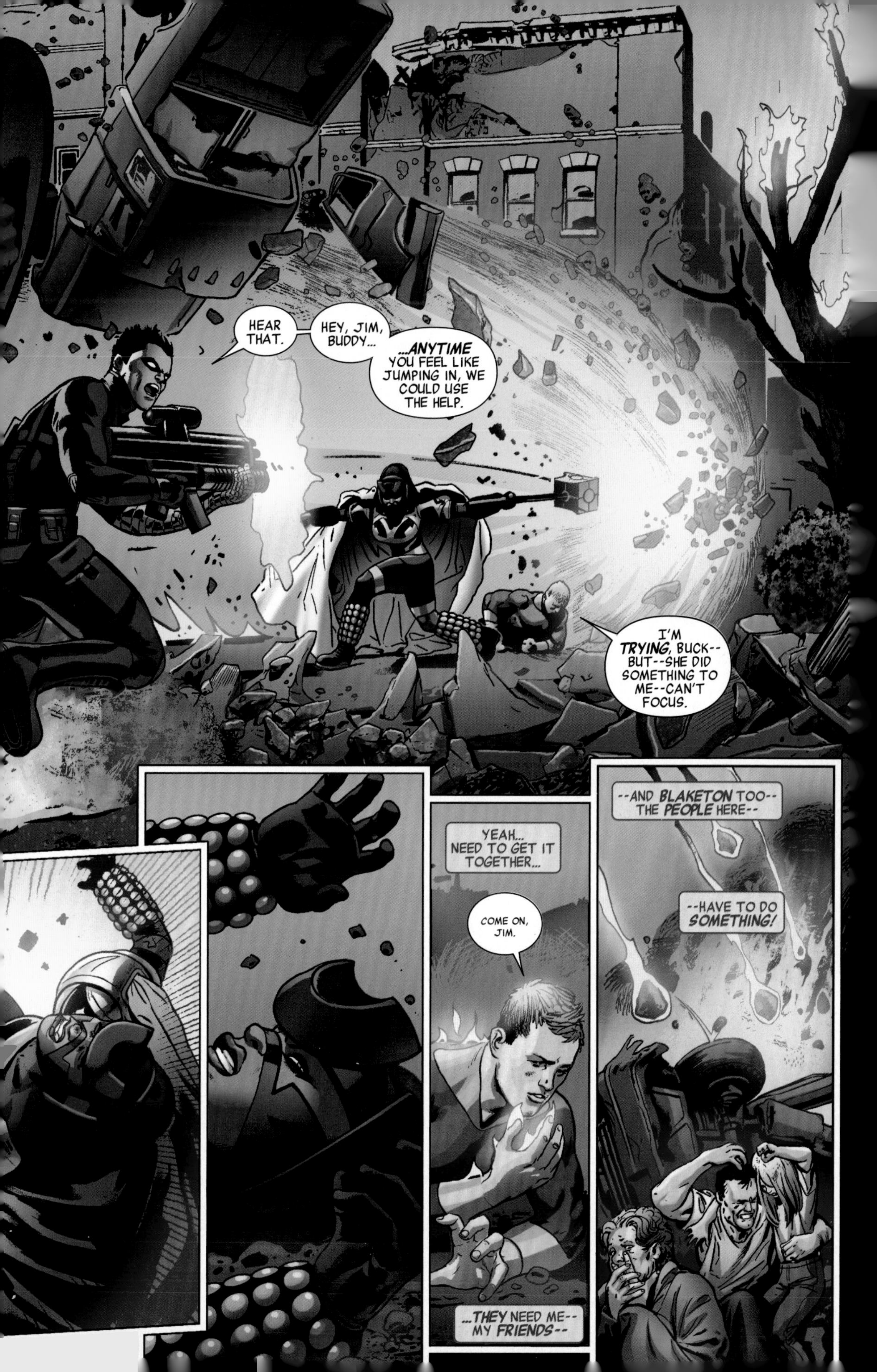
HEAR THAT.
HEY, JIM, BUDDY...
...ANYTIME YOU FEEL LIKE JUMPING IN, WE COULD USE THE HELP.
I'M TRYING, BUCK-- BUT--SHE DID SOMETHING TO ME--CAN'T FOCUS.
YEAH... NEED TO GET IT TOGETHER...
COME ON, JIM.
...THEY NEED ME-- MY FRIENDS--
--AND BLAKETON TOO-- THE PEOPLE HERE--
--HAVE TO DO SOMETHING!

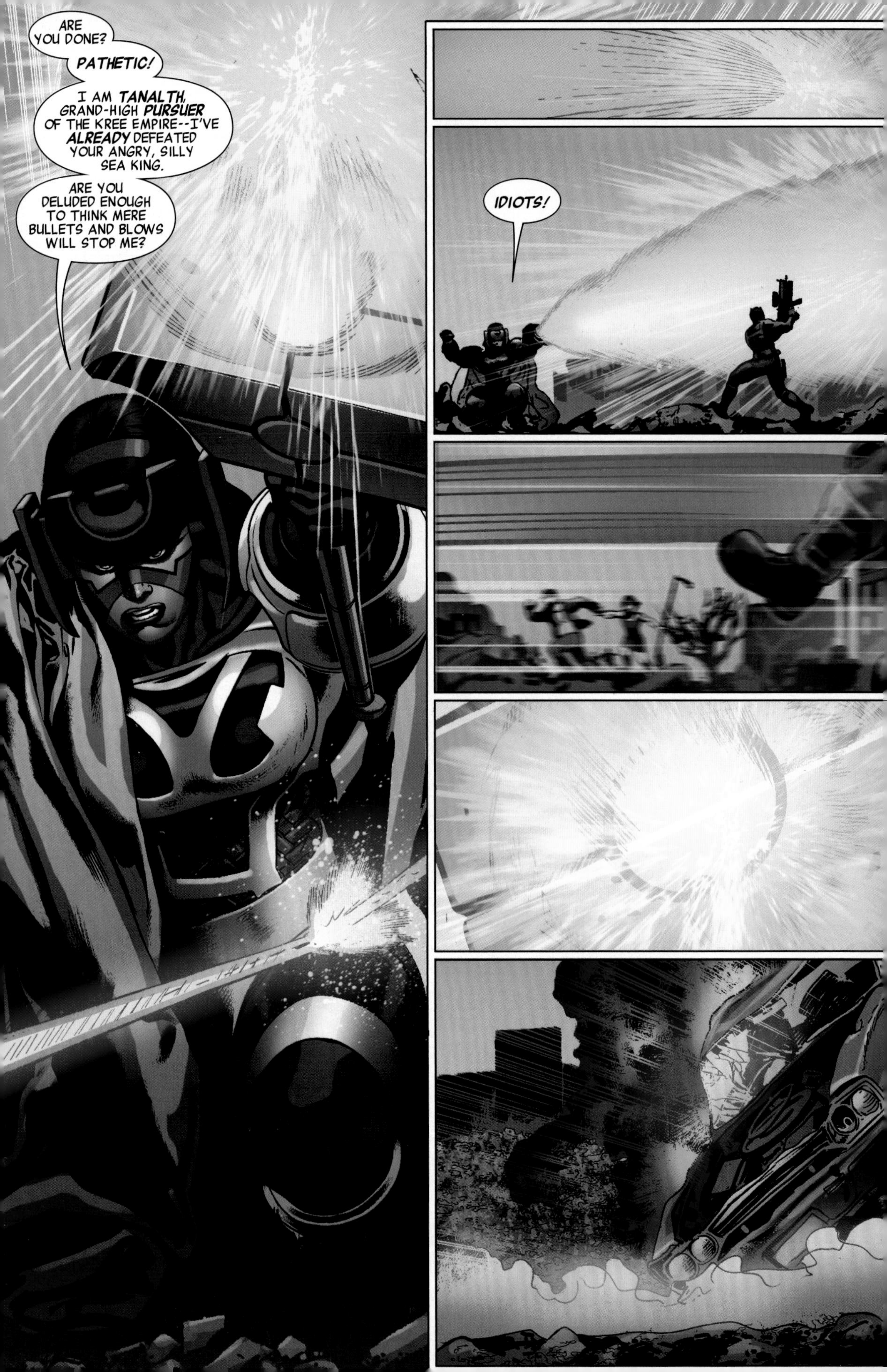
ARE YOU DONE?
PATHETIC!
I AM TANALTH, GRAND-HIGH PURSUER OF THE KREE EMPIRE--I'VE ALREADY DEFEATED YOUR ANGRY, SILLY SEA KING.
ARE YOU DELUDED ENOUGH TO THINK MERE BULLETS AND BLOWS WILL STOP ME?
IDIOTS!

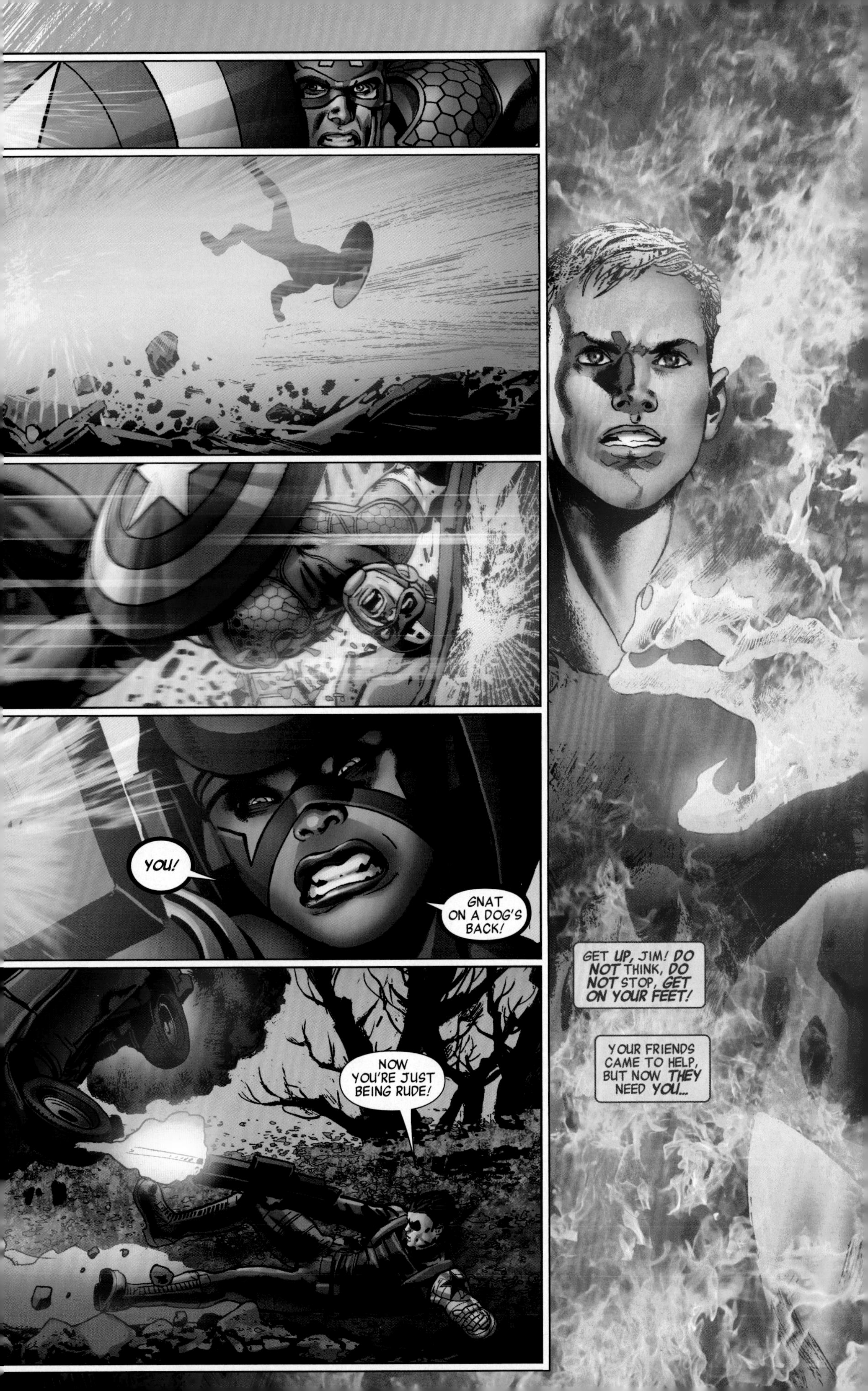
YOU!
GNAT ON A DOG'S BACK!
NOW YOU'RE JUST BEING RUDE!
GET UP, JIM! DO NOT THINK, DO NOT STOP, GET ON YOUR FEET!
YOUR FRIENDS CAME TO HELP, BUT NOW THEY NEED YOU...

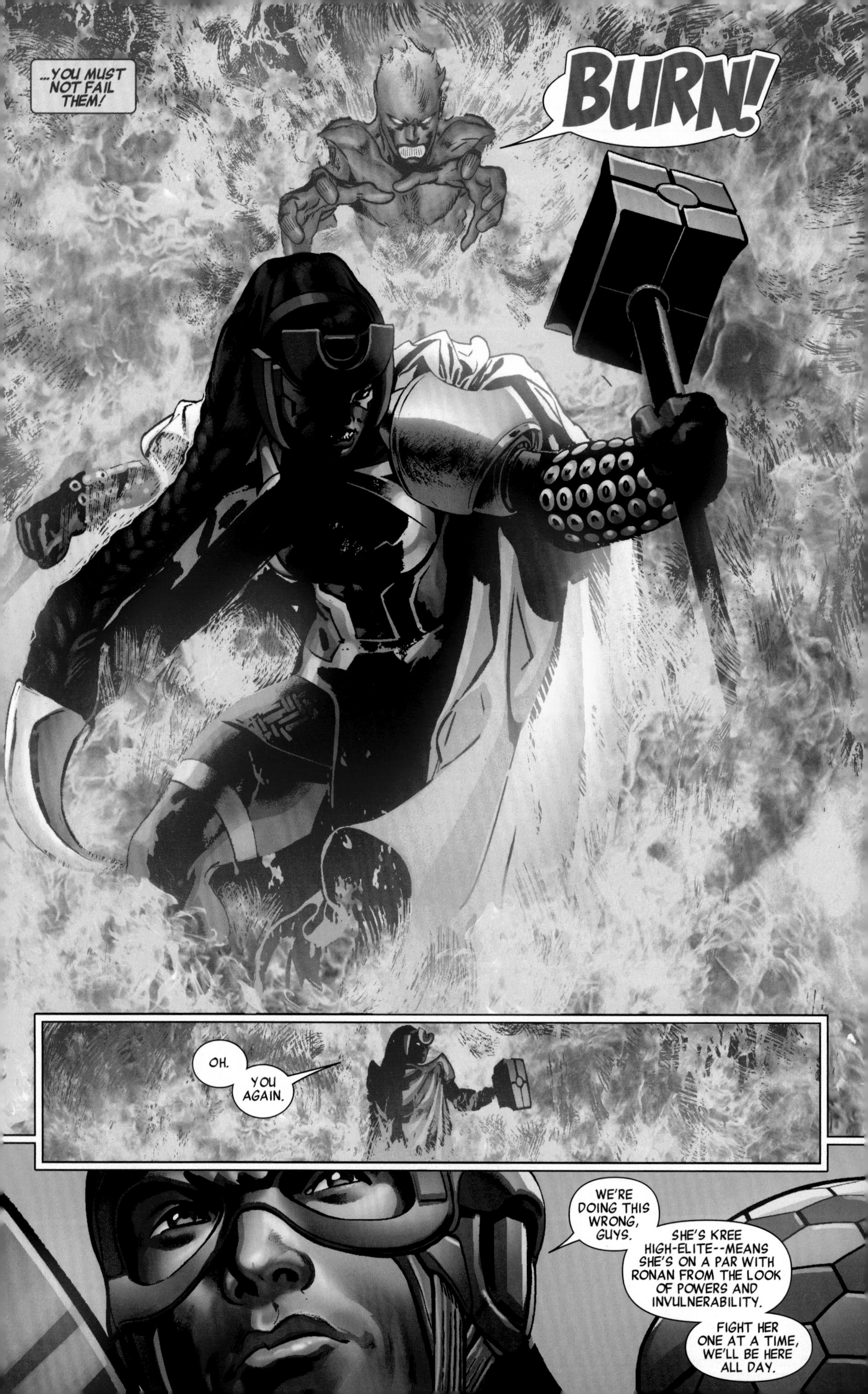
...YOU MUST NOT FAIL THEM!
BURN!
OH.
YOU AGAIN.
WE'RE DOING THIS WRONG, GUYS.
SHE'S KREE HIGH-ELITE--MEANS SHE'S ON A PAR WITH RONAN FROM THE LOOK OF POWERS AND INVULNERABILITY.
FIGHT HER ONE AT A TIME, WE'LL BE HERE ALL DAY.

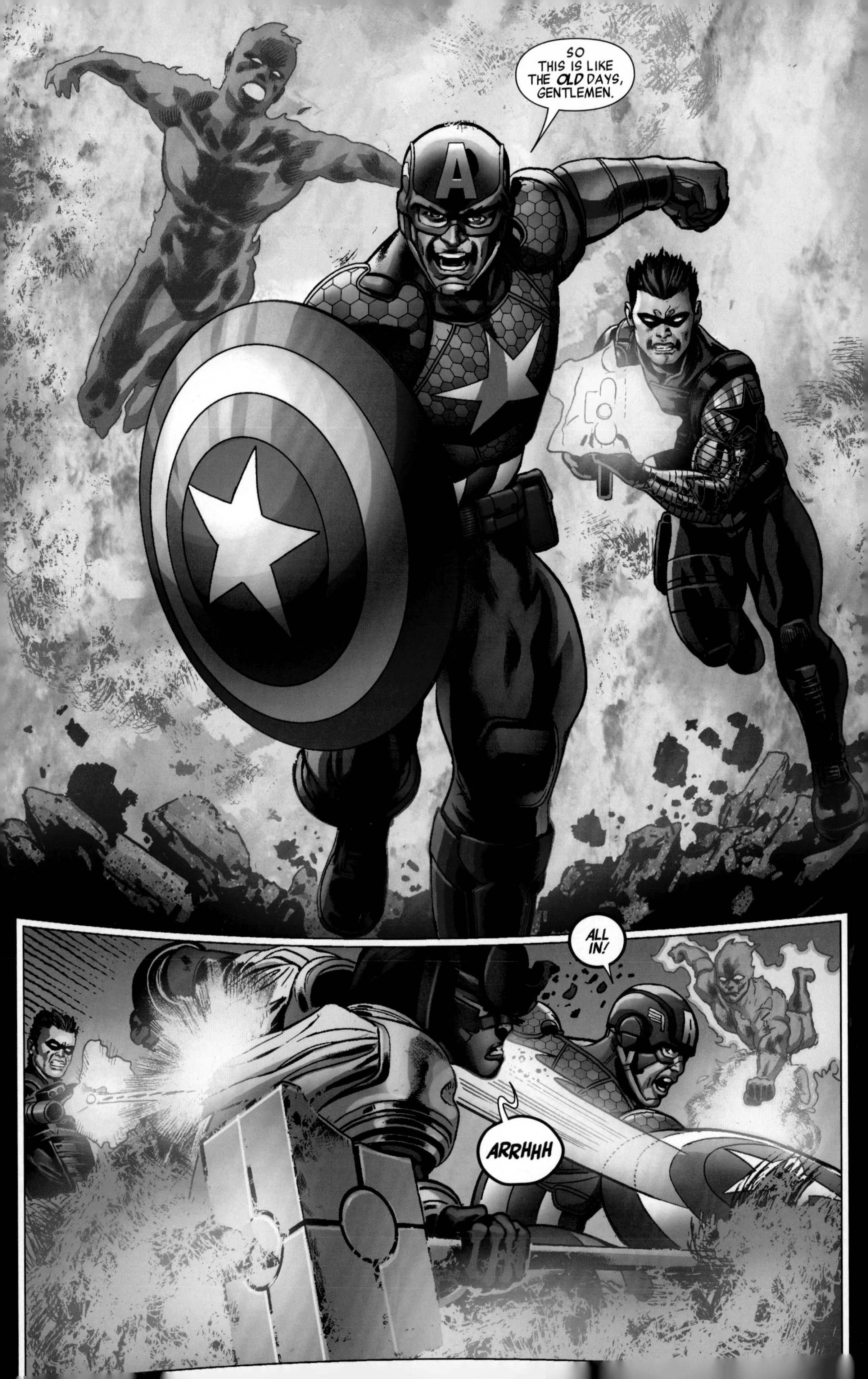
SO THIS IS LIKE THE OLD DAYS, GENTLEMEN.
ALL IN!
ARRHHH

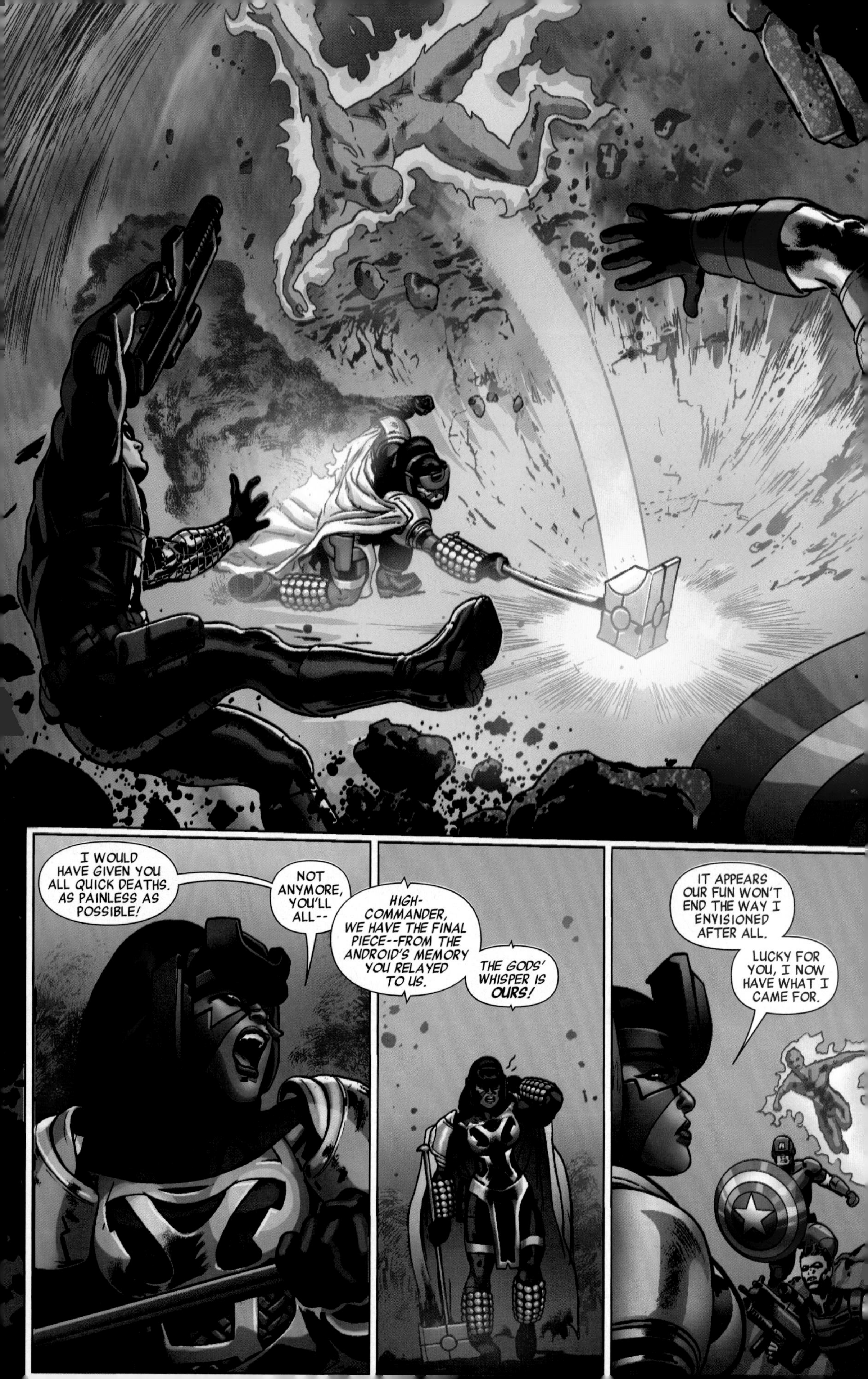
I WOULD HAVE GIVEN YOU ALL QUICK DEATHS. AS PAINLESS AS POSSIBLE!
NOT ANYMORE, YOU'LL ALL--
HIGH-COMMANDER, WE HAVE THE FINAL PIECE--FROM THE ANDROID'S MEMORY YOU RELAYED TO US.
THE GODS' WHISPER IS OURS!
IT APPEARS OUR FUN WON'T END THE WAY I ENVISIONED AFTER ALL.
LUCKY FOR YOU, I NOW HAVE WHAT I CAME FOR.

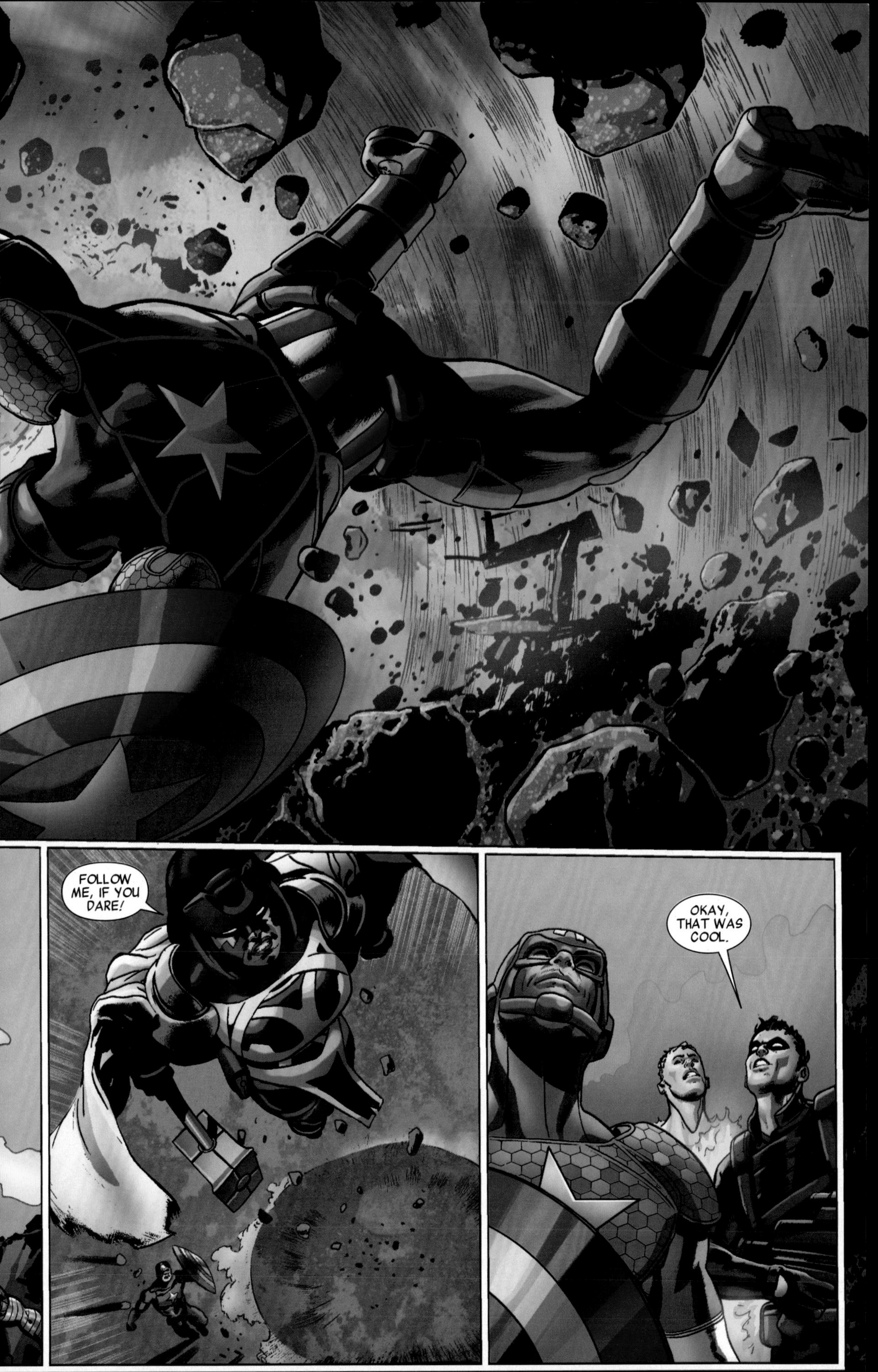
FOLLOW ME, IF YOU DARE!
OKAY, THAT WAS COOL.

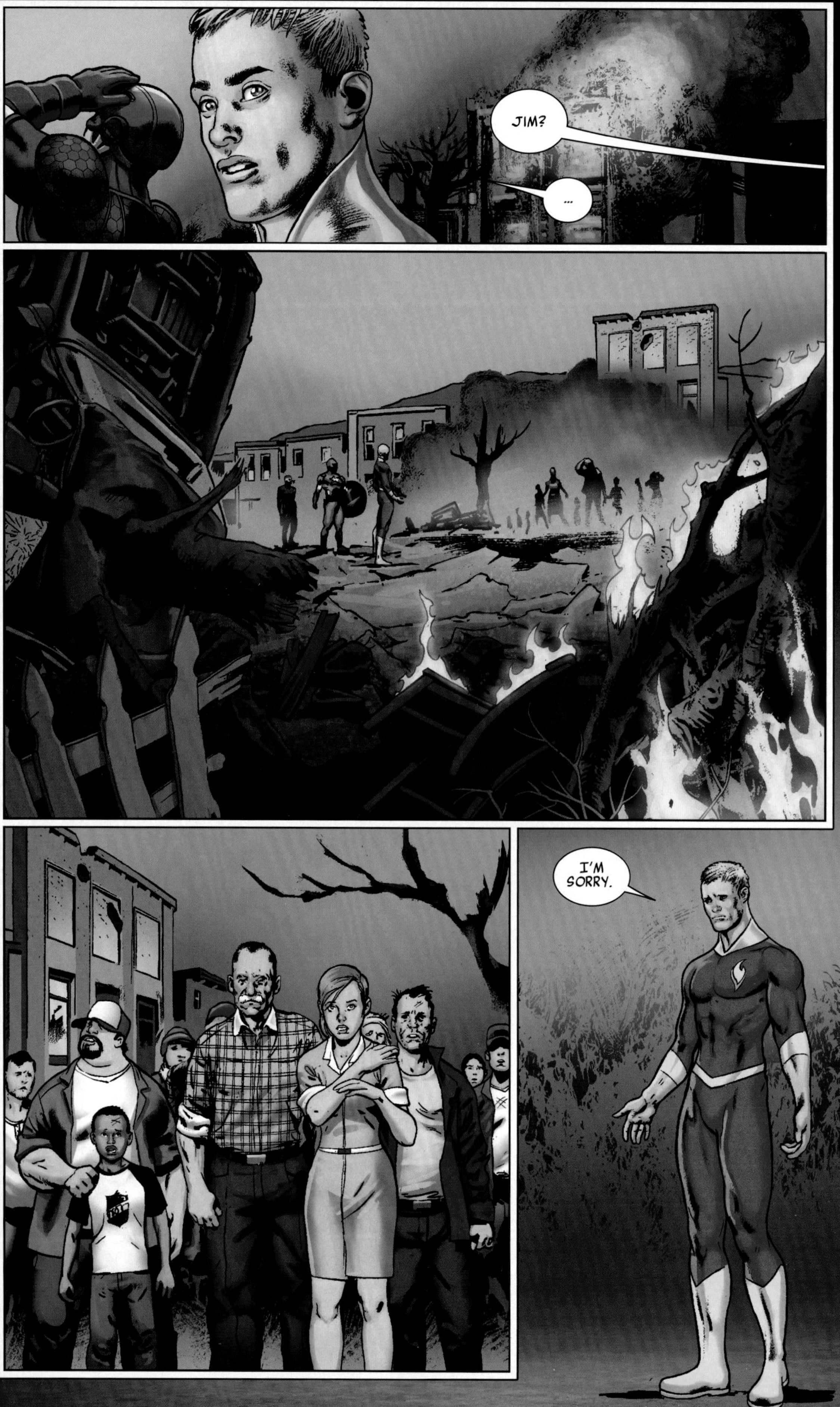
JIM?
...
I'M SORRY.

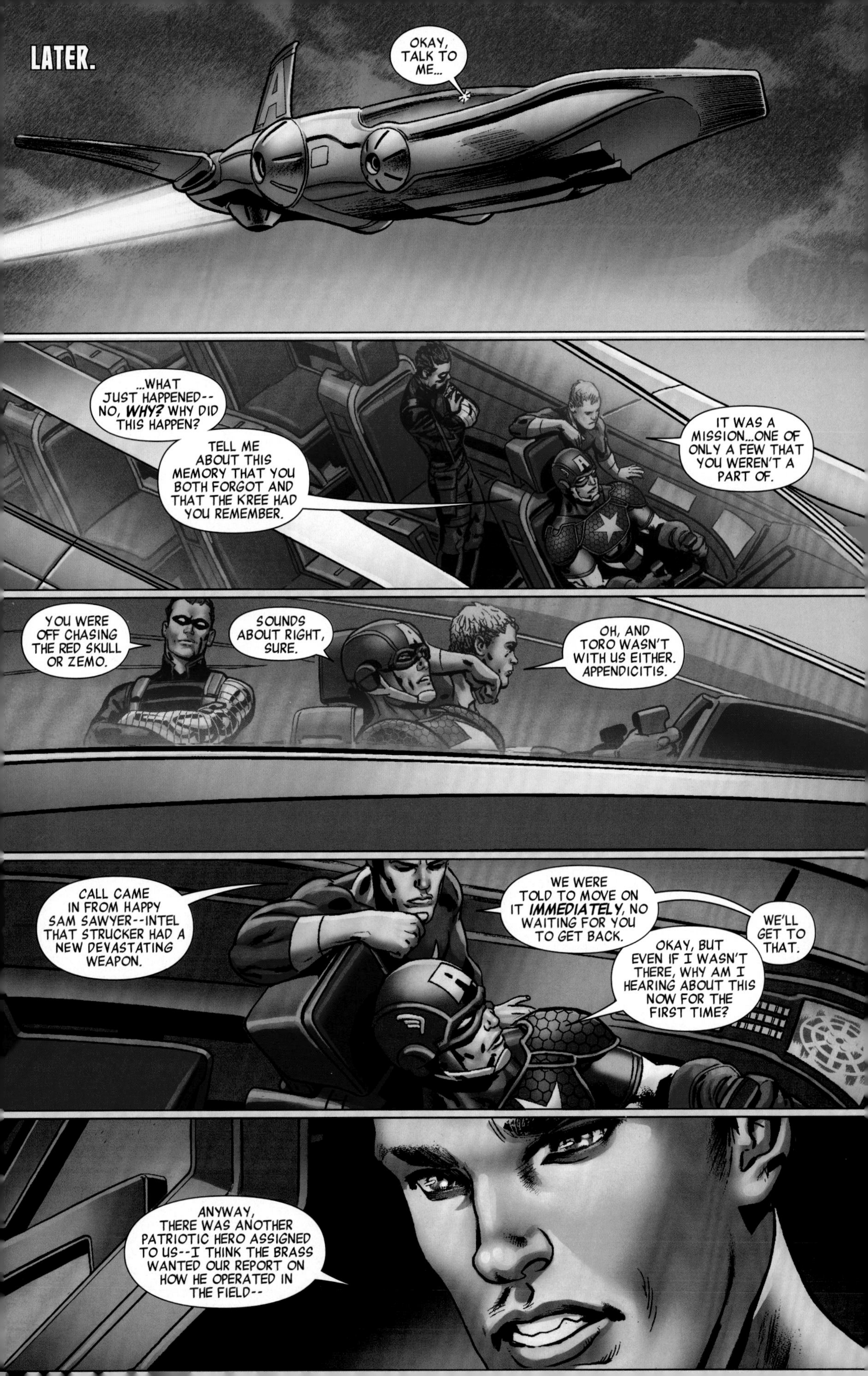
LATER.
OKAY, TALK TO ME...
...WHAT JUST HAPPENED-- NO, WHY? WHY DID THIS HAPPEN?
TELL ME ABOUT THIS MEMORY THAT YOU BOTH FORGOT AND THAT THE KREE HAD YOU REMEMBER.
IT WAS A MISSION...ONE OF ONLY A FEW THAT YOU WEREN'T A PART OF.
YOU WERE OFF CHASING THE RED SKULL OR ZEMO.
SOUNDS ABOUT RIGHT, SURE.
OH, AND TORO WASN'T WITH US EITHER. APPENDICITIS.
CALL CAME IN FROM HAPPY SAM SAWYER--INTEL THAT STRUCKER HAD A NEW DEVASTATING WEAPON.
WE WERE TOLD TO MOVE ON IT IMMEDIATELY, NO WAITING FOR YOU TO GET BACK.
WE'LL GET TO THAT.
OKAY, BUT EVEN IF I WASN'T THERE, WHY AM I HEARING ABOUT THIS NOW FOR THE FIRST TIME?
ANYWAY, THERE WAS ANOTHER PATRIOTIC HERO ASSIGNED TO US--I THINK THE BRASS WANTED OUR REPORT ON HOW HE OPERATED IN THE FIELD--

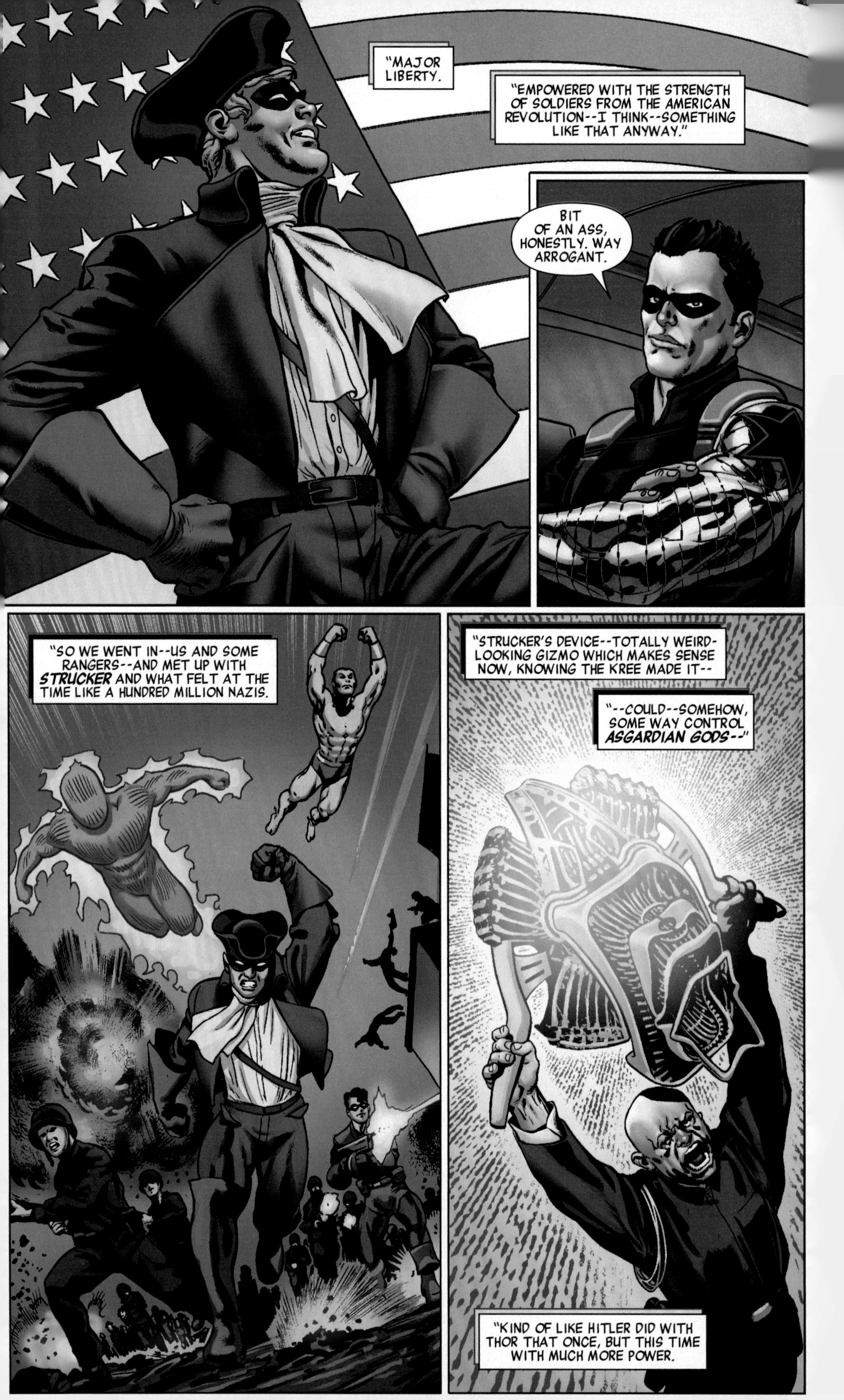

"MAJOR LIBERTY.
"EMPOWERED WITH THE STRENGTH OF SOLDIERS FROM THE AMERICAN REVOLUTION--I THINK--SOMETHING LIKE THAT ANYWAY."
BIT OF AN ASS, HONESTLY. WAY ARROGANT.
"SO WE WENT IN--US AND SOME RANGERS--AND MET UP WITH STRUCKER AND WHAT FELT AT THE TIME LIKE A HUNDRED MILLION NAZIS.
"STRUCKER'S DEVICE--TOTALLY WEIRD-LOOKING GIZMO WHICH MAKES SENSE NOW, KNOWING THE KREE MADE IT--
"--COULD--SOMEHOW, SOME WAY CONTROL ASGARDIAN GODS--"
"KIND OF LIKE HITLER DID WITH THOR THAT ONCE, BUT THIS TIME WITH MUCH MORE POWER.

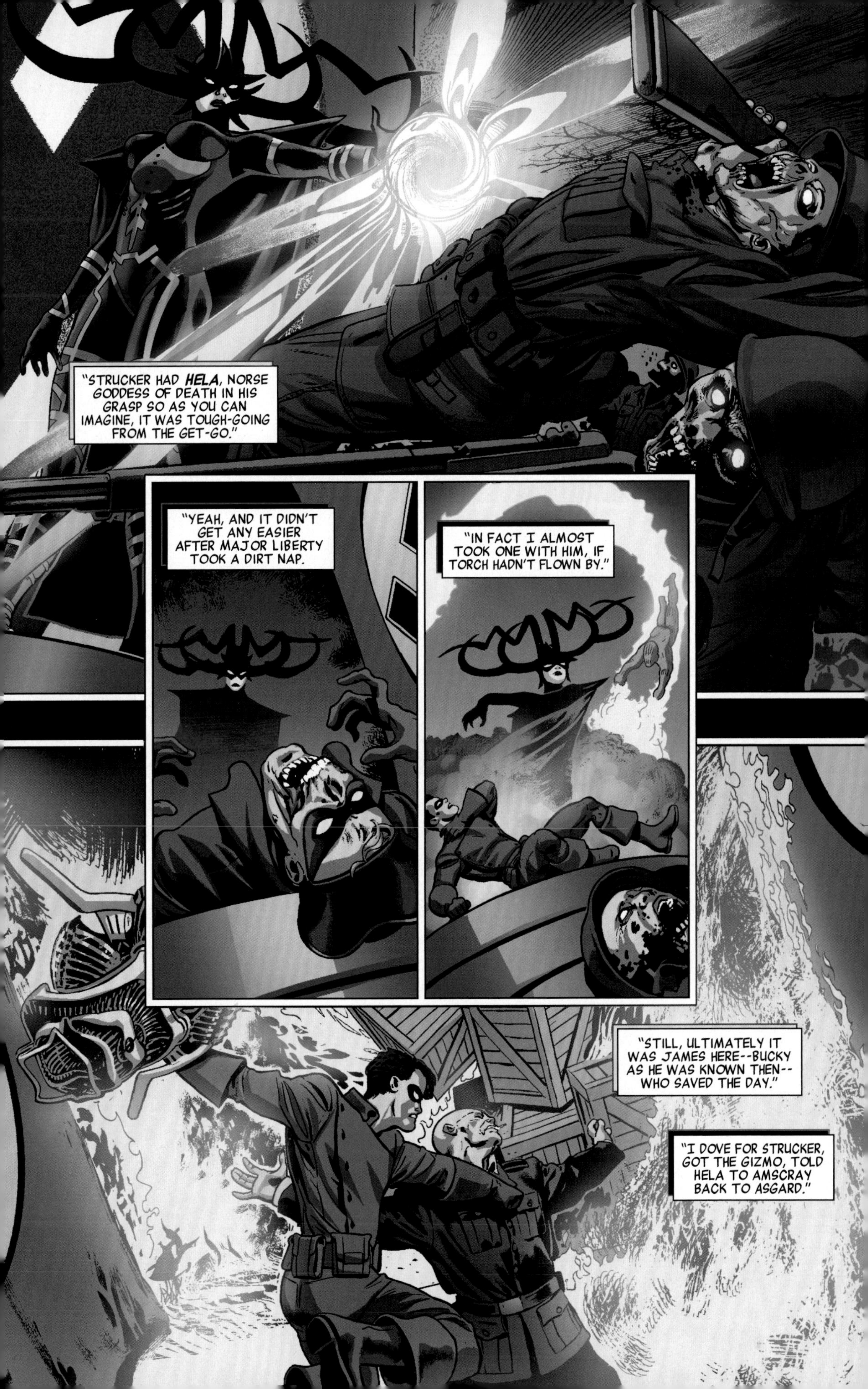
"STRUCKER HAD HELA, NORSE GODDESS OF DEATH IN HIS GRASP SO AS YOU CAN IMAGINE, IT WAS TOUGH-GOING FROM THE GET-GO."
"YEAH, AND IT DIDN'T GET ANY EASIER AFTER MAJOR LIBERTY TOOK A DIRT NAP.
"IN FACT I ALMOST TOOK ONE WITH HIM, IF TORCH HADN'T FLOWN BY."
"STILL, ULTIMATELY IT WAS JAMES HERE--BUCKY AS HE WAS KNOWN THEN--WHO SAVED THE DAY."
"I DOVE FOR STRUCKER, GOT THE GIZMO, TOLD HELA TO AMSCRAY BACK TO ASGARD."

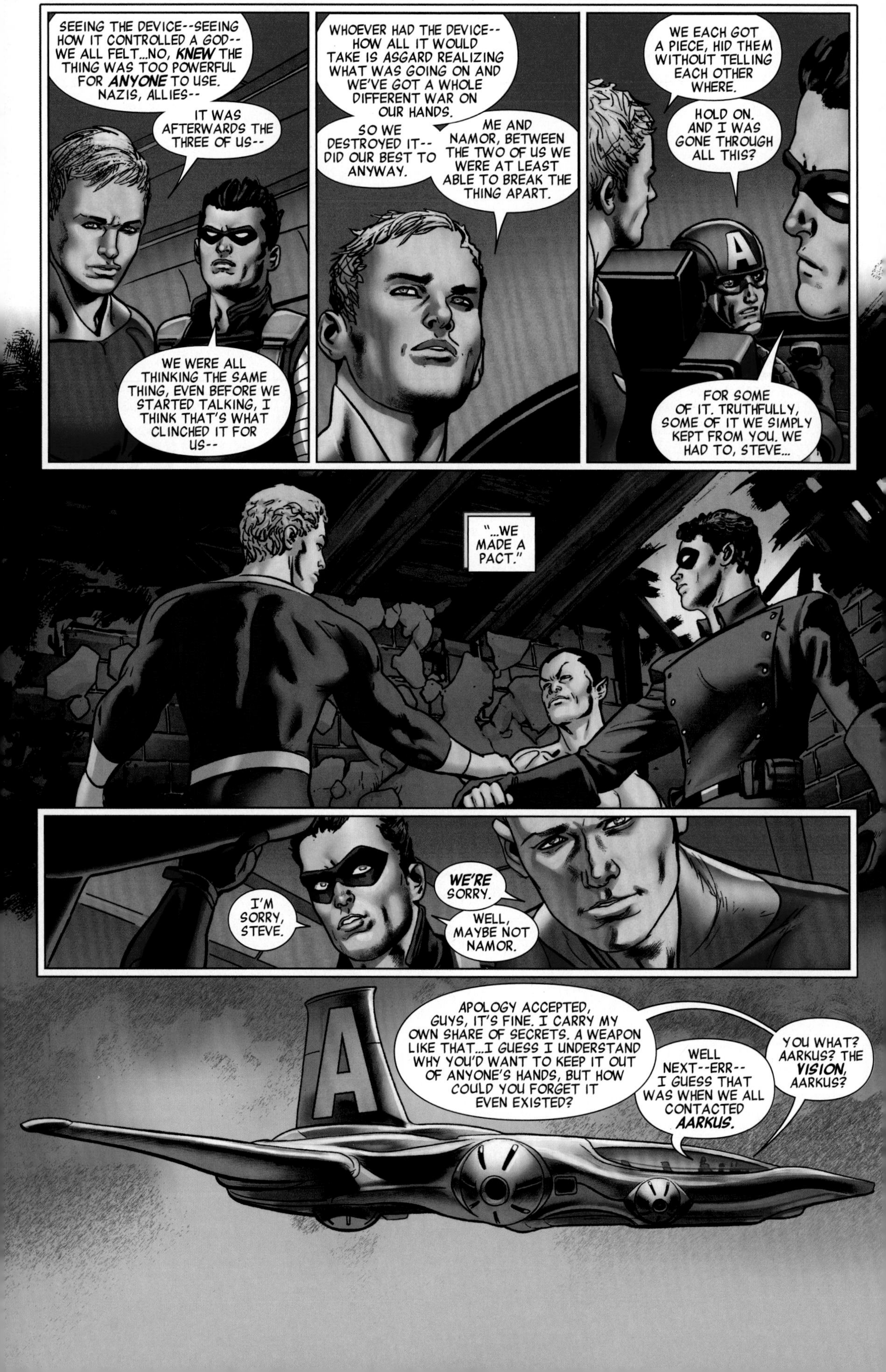
SEEING THE DEVICE--SEEING HOW IT CONTROLLED A GOD--WE ALL FELT...NO, *KNEW* THE THING WAS TOO POWERFUL FOR *ANYONE* TO USE. NAZIS, ALLIES--
IT WAS AFTERWARDS THE THREE OF US--
WE WERE ALL THINKING THE SAME THING, EVEN BEFORE WE STARTED TALKING, I THINK THAT'S WHAT CLINCHED IT FOR US--
WHOEVER HAD THE DEVICE--HOW ALL IT WOULD TAKE IS ASGARD REALIZING WHAT WAS GOING ON AND WE'VE GOT A WHOLE DIFFERENT WAR ON OUR HANDS.
SO WE DESTROYED IT--DID OUR BEST TO ANYWAY.
ME AND NAMOR, BETWEEN THE TWO OF US WE WERE AT LEAST ABLE TO BREAK THE THING APART.
WE EACH GOT A PIECE, HID THEM WITHOUT TELLING EACH OTHER WHERE.
HOLD ON. AND I WAS GONE THROUGH ALL THIS?
FOR SOME OF IT. TRUTHFULLY, SOME OF IT WE SIMPLY KEPT FROM YOU. WE HAD TO, STEVE...
"...WE MADE A PACT."
I'M SORRY, STEVE.
WE'RE SORRY.
WELL, MAYBE NOT NAMOR.
APOLOGY ACCEPTED, GUYS, IT'S FINE. I CARRY MY OWN SHARE OF SECRETS. A WEAPON LIKE THAT...I GUESS I UNDERSTAND WHY YOU'D WANT TO KEEP IT OUT OF ANYONE'S HANDS, BUT HOW COULD YOU FORGET IT EVEN EXISTED?
WELL NEXT--ERR--I GUESS THAT WAS WHEN WE ALL CONTACTED *AARKUS.*
YOU WHAT? AARKUS? THE *VISION*, AARKUS?

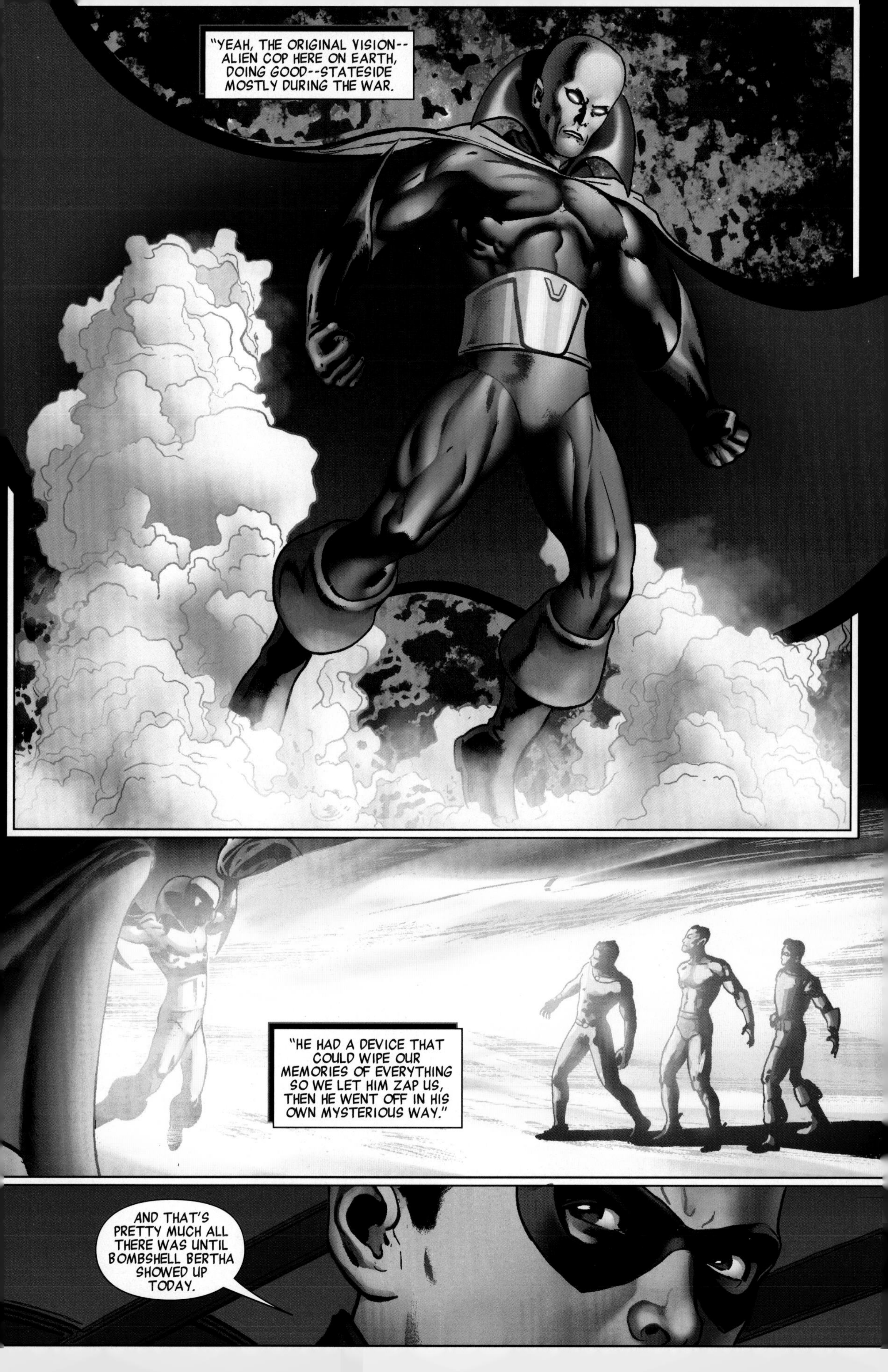
"YEAH, THE ORIGINAL VISION--ALIEN COP HERE ON EARTH, DOING GOOD--STATESIDE MOSTLY DURING THE WAR.
"HE HAD A DEVICE THAT COULD WIPE OUR MEMORIES OF EVERYTHING SO WE LET HIM ZAP US, THEN HE WENT OFF IN HIS OWN MYSTERIOUS WAY."
AND THAT'S PRETTY MUCH ALL THERE WAS UNTIL BOMBSHELL BERTHA SHOWED UP TODAY.

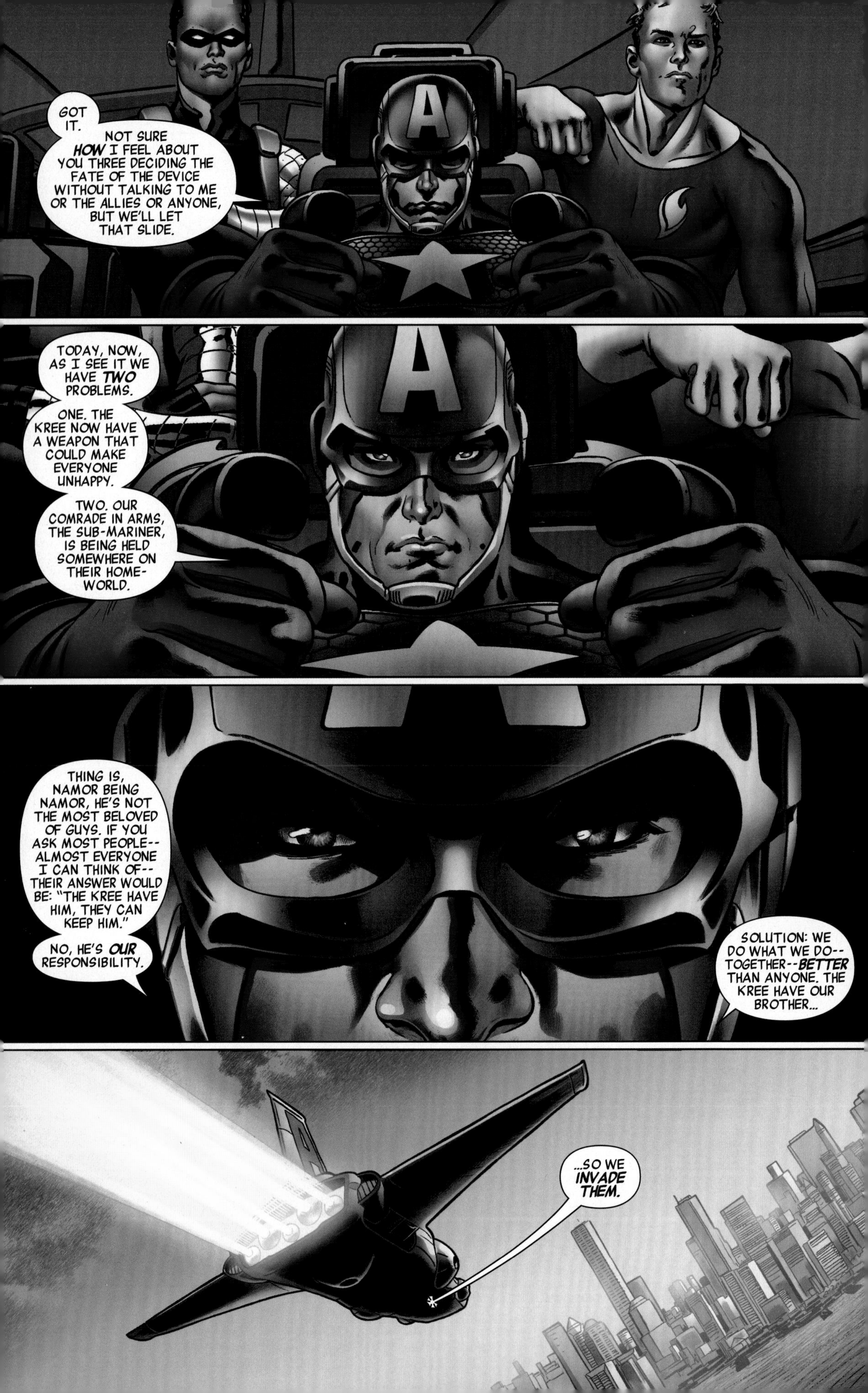
GOT IT.
NOT SURE HOW I FEEL ABOUT YOU THREE DECIDING THE FATE OF THE DEVICE WITHOUT TALKING TO ME OR THE ALLIES OR ANYONE, BUT WE'LL LET THAT SLIDE.
TODAY, NOW, AS I SEE IT WE HAVE TWO PROBLEMS.
ONE. THE KREE NOW HAVE A WEAPON THAT COULD MAKE EVERYONE UNHAPPY.
TWO. OUR COMRADE IN ARMS, THE SUB-MARINER, IS BEING HELD SOMEWHERE ON THEIR HOME-WORLD.
THING IS, NAMOR BEING NAMOR, HE'S NOT THE MOST BELOVED OF GUYS. IF YOU ASK MOST PEOPLE--ALMOST EVERYONE I CAN THINK OF--THEIR ANSWER WOULD BE: "THE KREE HAVE HIM, THEY CAN KEEP HIM."
NO, HE'S OUR RESPONSIBILITY.
SOLUTION: WE DO WHAT WE DO--TOGETHER--BETTER THAN ANYONE. THE KREE HAVE OUR BROTHER...
...SO WE INVADE THEM.

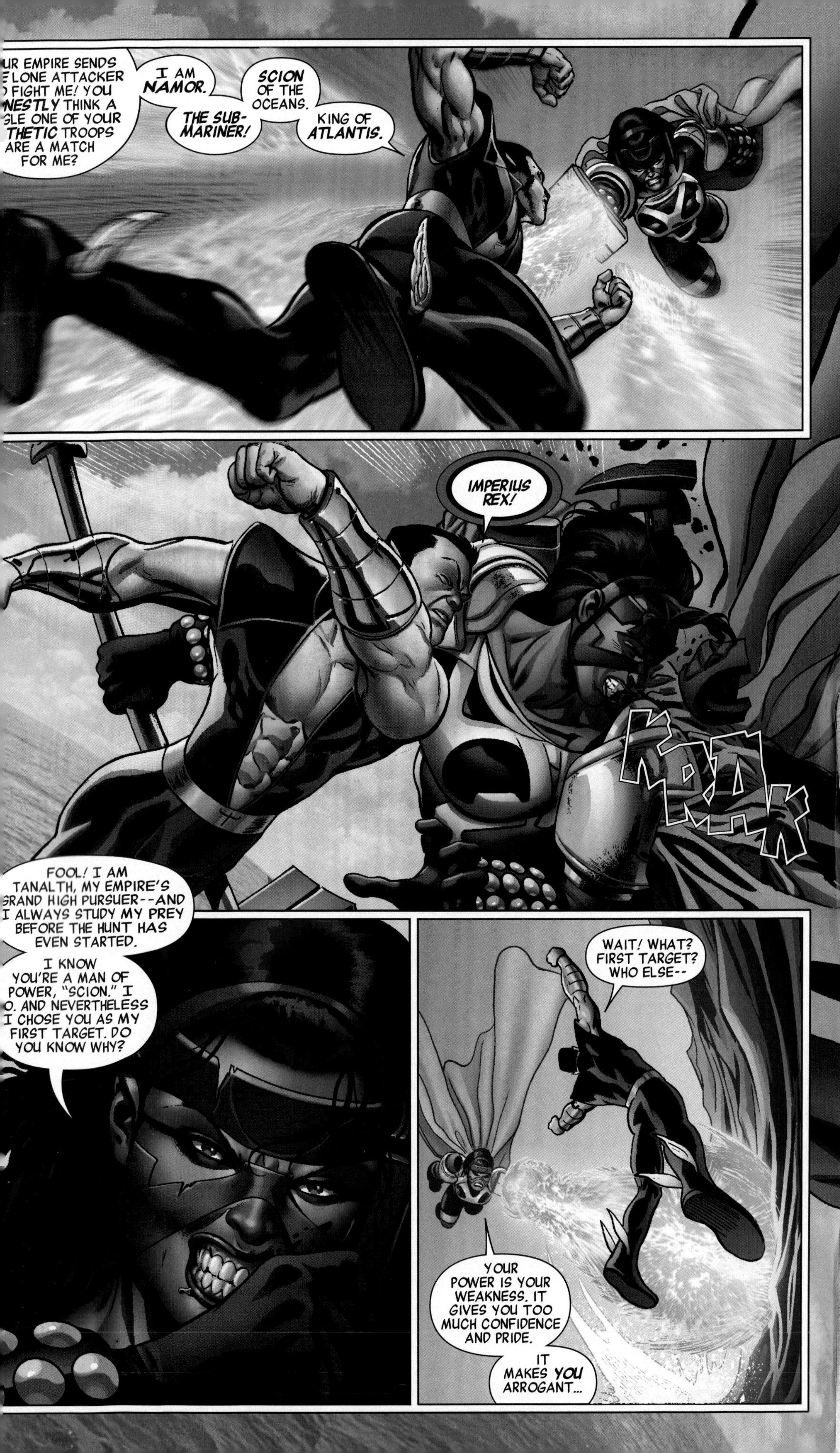
UR EMPIRE SENDS E LONE ATTACKER O FIGHT ME! YOU NESTLY THINK A GLE ONE OF YOUR THETIC TROOPS ARE A MATCH FOR ME?
I AM NAMOR.
THE SUB-MARINER!
SCION OF THE OCEANS.
KING OF ATLANTIS.
IMPERIUS REX!
FOOL! I AM TANALTH, MY EMPIRE'S GRAND HIGH PURSUER--AND I ALWAYS STUDY MY PREY BEFORE THE HUNT HAS EVEN STARTED.
I KNOW YOU'RE A MAN OF POWER, "SCION." I O. AND NEVERTHELESS I CHOSE YOU AS MY FIRST TARGET. DO YOU KNOW WHY?
WAIT! WHAT? FIRST TARGET? WHO ELSE--
YOUR POWER IS YOUR WEAKNESS. IT GIVES YOU TOO MUCH CONFIDENCE AND PRIDE.
IT MAKES YOU ARROGANT...

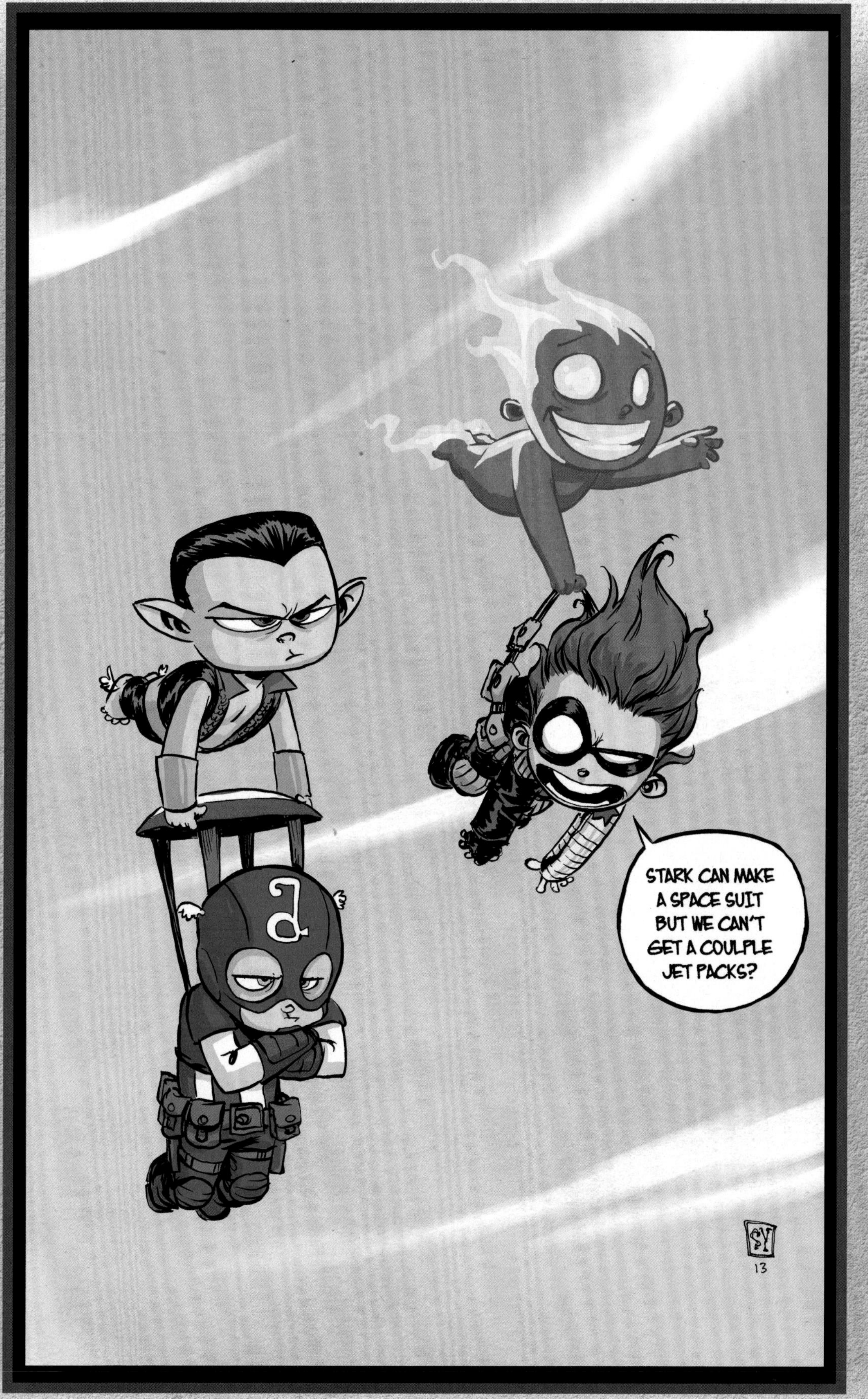
STARK CAN MAKE A SPACE SUIT BUT WE CAN'T GET A COULPLE JET PACKS?
SY 13

#1 Variant by Skottie Young

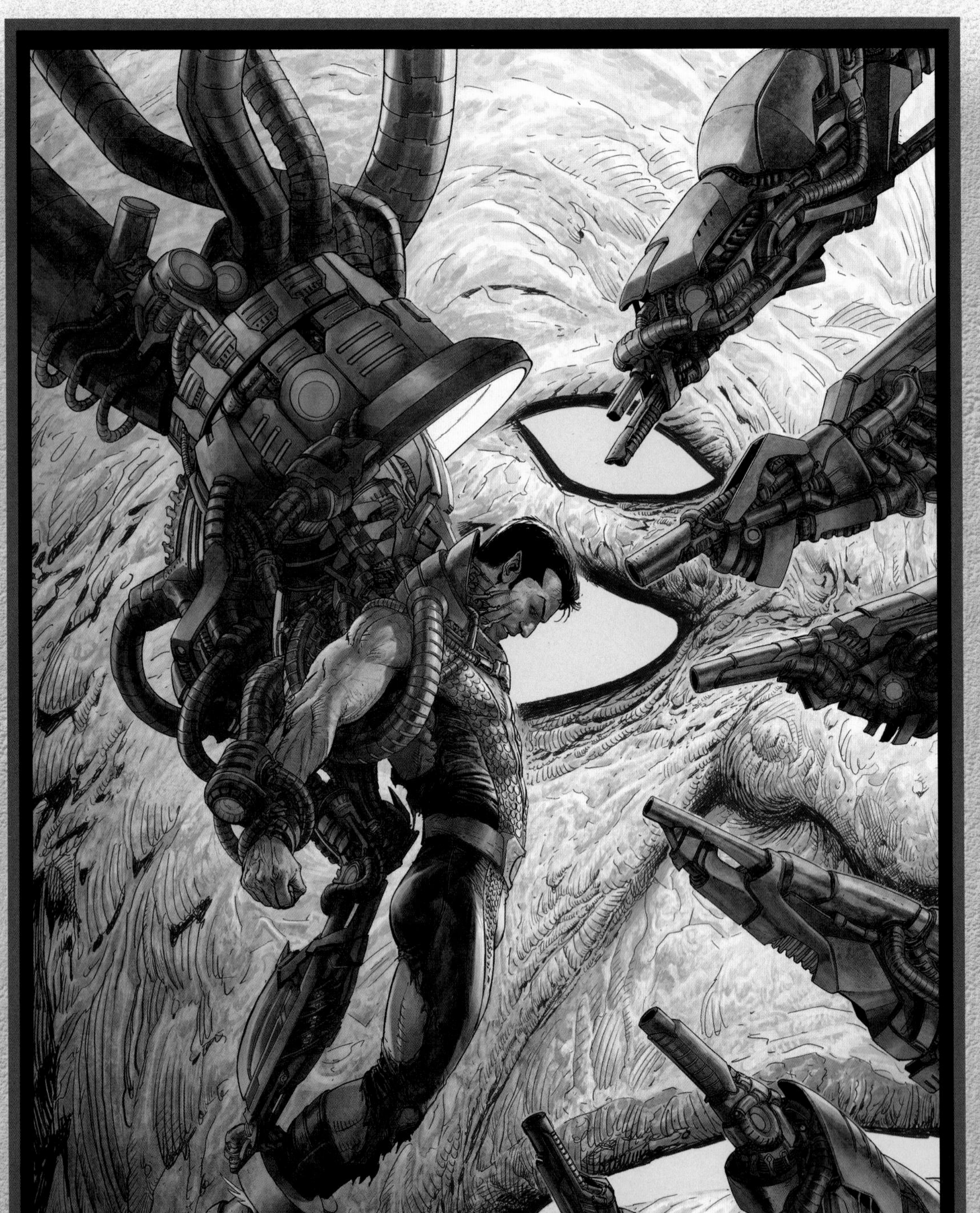

#3

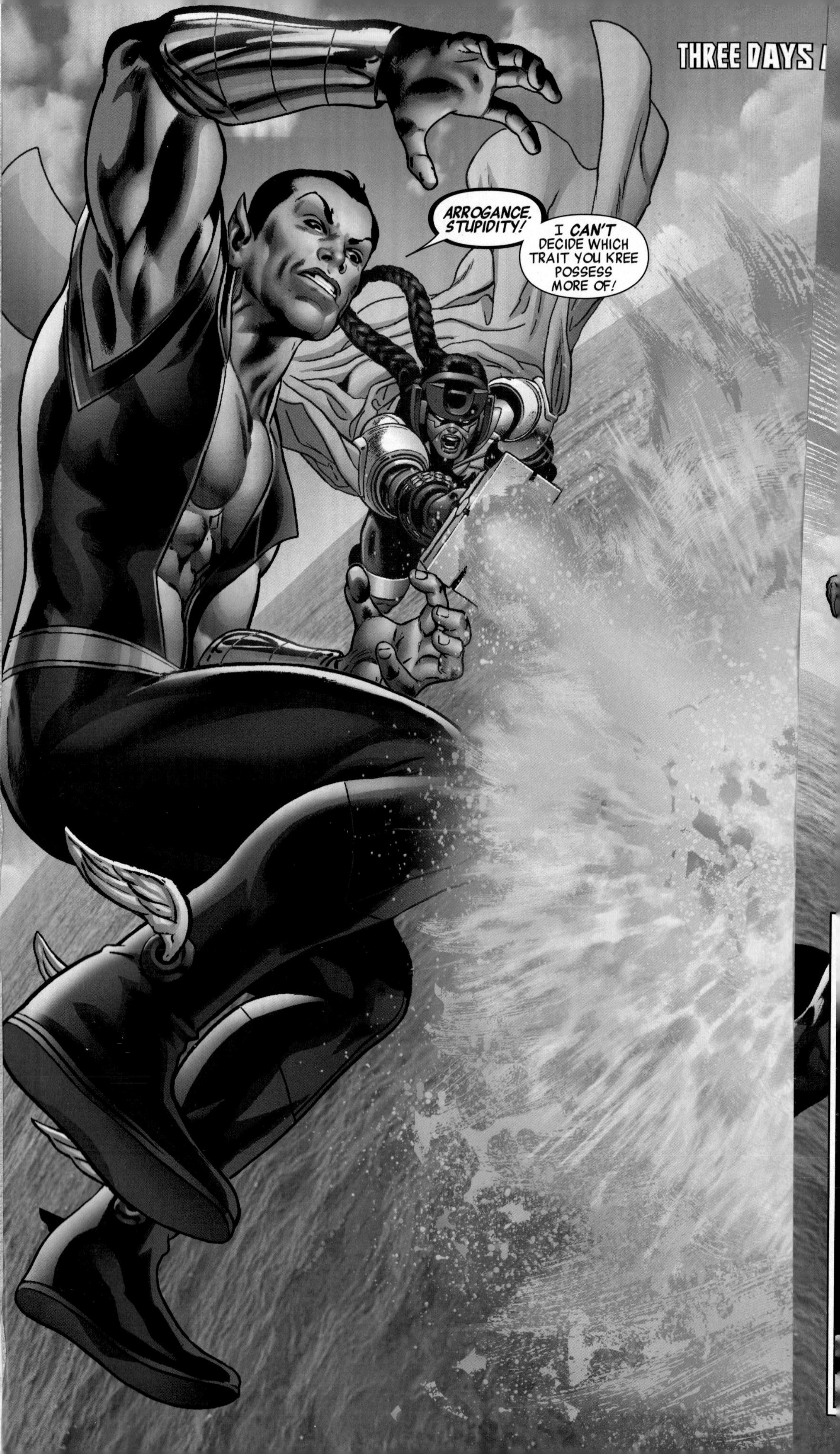

THREE DAYS
ARROGANCE. STUPIDITY!
I CAN'T DECIDE WHICH TRAIT YOU KREE POSSESS MORE OF!

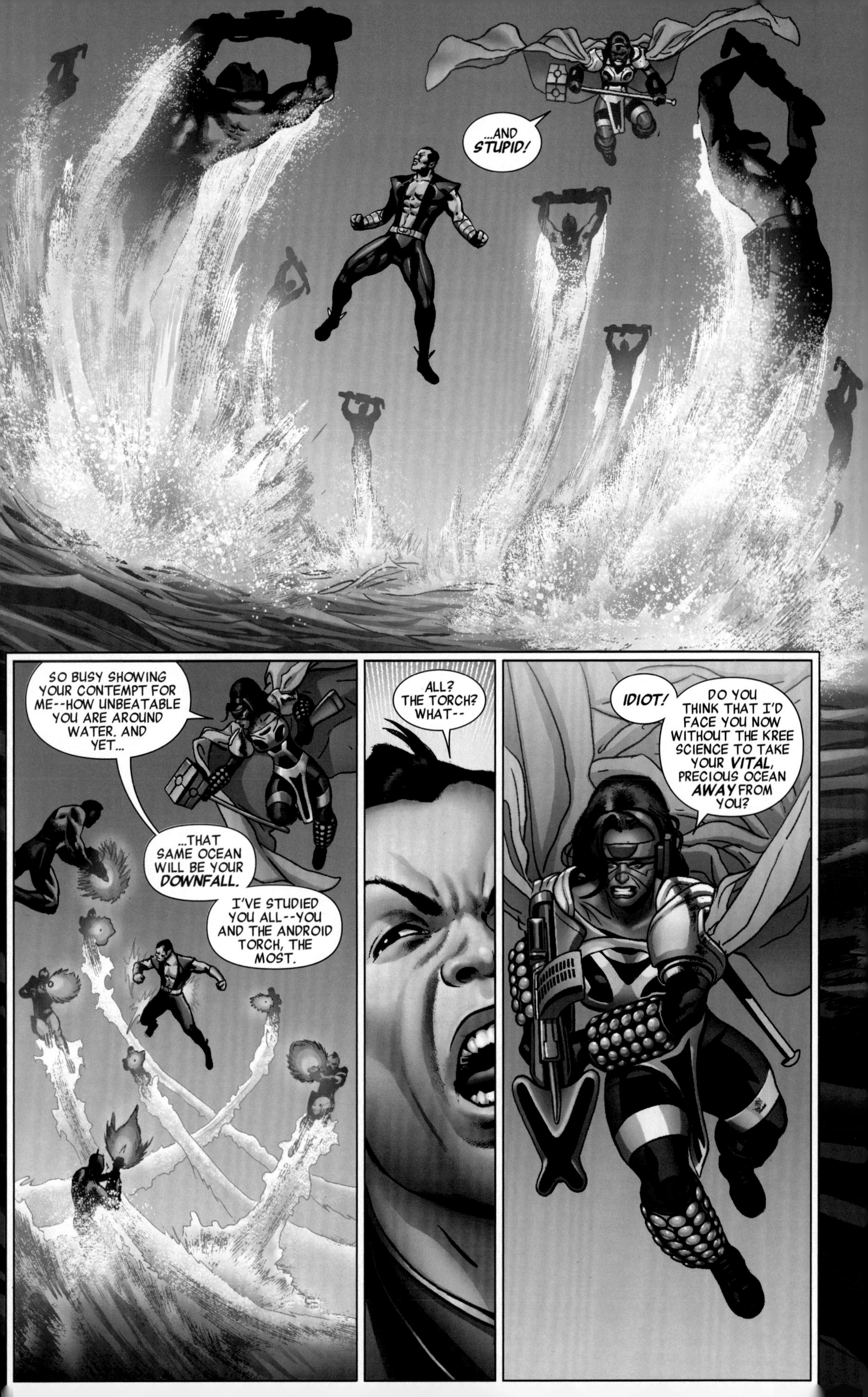
...AND STUPID!
SO BUSY SHOWING YOUR CONTEMPT FOR ME--HOW UNBEATABLE YOU ARE AROUND WATER. AND YET...
...THAT SAME OCEAN WILL BE YOUR DOWNFALL.
I'VE STUDIED YOU ALL--YOU AND THE ANDROID TORCH, THE MOST.
ALL? THE TORCH? WHAT--
IDIOT!
DO YOU THINK THAT I'D FACE YOU NOW WITHOUT THE KREE SCIENCE TO TAKE YOUR VITAL, PRECIOUS OCEAN AWAY FROM YOU?

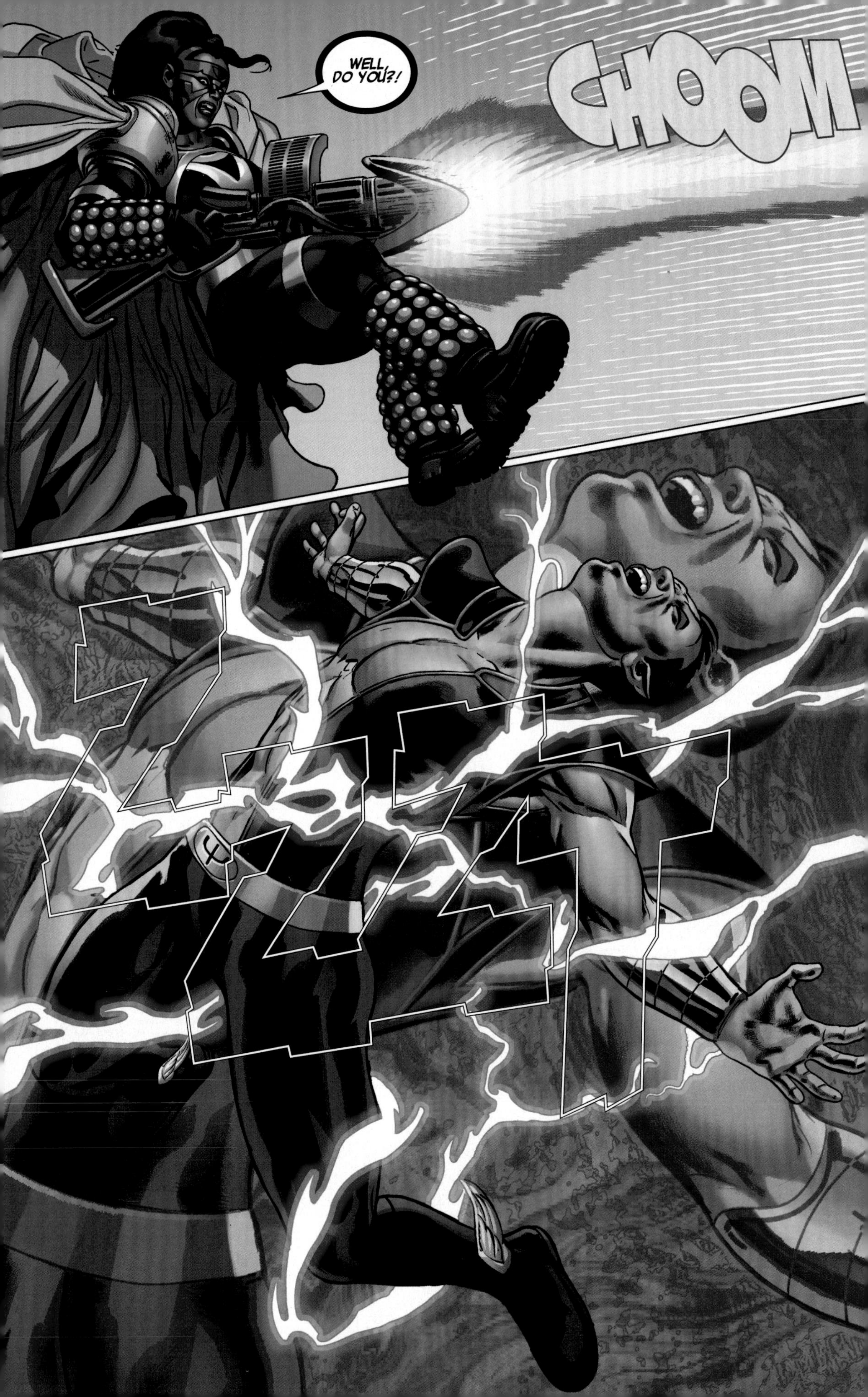
WELL, DO YOU?!
CHOOM
ZZST

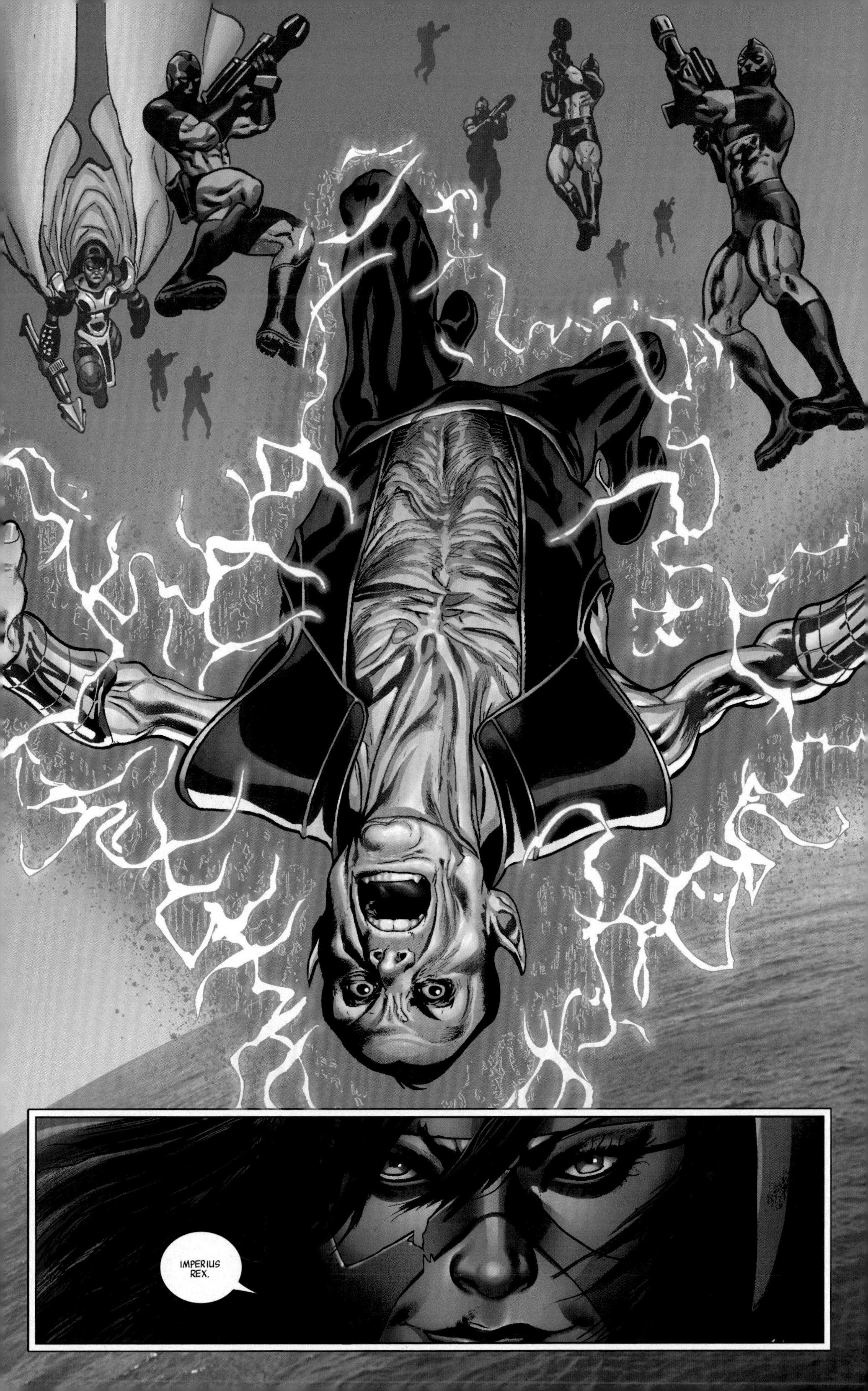
IMPERIUS REX.

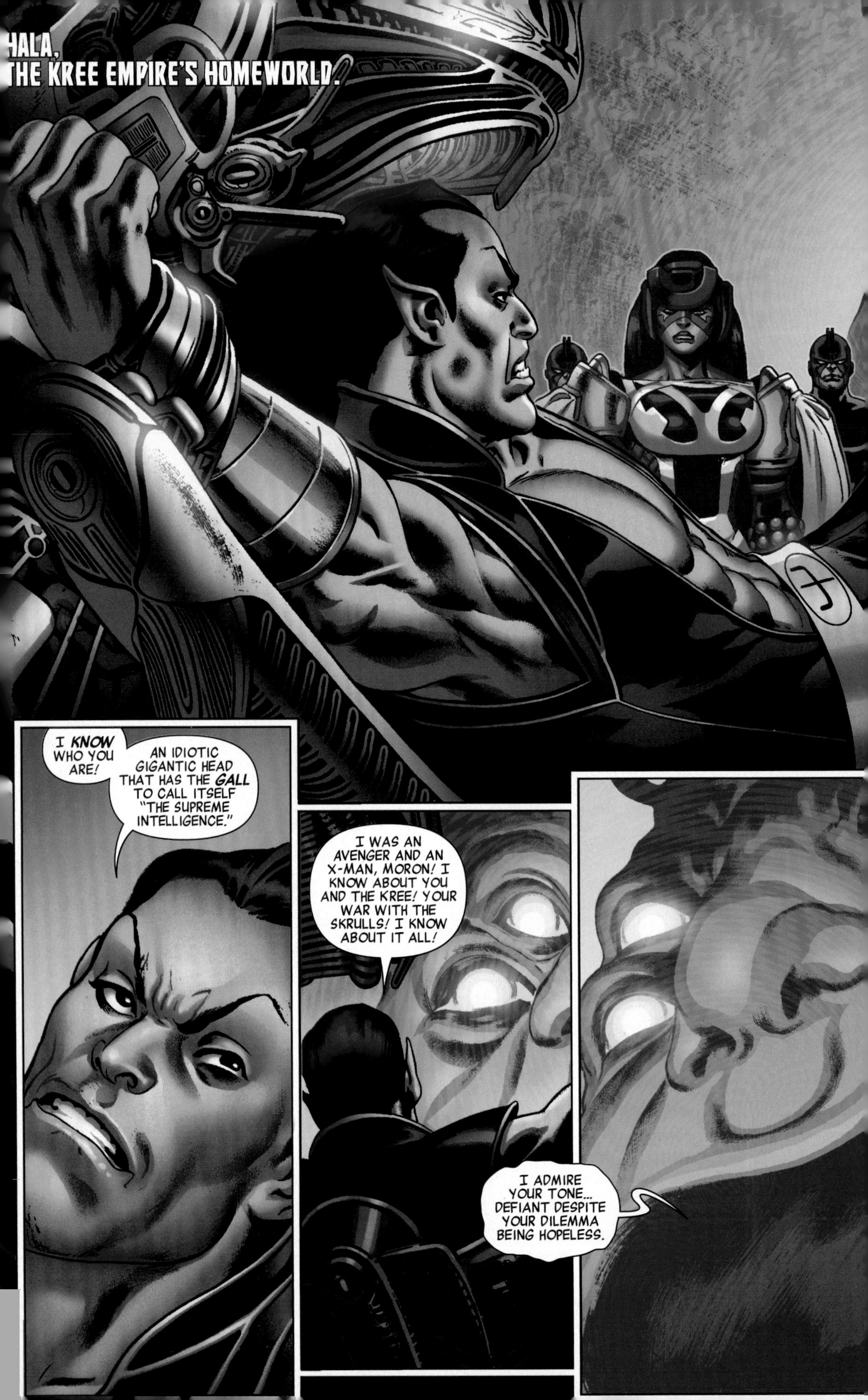
HALA,
THE KREE EMPIRE'S HOMEWORLD.
I KNOW WHO YOU ARE!
AN IDIOTIC GIGANTIC HEAD THAT HAS THE GALL TO CALL ITSELF "THE SUPREME INTELLIGENCE."
I WAS AN AVENGER AND AN X-MAN, MORON! I KNOW ABOUT YOU AND THE KREE! YOUR WAR WITH THE SKRULLS! I KNOW ABOUT IT ALL!
I ADMIRE YOUR TONE... DEFIANT DESPITE YOUR DILEMMA BEING HOPELESS.

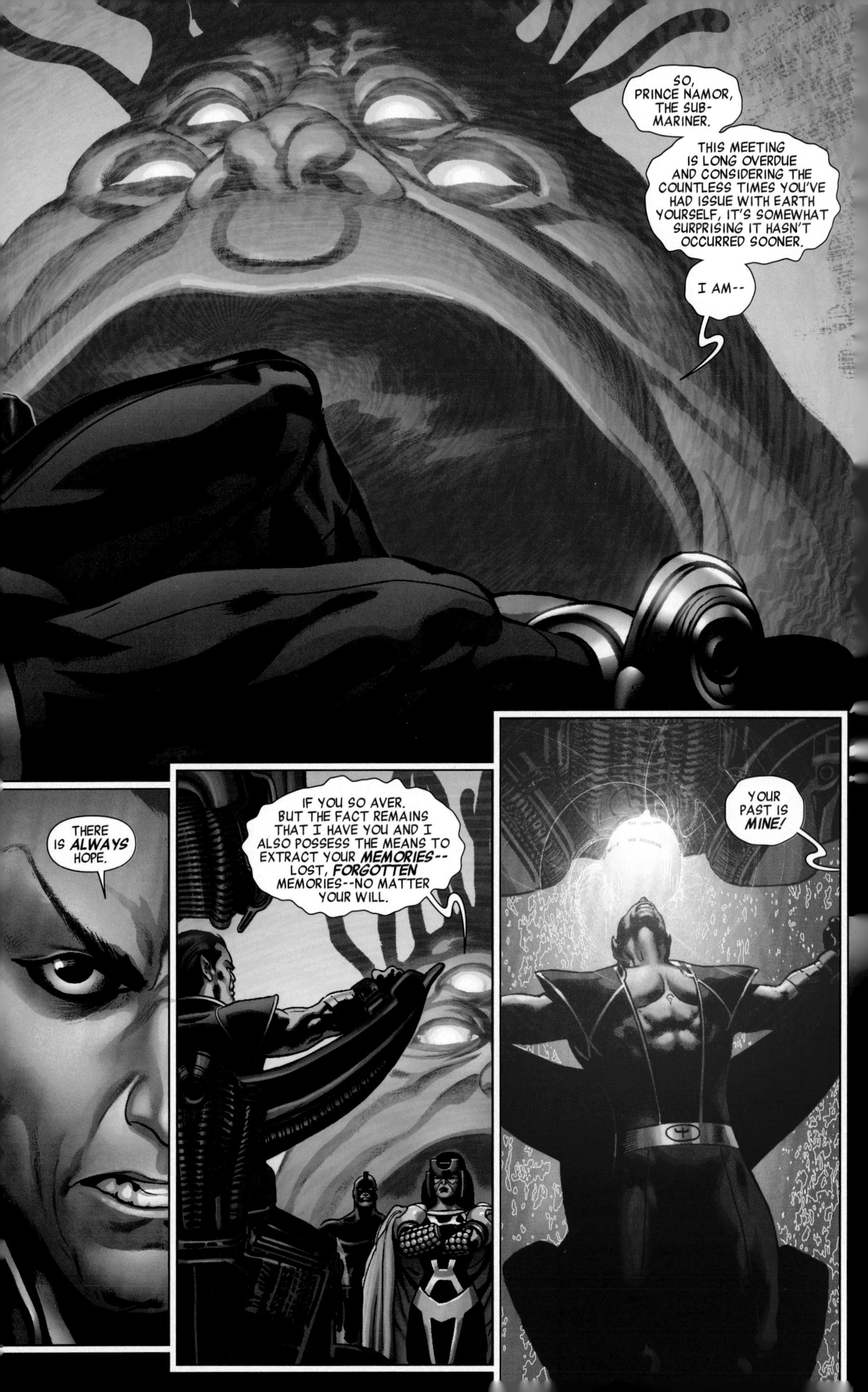

SO, PRINCE NAMOR, THE SUB-MARINER.
THIS MEETING IS LONG OVERDUE AND CONSIDERING THE COUNTLESS TIMES YOU'VE HAD ISSUE WITH EARTH YOURSELF, IT'S SOMEWHAT SURPRISING IT HASN'T OCCURRED SOONER.
I AM--
THERE IS ALWAYS HOPE.
IF YOU SO AVER. BUT THE FACT REMAINS THAT I HAVE YOU AND I ALSO POSSESS THE MEANS TO EXTRACT YOUR MEMORIES--LOST, FORGOTTEN MEMORIES--NO MATTER YOUR WILL.
YOUR PAST IS MINE!

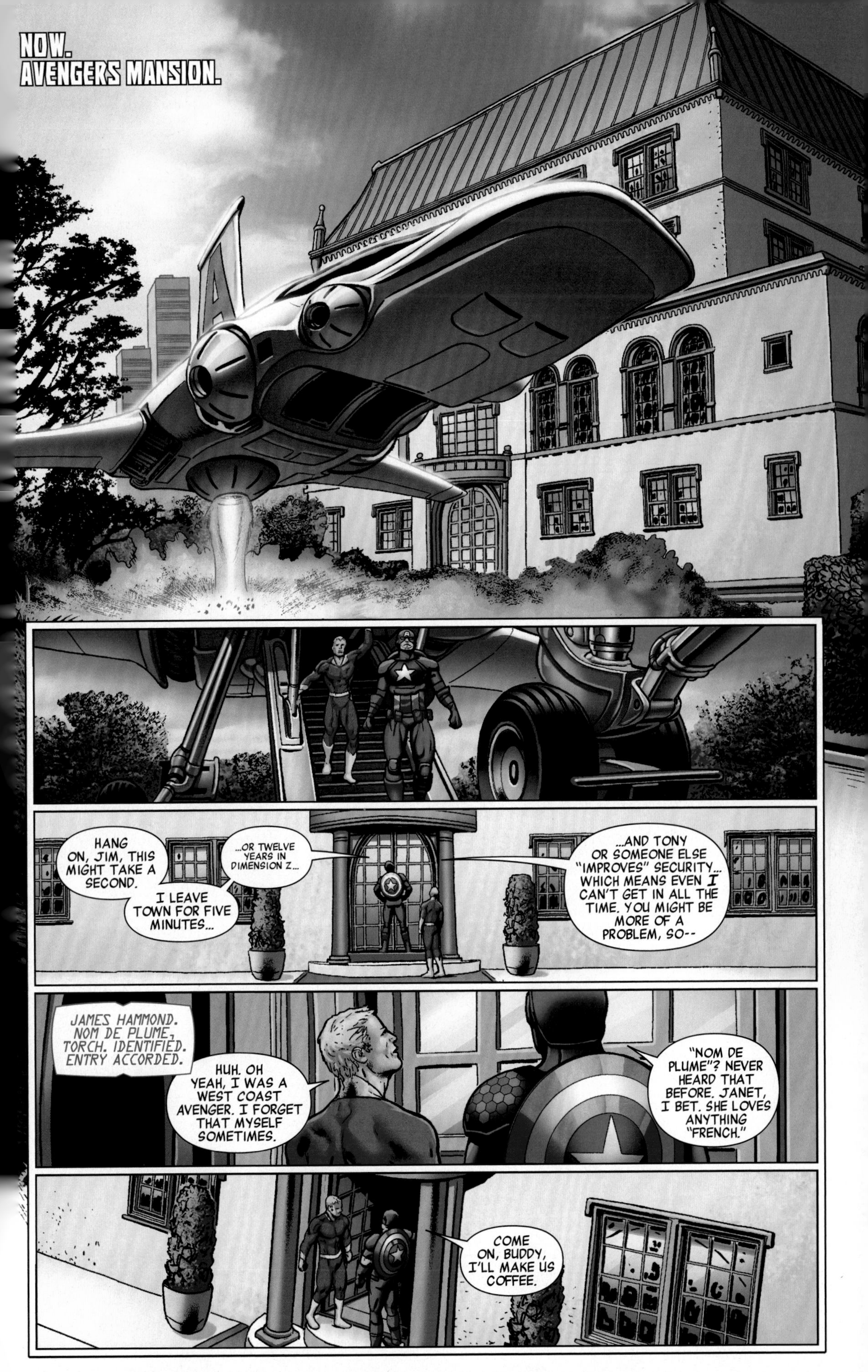
NOW.
AVENGERS MANSION.
HANG ON, JIM, THIS MIGHT TAKE A SECOND.
I LEAVE TOWN FOR FIVE MINUTES...
...OR TWELVE YEARS IN DIMENSION Z...
...AND TONY OR SOMEONE ELSE "IMPROVES" SECURITY... WHICH MEANS EVEN I CAN'T GET IN ALL THE TIME. YOU MIGHT BE MORE OF A PROBLEM, SO--
JAMES HAMMOND. NOM DE PLUME, TORCH. IDENTIFIED. ENTRY ACCORDED.
HUH. OH YEAH, I WAS A WEST COAST AVENGER. I FORGET THAT MYSELF SOMETIMES.
"NOM DE PLUME"? NEVER HEARD THAT BEFORE. JANET, I BET. SHE LOVES ANYTHING "FRENCH."
COME ON, BUDDY, I'LL MAKE US COFFEE.

SO BUCKY IS OFF UNDERTAKING THE FIRST PART OF YOUR PLAN...AND I'M HERE AT GROUND ZERO FOR SUPER HEROES...

...ADMIRING HOW EXPERTLY AMERICA'S ULTIMATE SUPER-SOLDIER MAKES AN ESPRESSO.

I KNOW YOUR PLAN AND WHY WE'RE LOOKING FOR AARKUS, THE ORIGINAL VISION...

...BUT WHY SEND BUCKY BY HIMSELF WHEN WE COULD ALL BE THERE?

WELL, FOR ONE, BUCKY IS A "DEAD MAN," AT LEAST IN THE EYES OF THE AUTHORITIES, AS YOU WELL KNOW. HE'S WANTED BY THE WORLD COURTS... HE SHOWS HIS FACE, HE'S BACK BEHIND BARS AS A CRIMINAL.

SO, NO WAY HE GETS TO SET FOOT IN AN AVENGERS HQ. YOU EVER SEEN ONE OF THESE PLACES ON LOCKDOWN?

MAKES MORE SENSE TO THROW HIM BACK INTO THE FIELD.

WHILE WE'VE BEEN HERE, I CONTACTED A COUPLE OF AVENGERS TEAMMATES WHO ALSO HAPPEN TO BE X-MEN.

SO YOU WEREN'T JUST OFF MAKING COFFEE. OKAY, THEN HOW DO THE X-MEN HELP US?

SOMETHING WENT DOWN NOT LONG AGO BETWEEN CHARLES XAVIER'S WEIRD KID DAVID AND AARKUS--DON'T HAVE THE FULL STORY, BUT IT ENDED WITH AARKUS ON ICE, COMATOSE IN ONE OF THE JEAN GREY INSTITUTE'S MANY LABS.

ULTIMATELY, HE WAS SET FREE, SO I CALLED LOGAN AND ROGUE TO SEE IF THEY KNEW WHERE HE WENT.

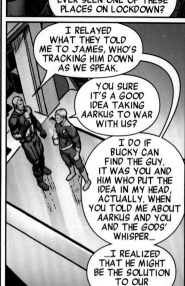

I RELAYED WHAT THEY TOLD ME TO JAMES, WHO'S TRACKING HIM DOWN AS WE SPEAK.

YOU SURE IT'S A GOOD IDEA TAKING AARKUS TO WAR WITH US?

I DO IF BUCKY CAN FIND THE GUY. IT WAS YOU AND HIM WHO PUT THE IDEA IN MY HEAD, ACTUALLY, WHEN YOU TOLD ME ABOUT AARKUS AND YOU AND THE GODS' WHISPER...

...I REALIZED THAT HE MIGHT BE THE SOLUTION TO OUR PROBLEM.

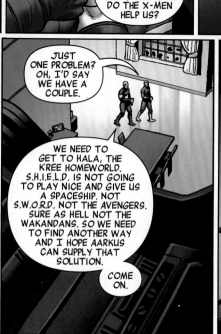

JUST ONE PROBLEM? OH, I'D SAY WE HAVE A COUPLE.

WE NEED TO GET TO HALA, THE KREE HOMEWORLD. S.H.I.E.L.D. IS NOT GOING TO PLAY NICE AND GIVE US A SPACESHIP. NOT S.W.O.R.D. NOT THE AVENGERS. SURE AS HELL NOT THE WAKANDANS. SO WE NEED TO FIND ANOTHER WAY AND I HOPE AARKUS CAN SUPPLY THAT SOLUTION.

COME ON.

WHILE WE WAIT FOR BUCK TO, HOPEFULLY, DO HIS THING, THERE'S SOMETHING ELSE THAT SHOULD GET DONE.

LEAD ON, BUDDY...

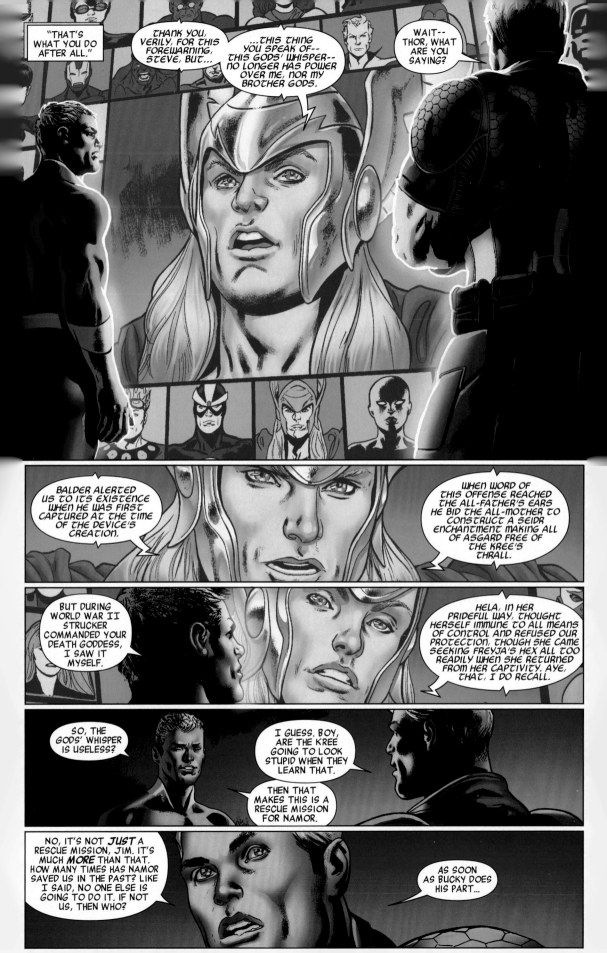

"THAT'S WHAT YOU DO AFTER ALL."

THANK YOU, VERILY, FOR THIS FOREWARNING, STEVE, BUT...

...THIS THING YOU SPEAK OF-- THIS GODS' WHISPER-- NO LONGER HAS POWER OVER ME, NOR MY BROTHER GODS.

WAIT-- THOR, WHAT ARE YOU SAYING?

BALDER ALERTED US TO ITS EXISTENCE WHEN HE WAS FIRST CAPTURED AT THE TIME OF THE DEVICE'S CREATION.

WHEN WORD OF THIS OFFENSE REACHED THE ALL-FATHER'S EARS HE BID THE ALL-MOTHER TO CONSTRUCT A SEIDR ENCHANTMENT MAKING ALL OF ASGARD FREE OF THE KREE'S THRALL.

BUT DURING WORLD WAR II STRUCKER COMMANDED YOUR DEATH GODDESS, I SAW IT MYSELF.

HELA, IN HER PRIDEFUL WAY, THOUGHT HERSELF IMMUNE TO ALL MEANS OF CONTROL AND REFUSED OUR PROTECTION, THOUGH SHE CAME SEEKING FREYJA'S HEX ALL TOO READILY WHEN SHE RETURNED FROM HER CAPTIVITY. AYE, THAT, I DO RECALL.

SO, THE GODS' WHISPER IS USELESS?

I GUESS. BOY, ARE THE KREE GOING TO LOOK STUPID WHEN THEY LEARN THAT.

THEN THAT MAKES THIS IS A RESCUE MISSION FOR NAMOR.

NO, IT'S NOT JUST A RESCUE MISSION, JIM. IT'S MUCH MORE THAN THAT. HOW MANY TIMES HAS NAMOR SAVED US IN THE PAST? LIKE I SAID, NO ONE ELSE IS GOING TO DO IT. IF NOT US, THEN WHO?

AS SOON AS BUCKY DOES HIS PART...

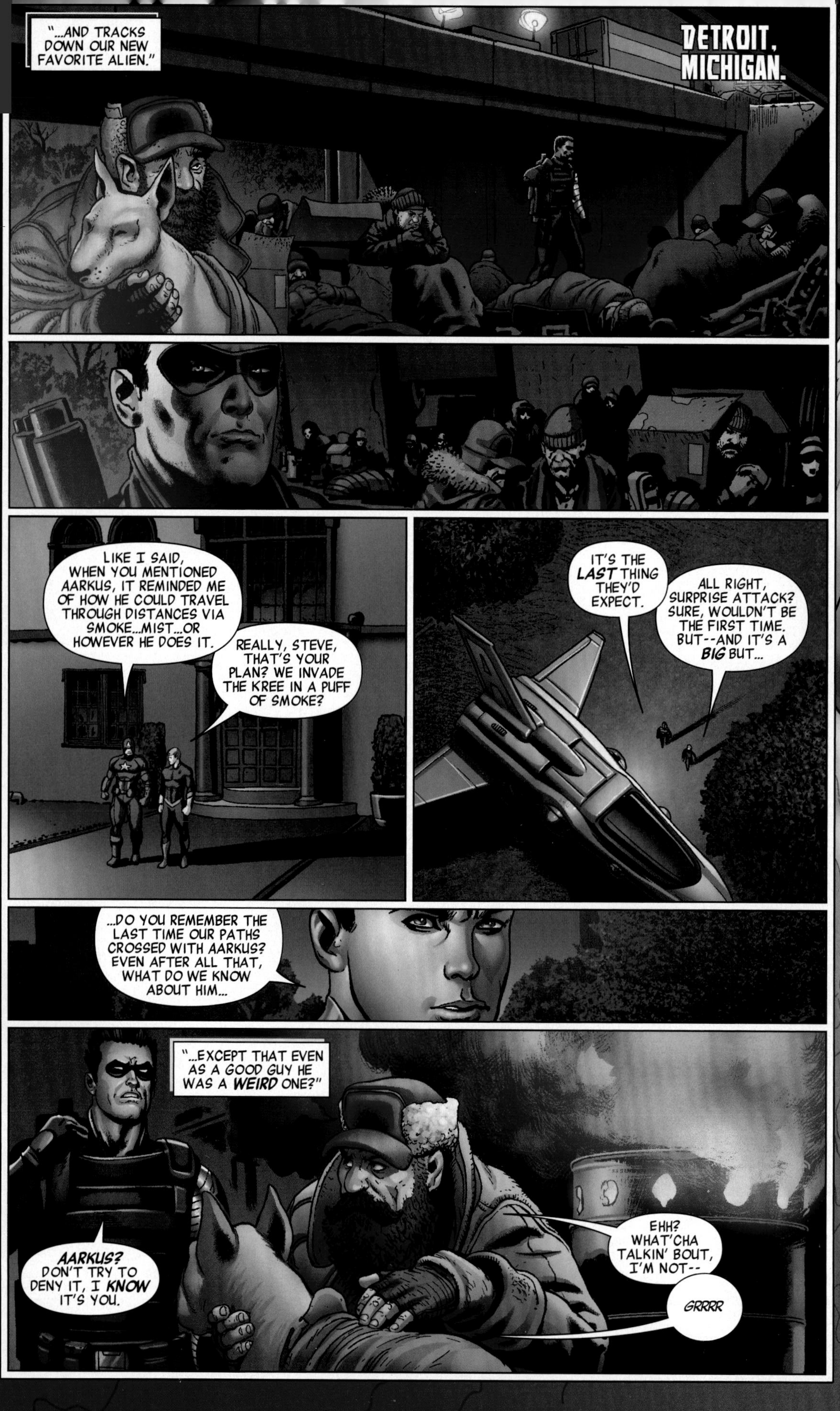
"...AND TRACKS DOWN OUR NEW FAVORITE ALIEN."
DETROIT, MICHIGAN.
LIKE I SAID, WHEN YOU MENTIONED AARKUS, IT REMINDED ME OF HOW HE COULD TRAVEL THROUGH DISTANCES VIA SMOKE...MIST...OR HOWEVER HE DOES IT.
REALLY, STEVE, THAT'S YOUR PLAN? WE INVADE THE KREE IN A PUFF OF SMOKE?
IT'S THE LAST THING THEY'D EXPECT.
ALL RIGHT, SURPRISE ATTACK? SURE, WOULDN'T BE THE FIRST TIME. BUT--AND IT'S A BIG BUT...
...DO YOU REMEMBER THE LAST TIME OUR PATHS CROSSED WITH AARKUS? EVEN AFTER ALL THAT, WHAT DO WE KNOW ABOUT HIM...
"...EXCEPT THAT EVEN AS A GOOD GUY HE WAS A WEIRD ONE?"
AARKUS? DON'T TRY TO DENY IT, I KNOW IT'S YOU.
EHH? WHAT'CHA TALKIN' BOUT, I'M NOT--
GRRRR

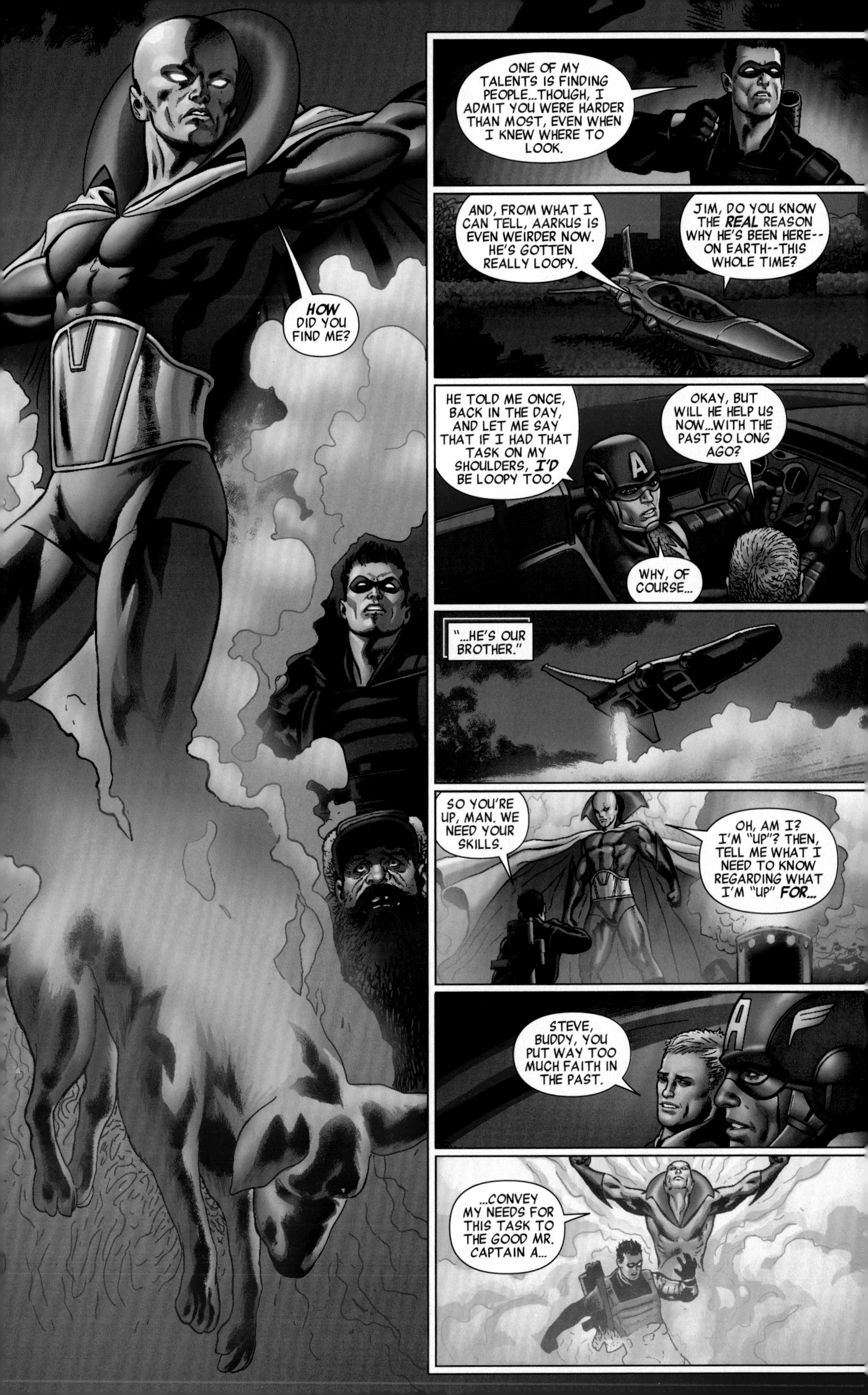
HOW DID YOU FIND ME?
ONE OF MY TALENTS IS FINDING PEOPLE...THOUGH, I ADMIT YOU WERE HARDER THAN MOST, EVEN WHEN I KNEW WHERE TO LOOK.
AND, FROM WHAT I CAN TELL, AARKUS IS EVEN WEIRDER NOW. HE'S GOTTEN REALLY LOOPY.
JIM, DO YOU KNOW THE REAL REASON WHY HE'S BEEN HERE--ON EARTH--THIS WHOLE TIME?
HE TOLD ME ONCE, BACK IN THE DAY, AND LET ME SAY THAT IF I HAD THAT TASK ON MY SHOULDERS, I'D BE LOOPY TOO.
OKAY, BUT WILL HE HELP US NOW...WITH THE PAST SO LONG AGO?
WHY, OF COURSE...
"...HE'S OUR BROTHER."
SO YOU'RE UP, MAN. WE NEED YOUR SKILLS.
OH, AM I? I'M "UP"? THEN, TELL ME WHAT I NEED TO KNOW REGARDING WHAT I'M "UP" FOR...
STEVE, BUDDY, YOU PUT WAY TOO MUCH FAITH IN THE PAST.
...CONVEY MY NEEDS FOR THIS TASK TO THE GOOD MR. CAPTAIN A...

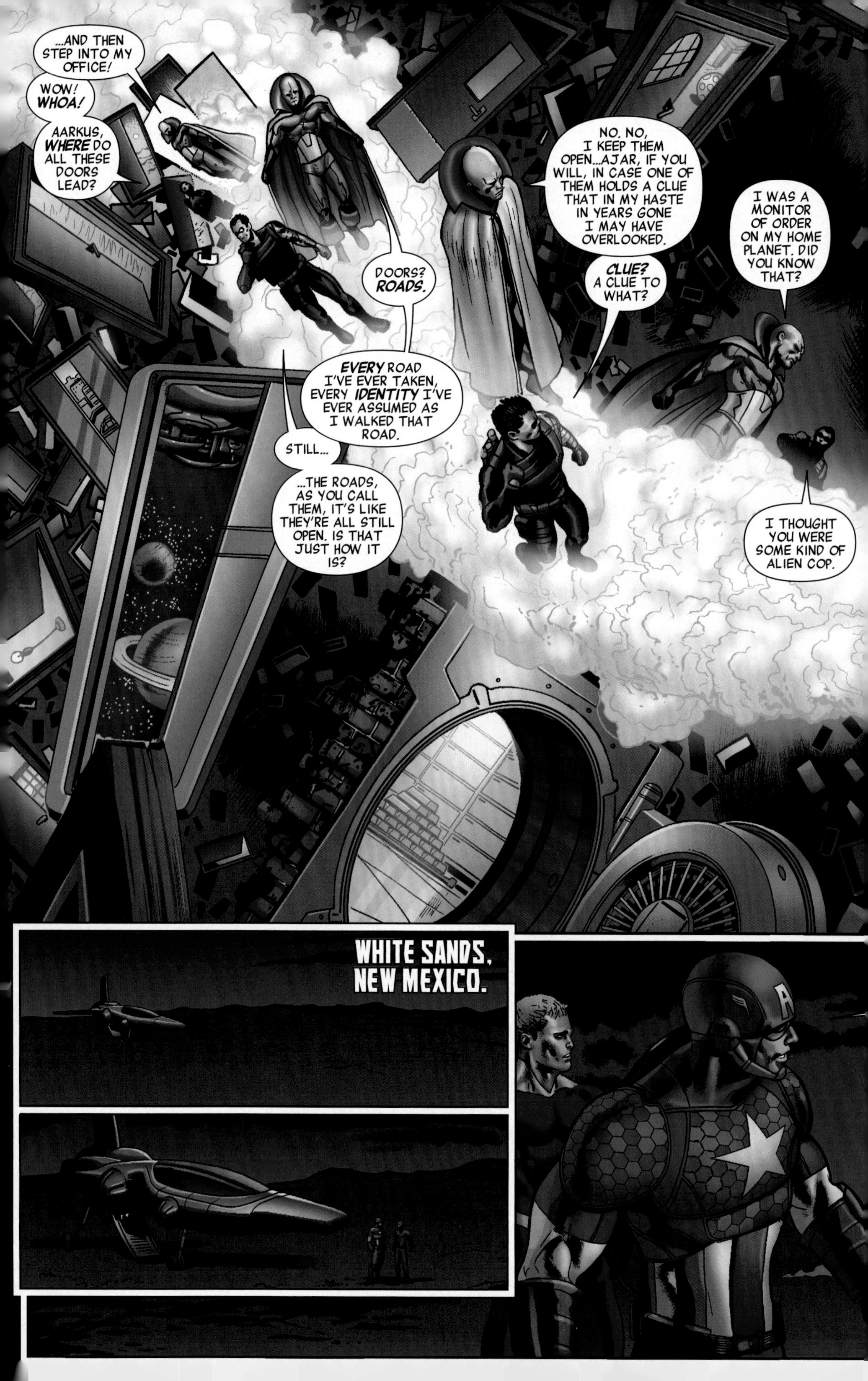
...AND THEN STEP INTO MY OFFICE!
WOW! WHOA!
AARKUS, WHERE DO ALL THESE DOORS LEAD?
DOORS? ROADS.
EVERY ROAD I'VE EVER TAKEN, EVERY IDENTITY I'VE EVER ASSUMED AS I WALKED THAT ROAD.
STILL...
...THE ROADS, AS YOU CALL THEM, IT'S LIKE THEY'RE ALL STILL OPEN. IS THAT JUST HOW IT IS?
NO. NO, I KEEP THEM OPEN...AJAR, IF YOU WILL, IN CASE ONE OF THEM HOLDS A CLUE THAT IN MY HASTE IN YEARS GONE I MAY HAVE OVERLOOKED.
CLUE? A CLUE TO WHAT?
I WAS A MONITOR OF ORDER ON MY HOME PLANET. DID YOU KNOW THAT?
I THOUGHT YOU WERE SOME KIND OF ALIEN COP.
WHITE SANDS, NEW MEXICO.

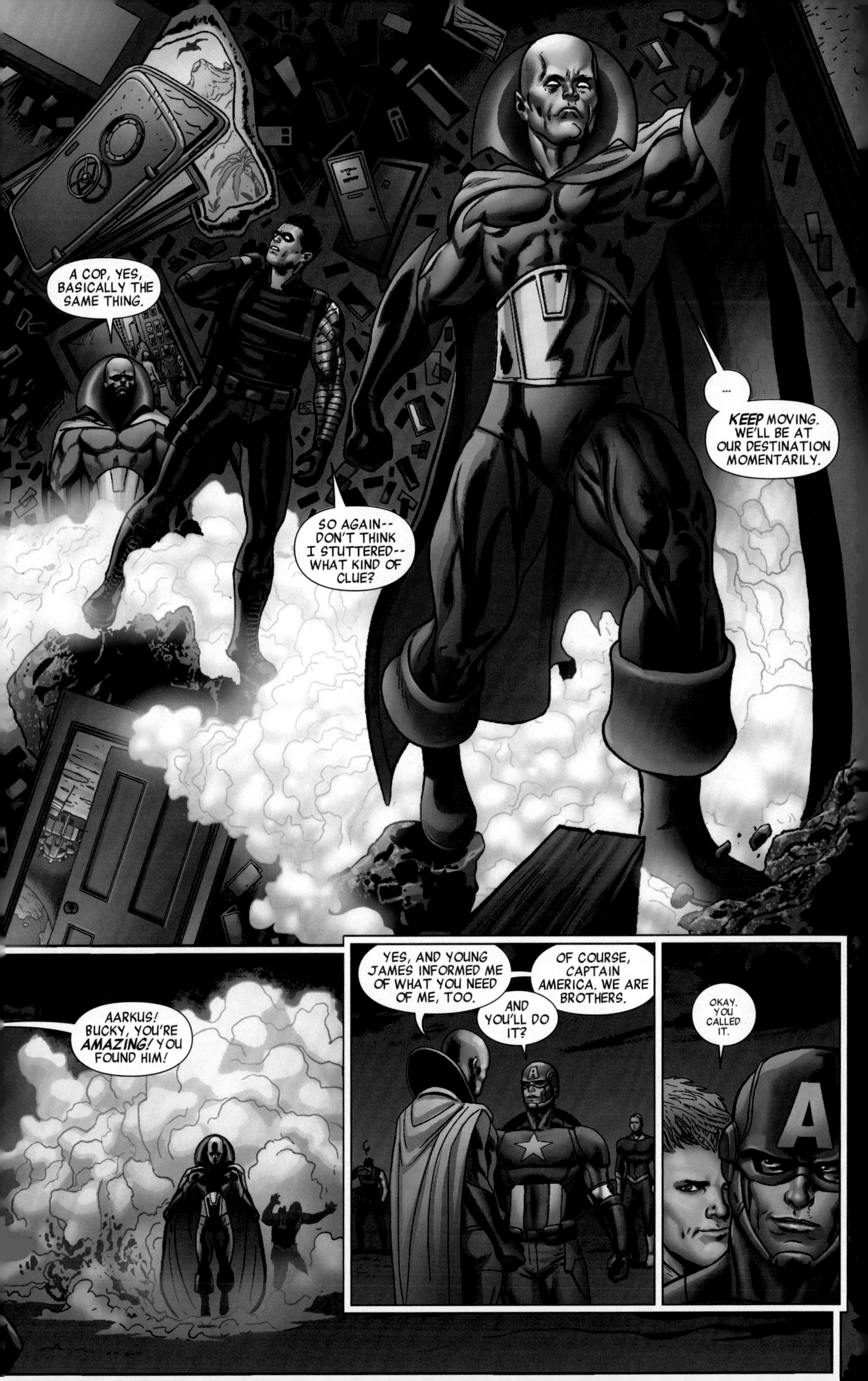
A COP, YES, BASICALLY THE SAME THING.
SO AGAIN-- DON'T THINK I STUTTERED-- WHAT KIND OF CLUE?
...
KEEP MOVING. WE'LL BE AT OUR DESTINATION MOMENTARILY.
AARKUS! BUCKY, YOU'RE AMAZING! YOU FOUND HIM!
YES, AND YOUNG JAMES INFORMED ME OF WHAT YOU NEED OF ME, TOO.
AND YOU'LL DO IT?
OF COURSE, CAPTAIN AMERICA. WE ARE BROTHERS.
OKAY. YOU CALLED IT.

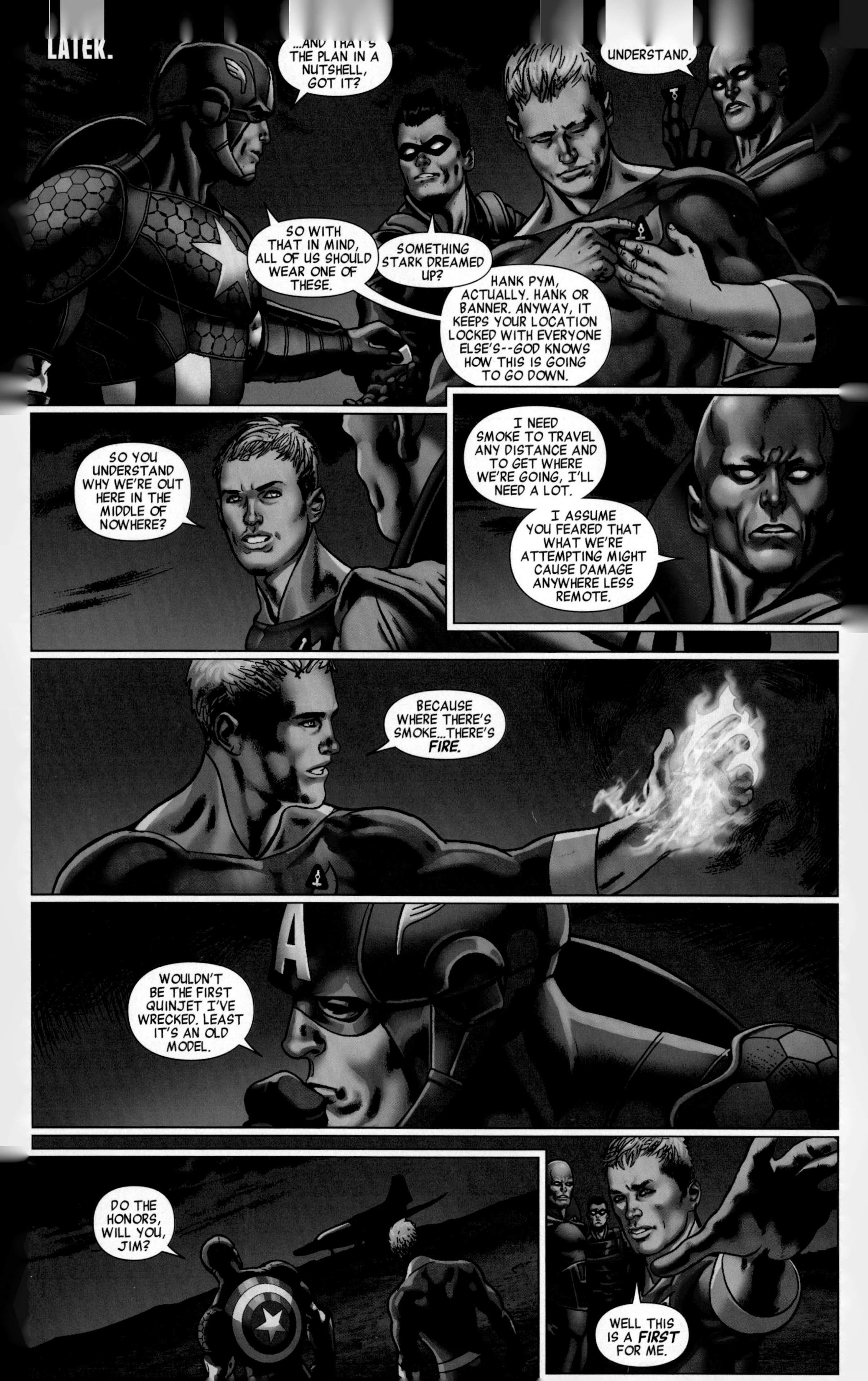
LATER.
...AND THAT'S THE PLAN IN A NUTSHELL, GOT IT?
UNDERSTAND.
SO WITH THAT IN MIND, ALL OF US SHOULD WEAR ONE OF THESE.
SOMETHING STARK DREAMED UP?
HANK PYM, ACTUALLY. HANK OR BANNER. ANYWAY, IT KEEPS YOUR LOCATION LOCKED WITH EVERYONE ELSE'S--GOD KNOWS HOW THIS IS GOING TO GO DOWN.
SO YOU UNDERSTAND WHY WE'RE OUT HERE IN THE MIDDLE OF NOWHERE?
I NEED SMOKE TO TRAVEL ANY DISTANCE AND TO GET WHERE WE'RE GOING, I'LL NEED A LOT.
I ASSUME YOU FEARED THAT WHAT WE'RE ATTEMPTING MIGHT CAUSE DAMAGE ANYWHERE LESS REMOTE.
BECAUSE WHERE THERE'S SMOKE...THERE'S FIRE.
WOULDN'T BE THE FIRST QUINJET I'VE WRECKED. LEAST IT'S AN OLD MODEL.
DO THE HONORS, WILL YOU, JIM?
WELL THIS IS A FIRST FOR ME.

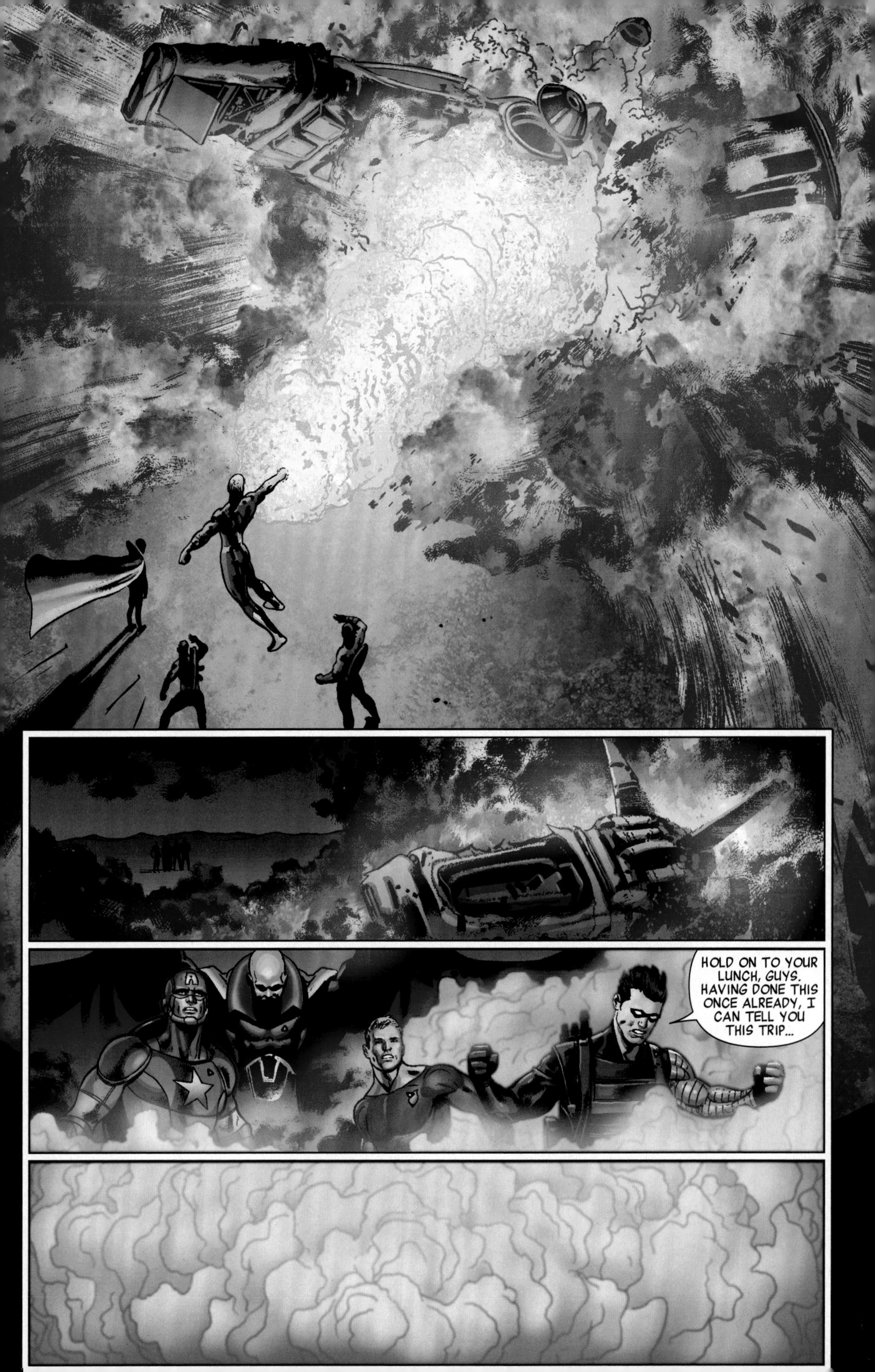
HOLD ON TO YOUR LUNCH, GUYS. HAVING DONE THIS ONCE ALREADY, I CAN TELL YOU THIS TRIP...

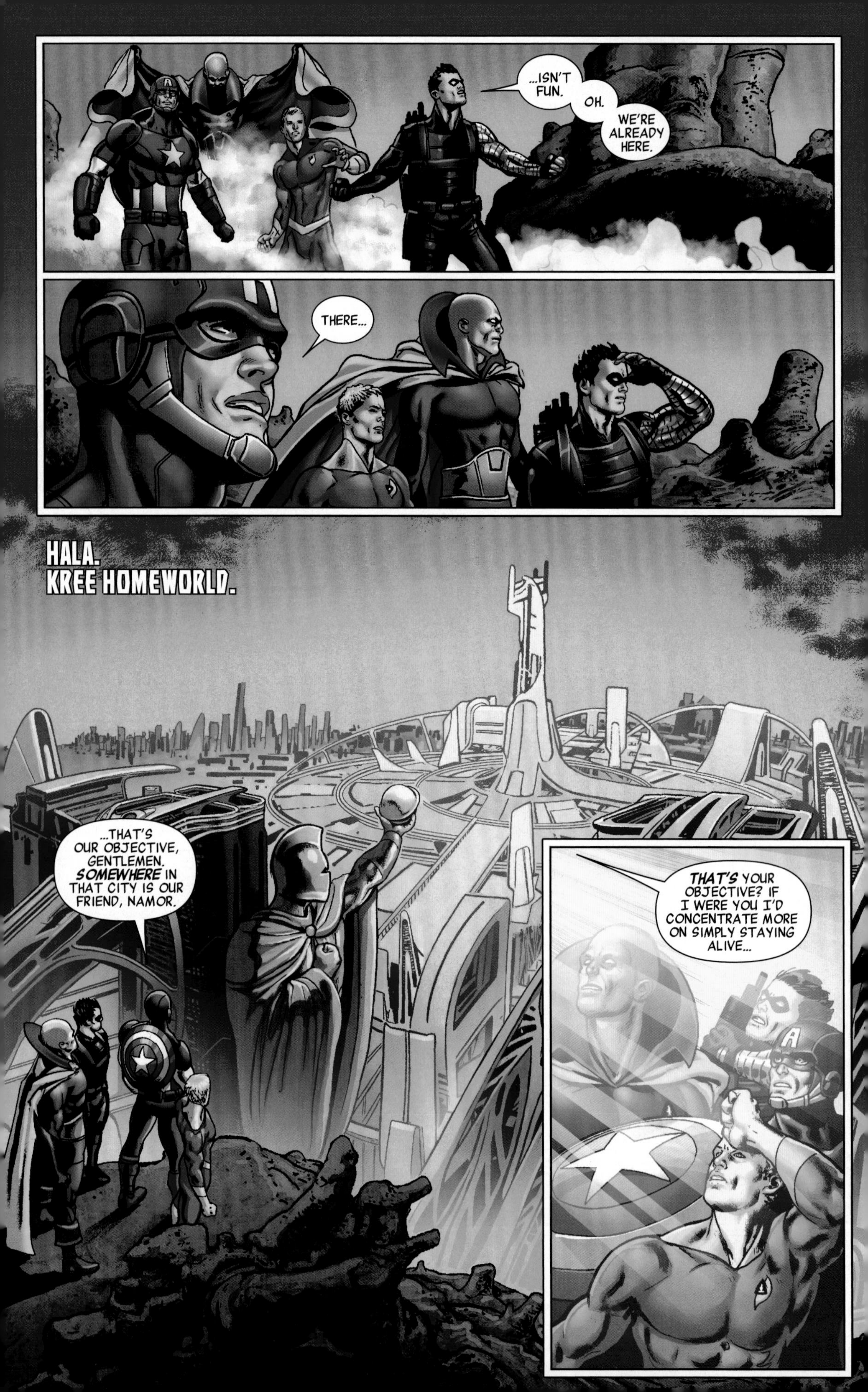

...ISN'T FUN.
OH.
WE'RE ALREADY HERE.
THERE...
HALA. KREE HOMEWORLD.
...THAT'S OUR OBJECTIVE, GENTLEMEN. SOMEWHERE IN THAT CITY IS OUR FRIEND, NAMOR.
THAT'S YOUR OBJECTIVE? IF I WERE YOU I'D CONCENTRATE MORE ON SIMPLY STAYING ALIVE...

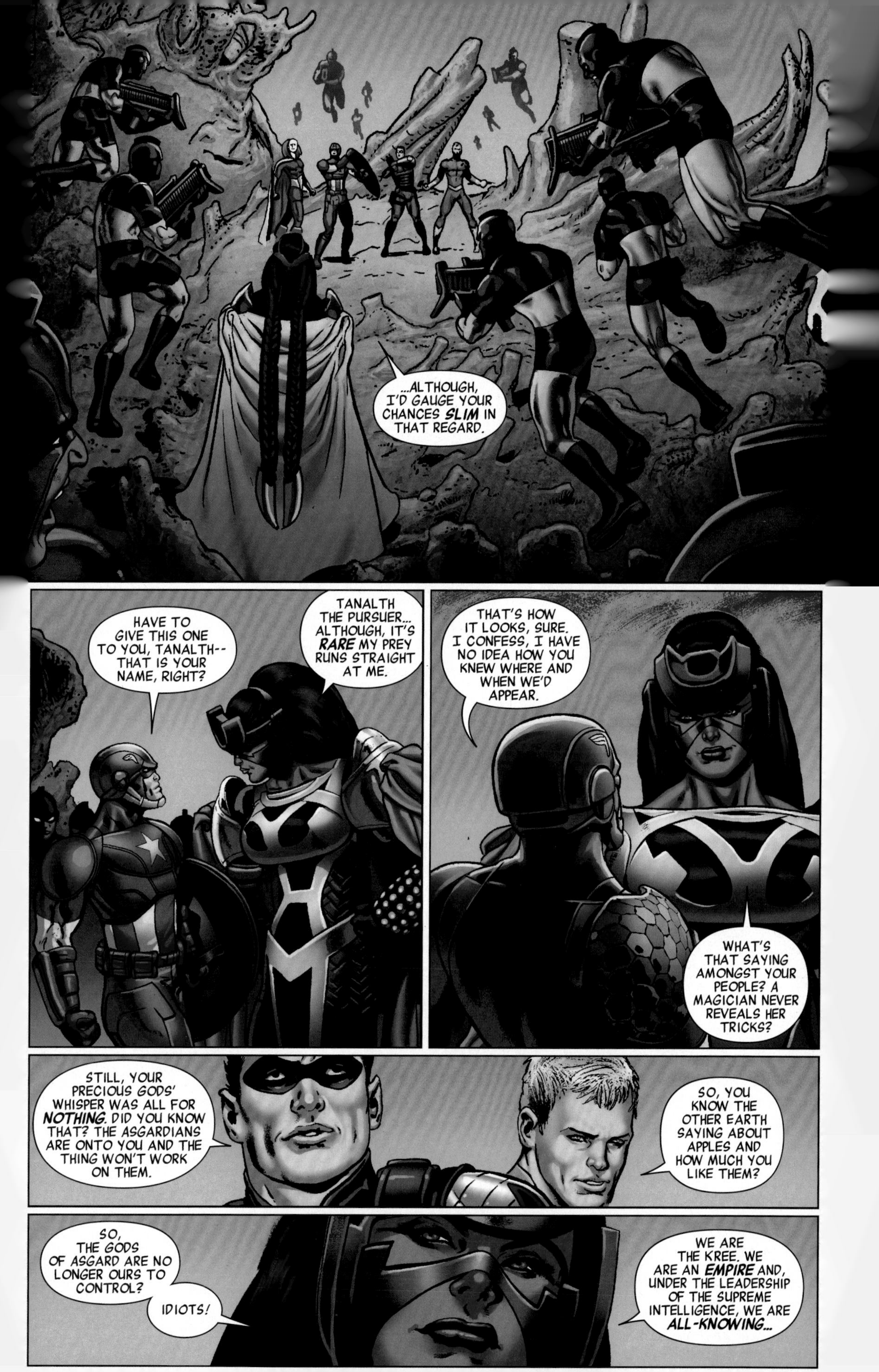
...ALTHOUGH, I'D GAUGE YOUR CHANCES SLIM IN THAT REGARD.
HAVE TO GIVE THIS ONE TO YOU, TANALTH-- THAT IS YOUR NAME, RIGHT?
TANALTH THE PURSUER... ALTHOUGH, IT'S RARE MY PREY RUNS STRAIGHT AT ME.
THAT'S HOW IT LOOKS, SURE. I CONFESS, I HAVE NO IDEA HOW YOU KNEW WHERE AND WHEN WE'D APPEAR.
WHAT'S THAT SAYING AMONGST YOUR PEOPLE? A MAGICIAN NEVER REVEALS HER TRICKS?
STILL, YOUR PRECIOUS GODS' WHISPER WAS ALL FOR NOTHING. DID YOU KNOW THAT? THE ASGARDIANS ARE ONTO YOU AND THE THING WON'T WORK ON THEM.
SO, YOU KNOW THE OTHER EARTH SAYING ABOUT APPLES AND HOW MUCH YOU LIKE THEM?
SO, THE GODS OF ASGARD ARE NO LONGER OURS TO CONTROL?
IDIOTS!
WE ARE THE KREE. WE ARE AN EMPIRE AND, UNDER THE LEADERSHIP OF THE SUPREME INTELLIGENCE, WE ARE ALL-KNOWING...

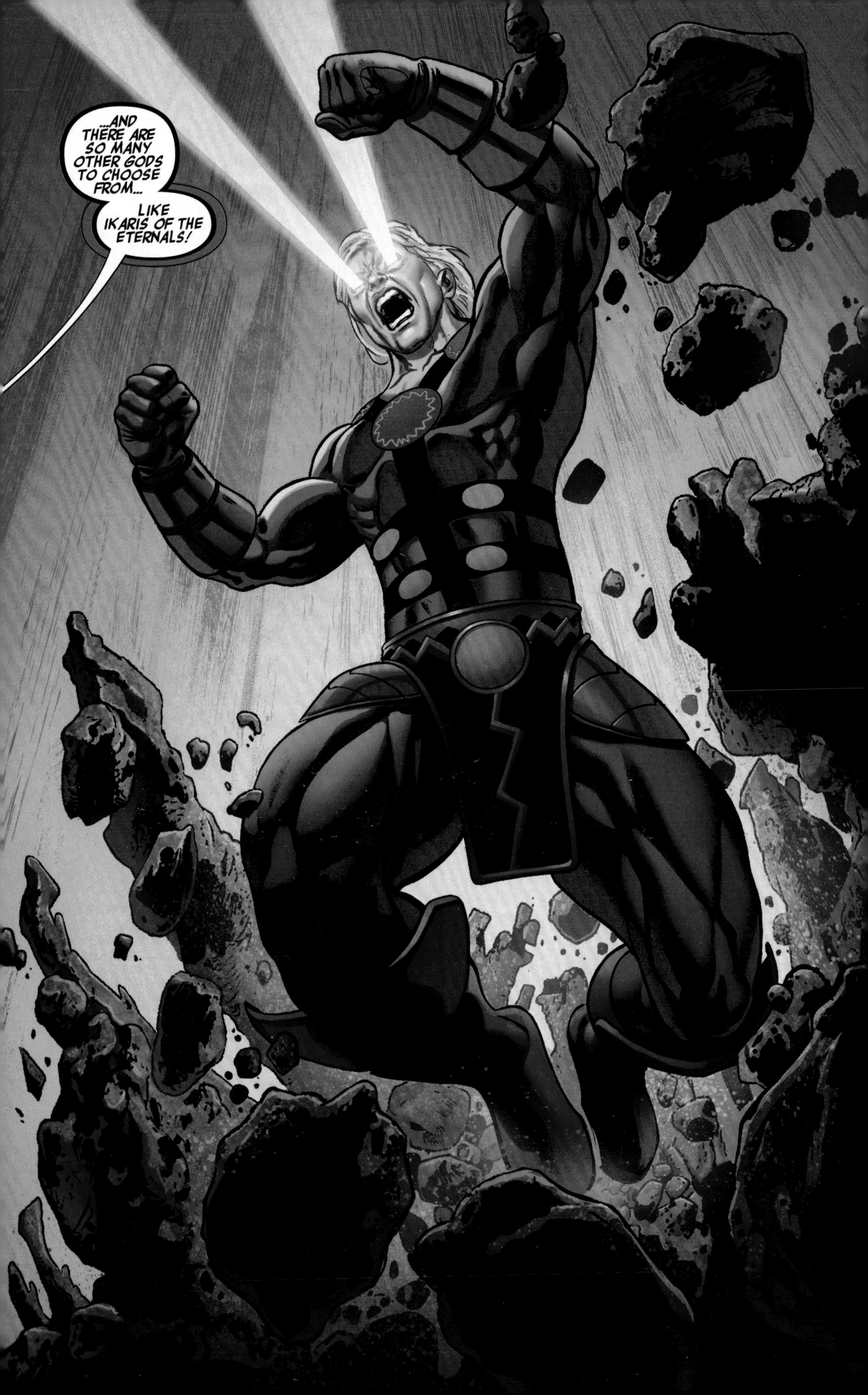
...AND THERE ARE SO MANY OTHER GODS TO CHOOSE FROM...
LIKE IKARIS OF THE ETERNALS!

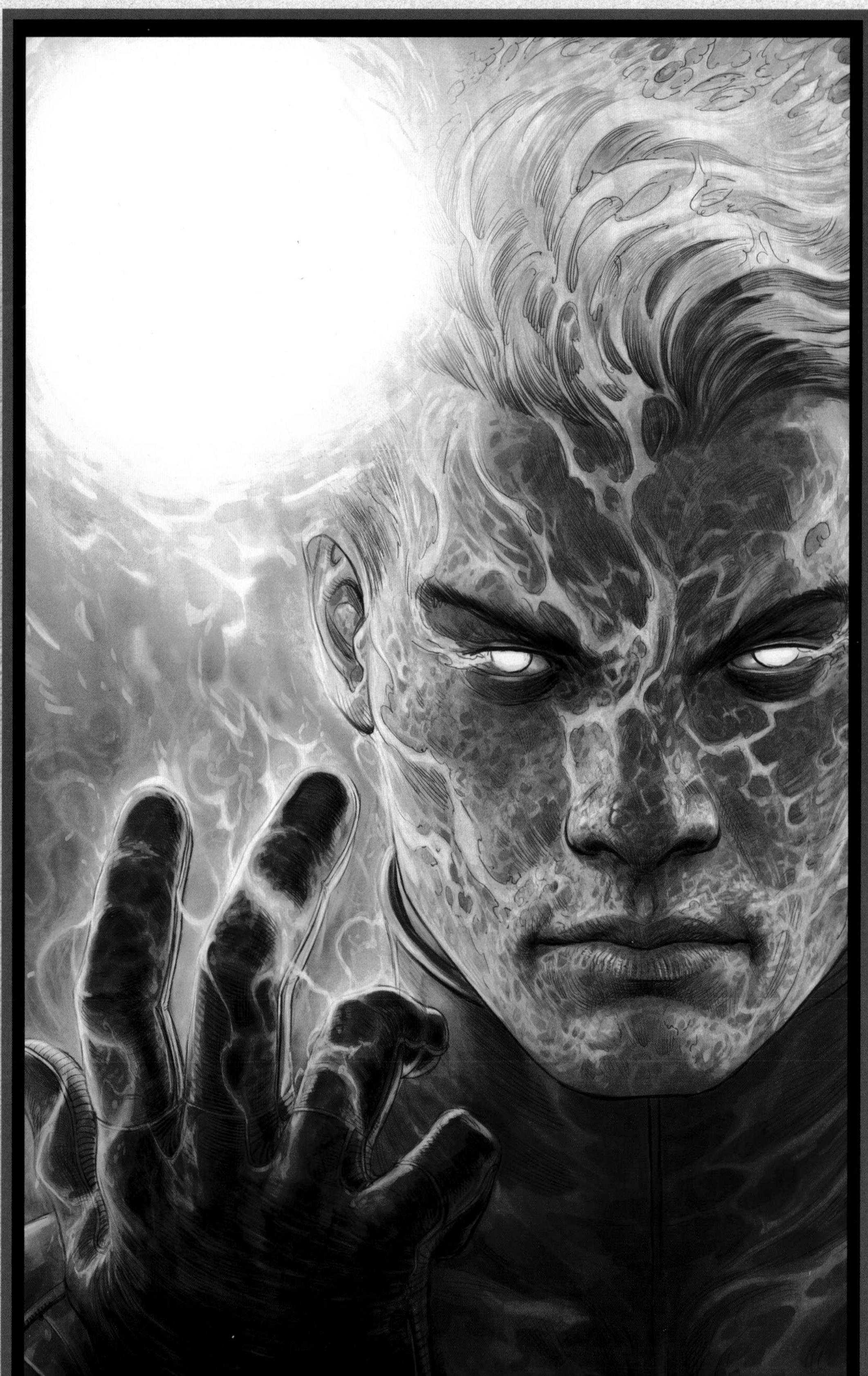

#4

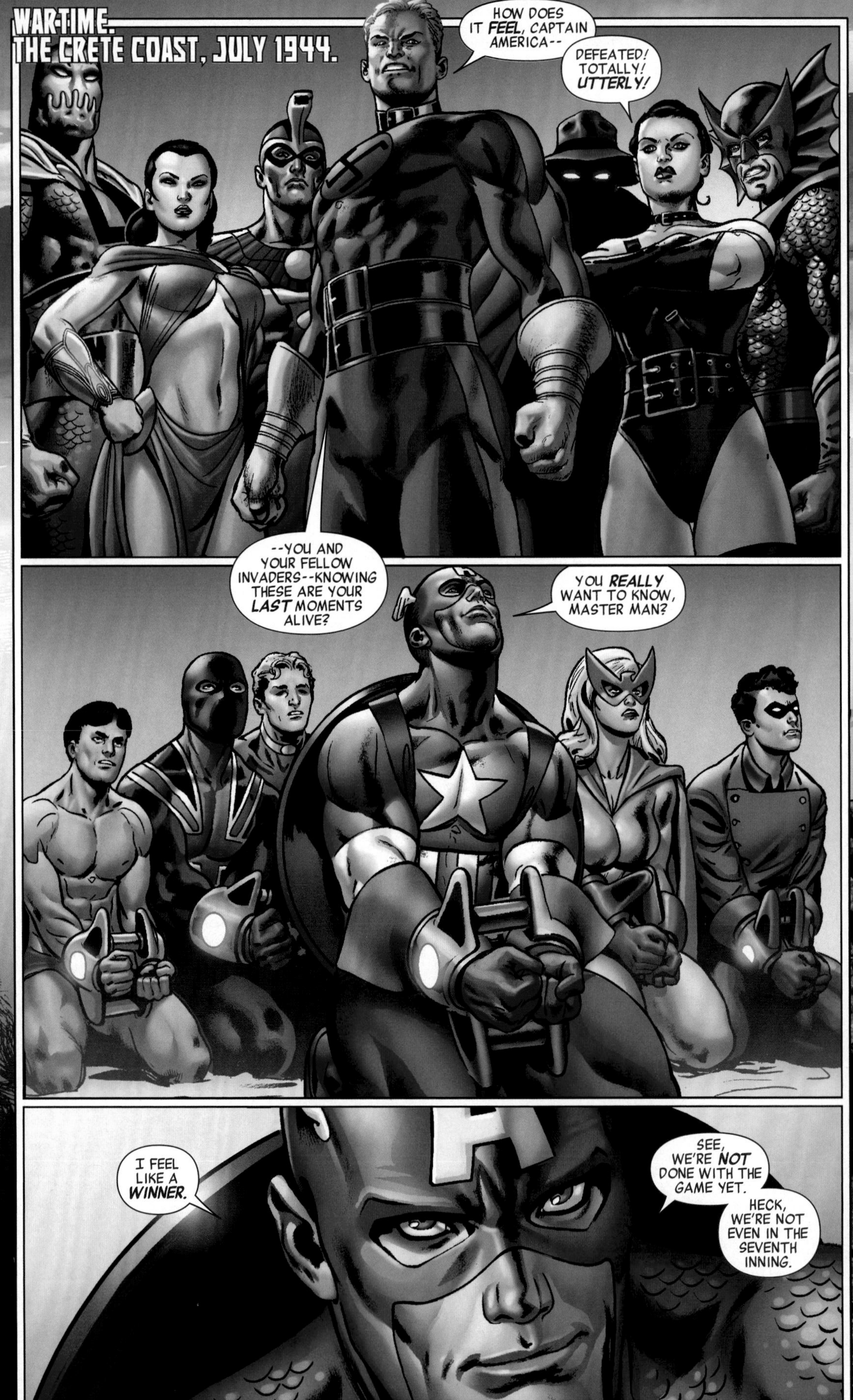
WAR-TIME.
THE CRETE COAST, JULY 1944.
HOW DOES IT FEEL, CAPTAIN AMERICA--
DEFEATED! TOTALLY! UTTERLY!
--YOU AND YOUR FELLOW INVADERS--KNOWING THESE ARE YOUR LAST MOMENTS ALIVE?
YOU REALLY WANT TO KNOW, MASTER MAN?
I FEEL LIKE A WINNER.
SEE, WE'RE NOT DONE WITH THE GAME YET.
HECK, WE'RE NOT EVEN IN THE SEVENTH INNING.

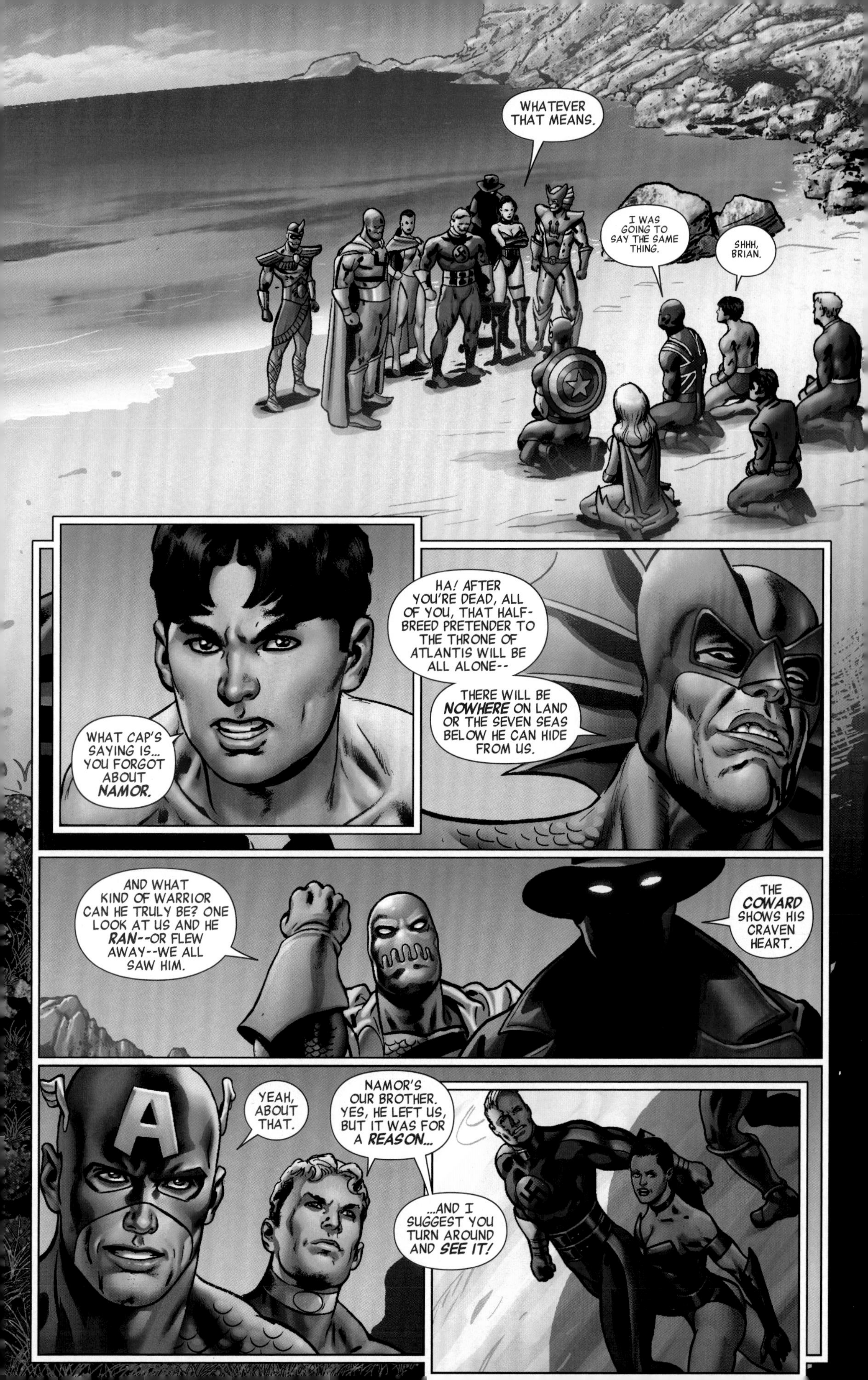
WHATEVER THAT MEANS.
I WAS GOING TO SAY THE SAME THING.
SHHH, BRIAN.
WHAT CAP'S SAYING IS... YOU FORGOT ABOUT NAMOR.
HA! AFTER YOU'RE DEAD, ALL OF YOU, THAT HALF-BREED PRETENDER TO THE THRONE OF ATLANTIS WILL BE ALL ALONE--
THERE WILL BE NOWHERE ON LAND OR THE SEVEN SEAS BELOW HE CAN HIDE FROM US.
AND WHAT KIND OF WARRIOR CAN HE TRULY BE? ONE LOOK AT US AND HE RAN--OR FLEW AWAY--WE ALL SAW HIM.
THE COWARD SHOWS HIS CRAVEN HEART.
YEAH, ABOUT THAT.
NAMOR'S OUR BROTHER. YES, HE LEFT US, BUT IT WAS FOR A REASON...
...AND I SUGGEST YOU TURN AROUND AND SEE IT!

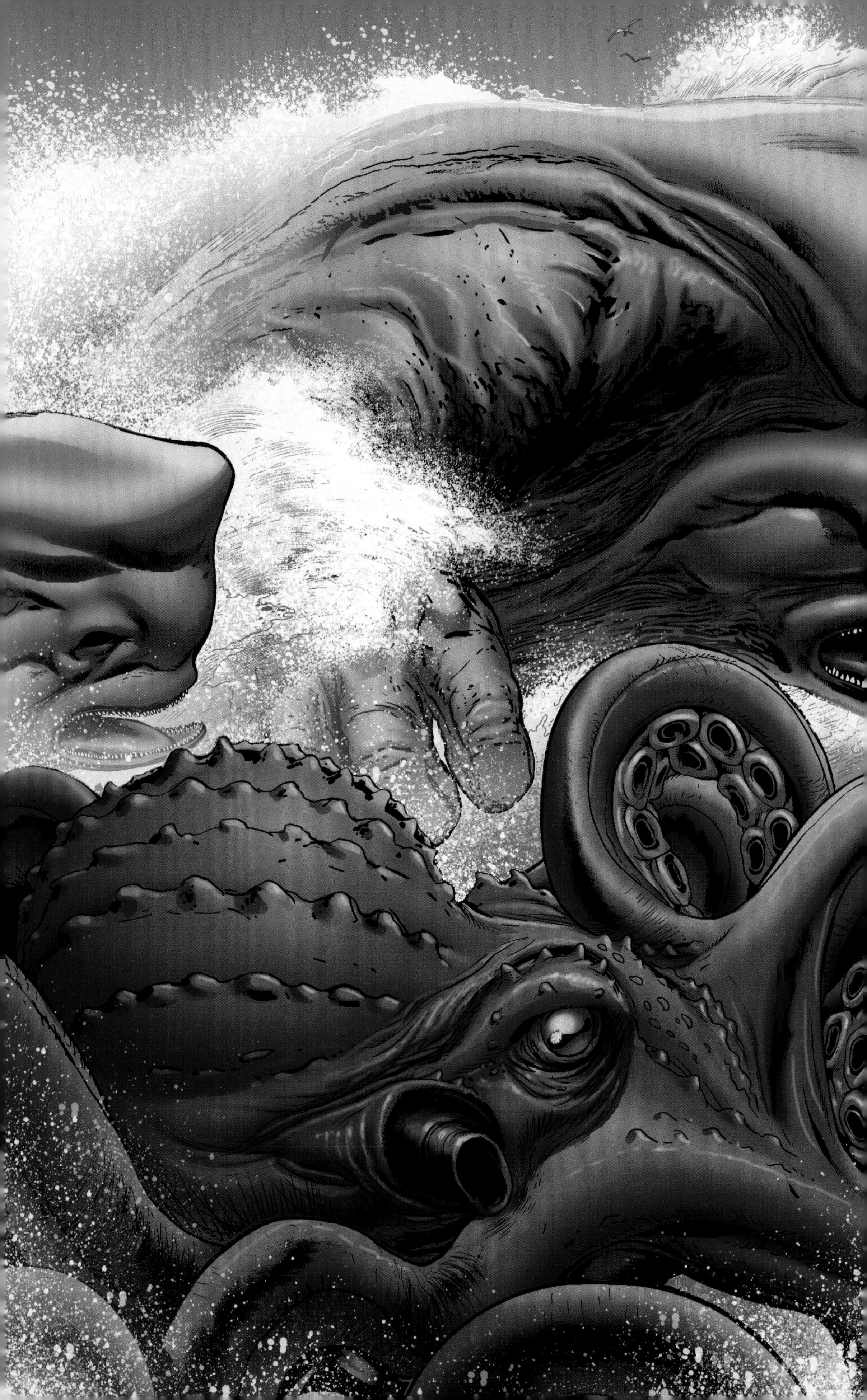

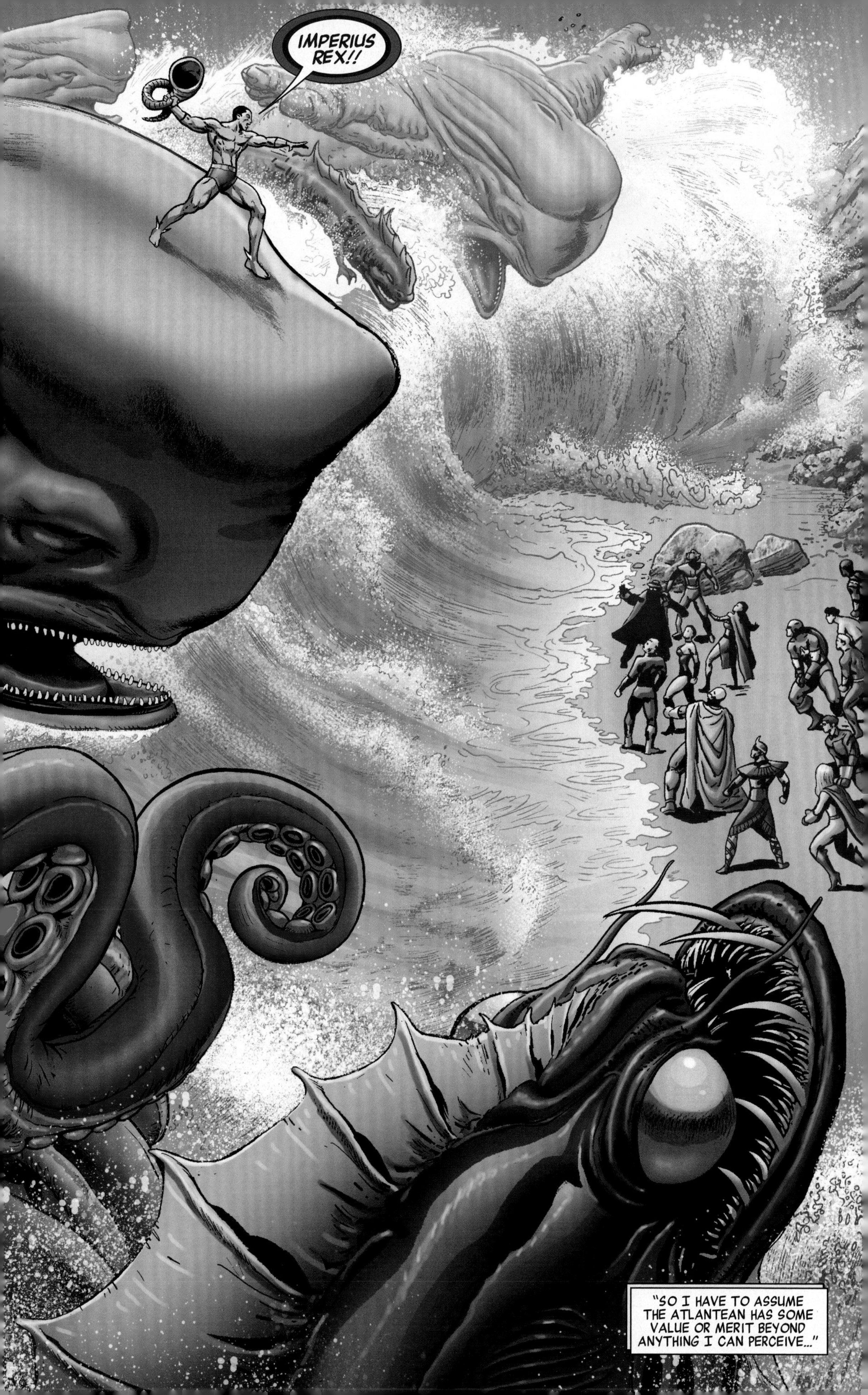
IMPERIUS REX!!
"SO I HAVE TO ASSUME THE ATLANTEAN HAS SOME VALUE OR MERIT BEYOND ANYTHING I CAN PERCEIVE..."

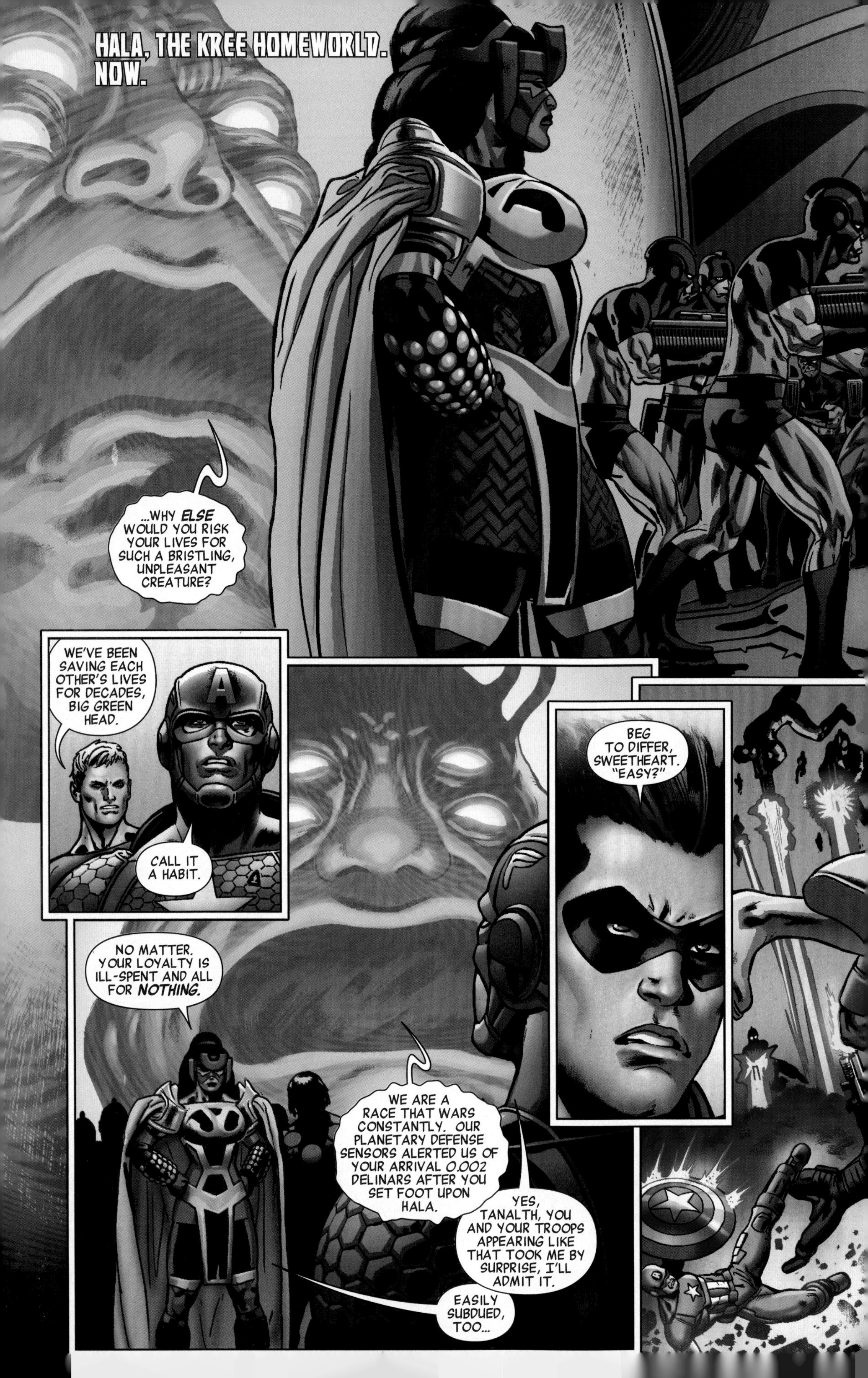
HALA, THE KREE HOMEWORLD. NOW.
...WHY ELSE WOULD YOU RISK YOUR LIVES FOR SUCH A BRISTLING, UNPLEASANT CREATURE?
WE'VE BEEN SAVING EACH OTHER'S LIVES FOR DECADES, BIG GREEN HEAD.
CALL IT A HABIT.
NO MATTER. YOUR LOYALTY IS ILL-SPENT AND ALL FOR NOTHING.
WE ARE A RACE THAT WARS CONSTANTLY. OUR PLANETARY DEFENSE SENSORS ALERTED US OF YOUR ARRIVAL 0.002 DELINARS AFTER YOU SET FOOT UPON HALA.
YES, TANALTH, YOU AND YOUR TROOPS APPEARING LIKE THAT TOOK ME BY SURPRISE, I'LL ADMIT IT.
EASILY SUBDUED, TOO...
BEG TO DIFFER, SWEETHEART. "EASY?"

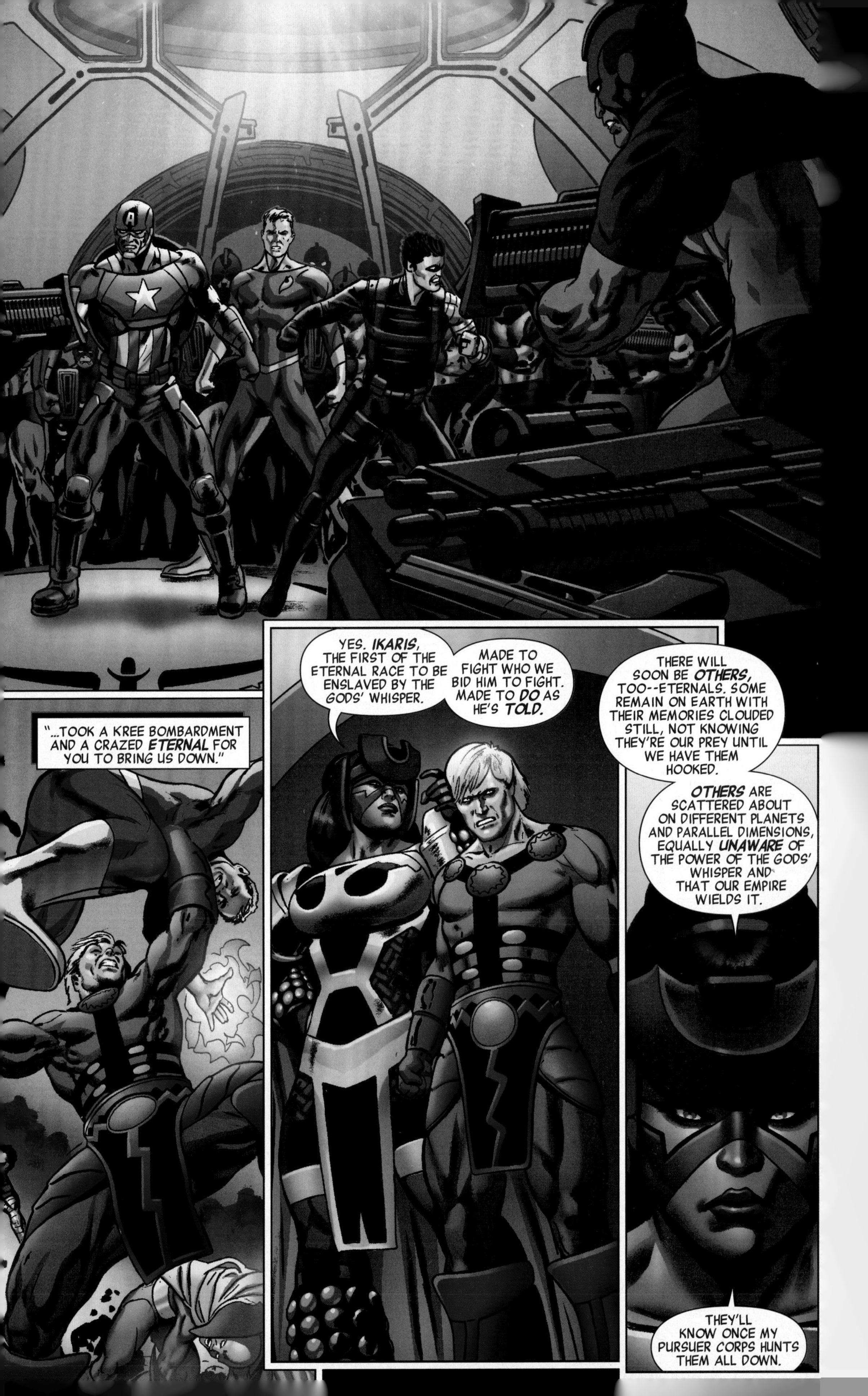

"...TOOK A KREE BOMBARDMENT AND A CRAZED ETERNAL FOR YOU TO BRING US DOWN."
YES. IKARIS, THE FIRST OF THE ETERNAL RACE TO BE ENSLAVED BY THE GODS' WHISPER.
MADE TO FIGHT WHO WE BID HIM TO FIGHT. MADE TO DO AS HE'S TOLD.
THERE WILL SOON BE OTHERS, TOO--ETERNALS. SOME REMAIN ON EARTH WITH THEIR MEMORIES CLOUDED STILL, NOT KNOWING THEY'RE OUR PREY UNTIL WE HAVE THEM HOOKED.
OTHERS ARE SCATTERED ABOUT ON DIFFERENT PLANETS AND PARALLEL DIMENSIONS, EQUALLY UNAWARE OF THE POWER OF THE GODS' WHISPER AND THAT OUR EMPIRE WIELDS IT.
THEY'LL KNOW ONCE MY PURSUER CORPS HUNTS THEM ALL DOWN.

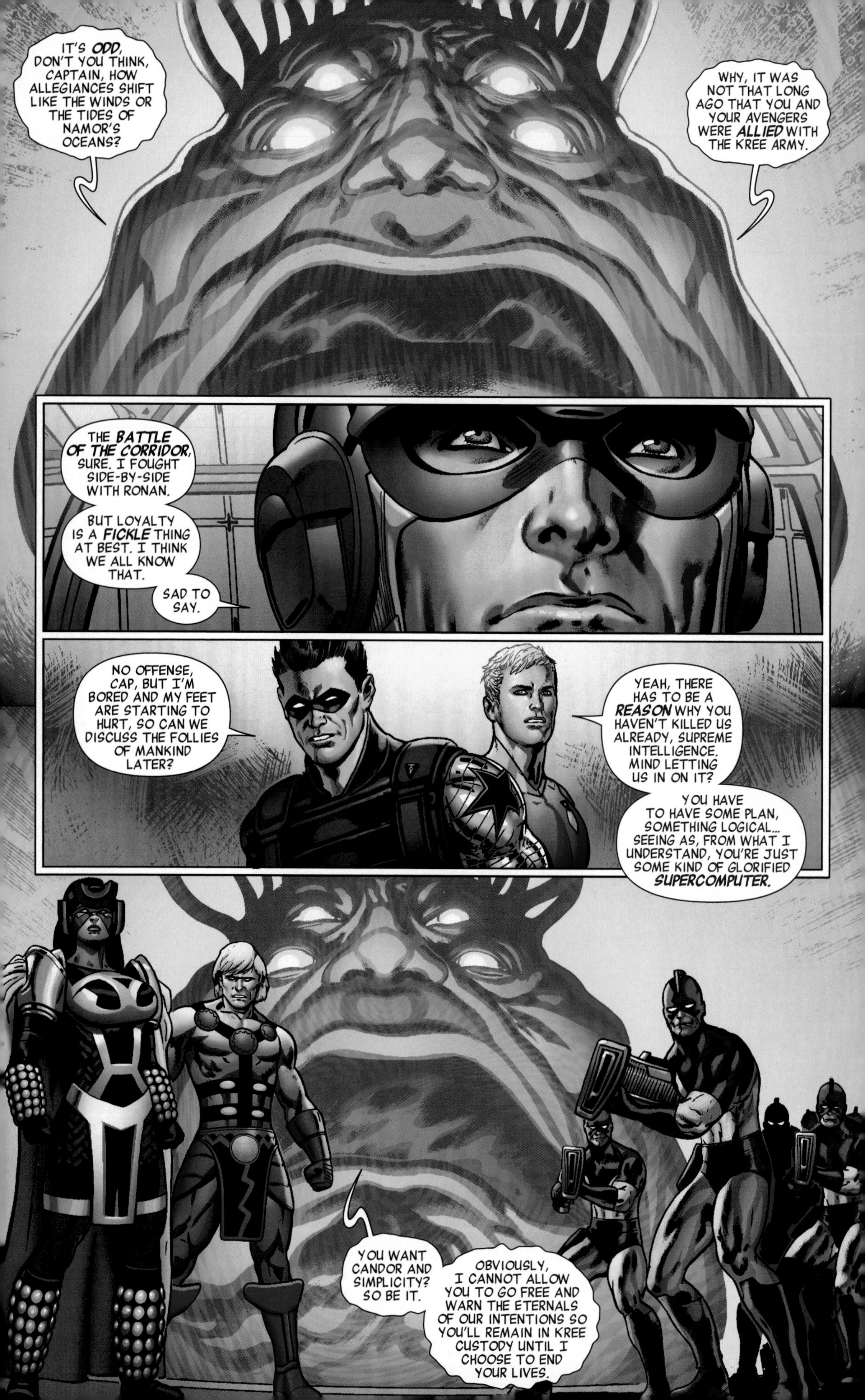
IT'S ODD, DON'T YOU THINK, CAPTAIN, HOW ALLEGIANCES SHIFT LIKE THE WINDS OR THE TIDES OF NAMOR'S OCEANS?
WHY, IT WAS NOT THAT LONG AGO THAT YOU AND YOUR AVENGERS WERE ALLIED WITH THE KREE ARMY.
THE BATTLE OF THE CORRIDOR, SURE. I FOUGHT SIDE-BY-SIDE WITH RONAN.
BUT LOYALTY IS A FICKLE THING AT BEST. I THINK WE ALL KNOW THAT.
SAD TO SAY.
NO OFFENSE, CAP, BUT I'M BORED AND MY FEET ARE STARTING TO HURT, SO CAN WE DISCUSS THE FOLLIES OF MANKIND LATER?
YEAH, THERE HAS TO BE A REASON WHY YOU HAVEN'T KILLED US ALREADY, SUPREME INTELLIGENCE. MIND LETTING US IN ON IT?
YOU HAVE TO HAVE SOME PLAN, SOMETHING LOGICAL... SEEING AS, FROM WHAT I UNDERSTAND, YOU'RE JUST SOME KIND OF GLORIFIED SUPERCOMPUTER.
YOU WANT CANDOR AND SIMPLICITY? SO BE IT.
OBVIOUSLY, I CANNOT ALLOW YOU TO GO FREE AND WARN THE ETERNALS OF OUR INTENTIONS SO YOU'LL REMAIN IN KREE CUSTODY UNTIL I CHOOSE TO END YOUR LIVES.

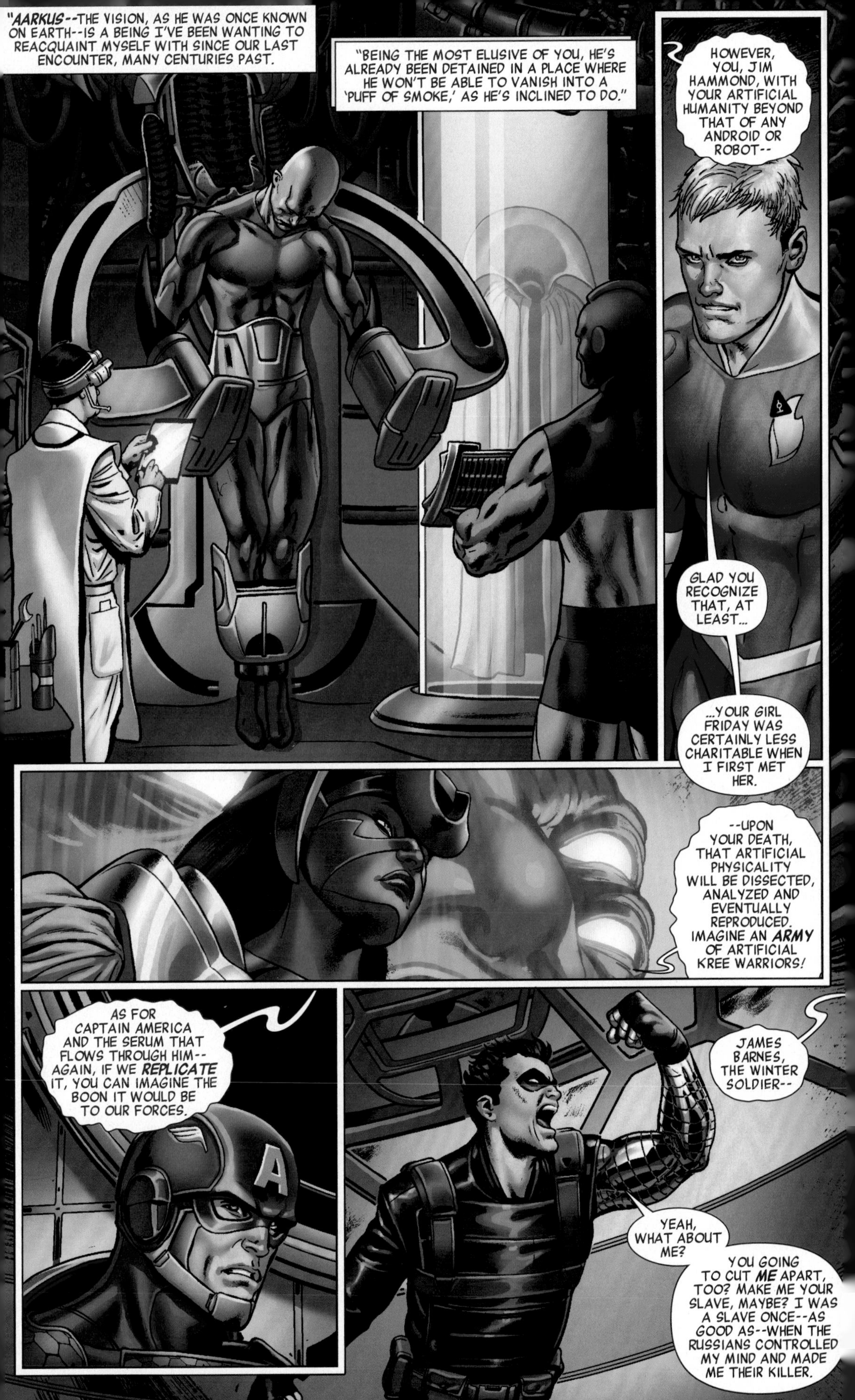
"AARKUS--THE VISION, AS HE WAS ONCE KNOWN ON EARTH--IS A BEING I'VE BEEN WANTING TO REACQUAINT MYSELF WITH SINCE OUR LAST ENCOUNTER, MANY CENTURIES PAST.
"BEING THE MOST ELUSIVE OF YOU, HE'S ALREADY BEEN DETAINED IN A PLACE WHERE HE WON'T BE ABLE TO VANISH INTO A 'PUFF OF SMOKE,' AS HE'S INCLINED TO DO."
HOWEVER, YOU, JIM HAMMOND, WITH YOUR ARTIFICIAL HUMANITY BEYOND THAT OF ANY ANDROID OR ROBOT--
GLAD YOU RECOGNIZE THAT, AT LEAST...
...YOUR GIRL FRIDAY WAS CERTAINLY LESS CHARITABLE WHEN I FIRST MET HER.
--UPON YOUR DEATH, THAT ARTIFICIAL PHYSICALITY WILL BE DISSECTED, ANALYZED AND EVENTUALLY REPRODUCED. IMAGINE AN ARMY OF ARTIFICIAL KREE WARRIORS!
AS FOR CAPTAIN AMERICA AND THE SERUM THAT FLOWS THROUGH HIM--AGAIN, IF WE REPLICATE IT, YOU CAN IMAGINE THE BOON IT WOULD BE TO OUR FORCES.
JAMES BARNES, THE WINTER SOLDIER--
YEAH, WHAT ABOUT ME?
YOU GOING TO CUT ME APART, TOO? MAKE ME YOUR SLAVE, MAYBE? I WAS A SLAVE ONCE--AS GOOD AS--WHEN THE RUSSIANS CONTROLLED MY MIND AND MADE ME THEIR KILLER.

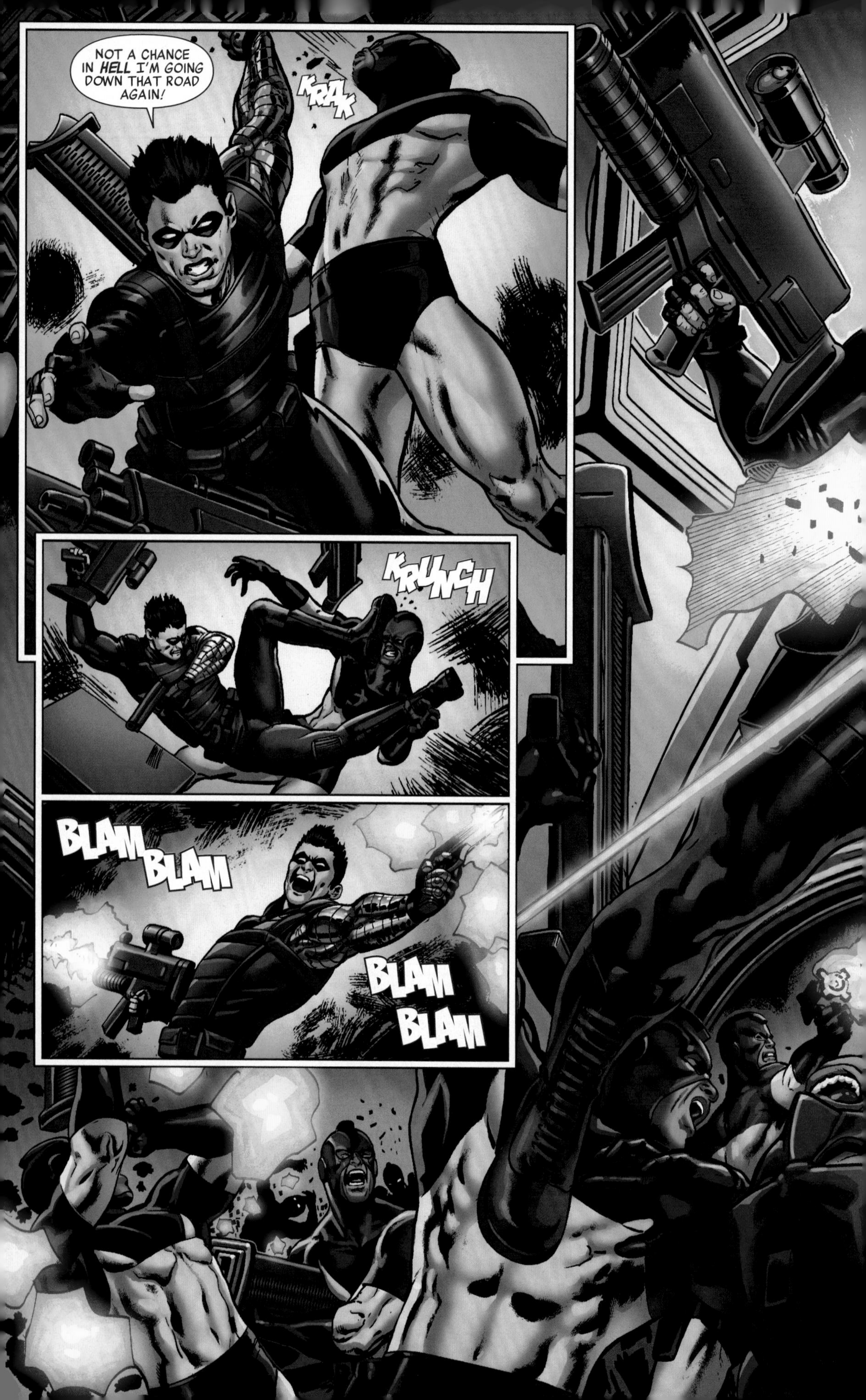
NOT A CHANCE IN HELL I'M GOING DOWN THAT ROAD AGAIN!
KRAK
KRUNCH
BLAM BLAM
BLAM BLAM

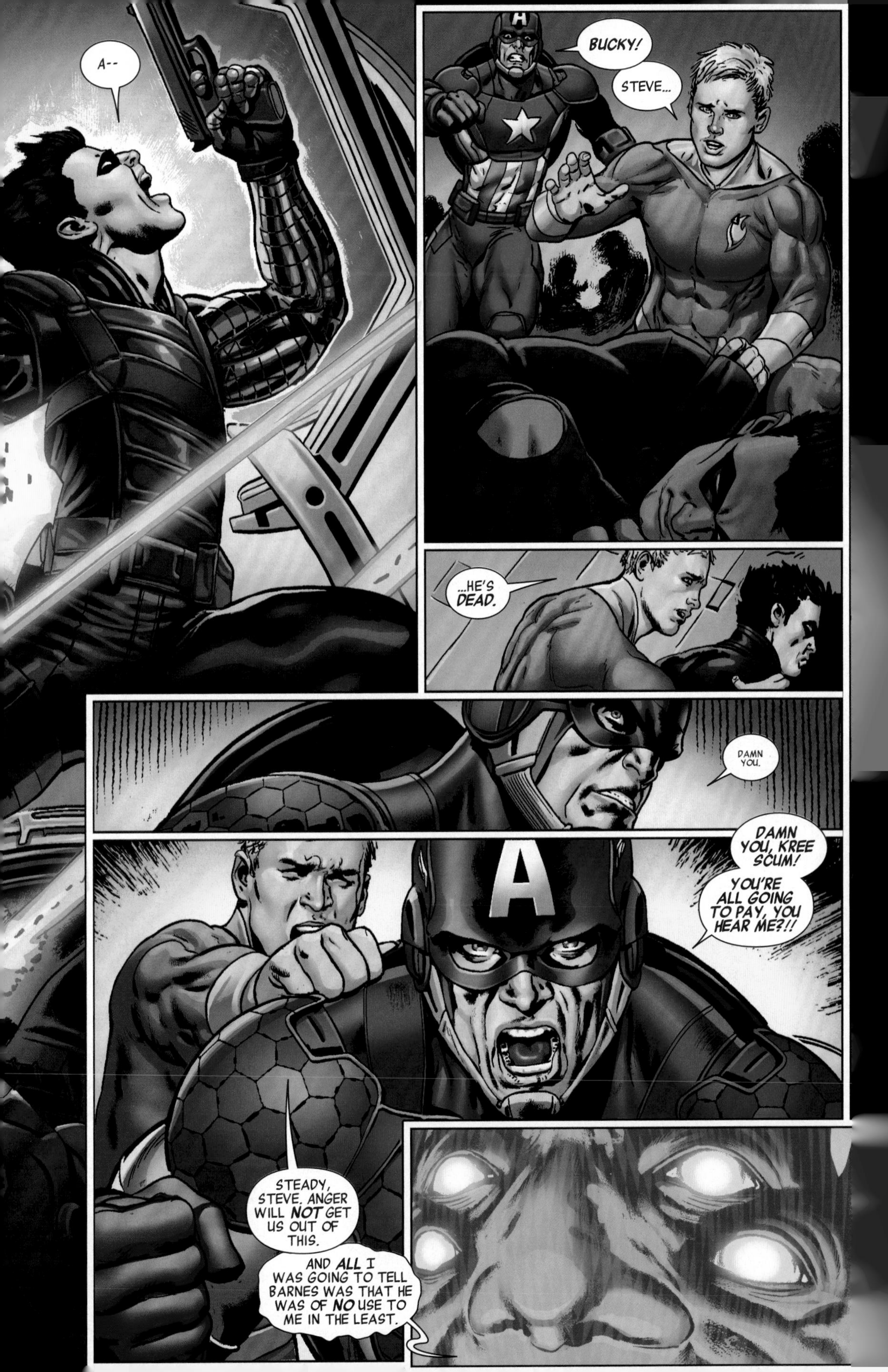
A--
BUCKY!
STEVE...
...HE'S DEAD.
DAMN YOU.
DAMN YOU, KREE SCUM!
YOU'RE ALL GOING TO PAY, YOU HEAR ME?!!
STEADY, STEVE. ANGER WILL NOT GET US OUT OF THIS.
AND ALL I WAS GOING TO TELL BARNES WAS THAT HE WAS OF NO USE TO ME IN THE LEAST.

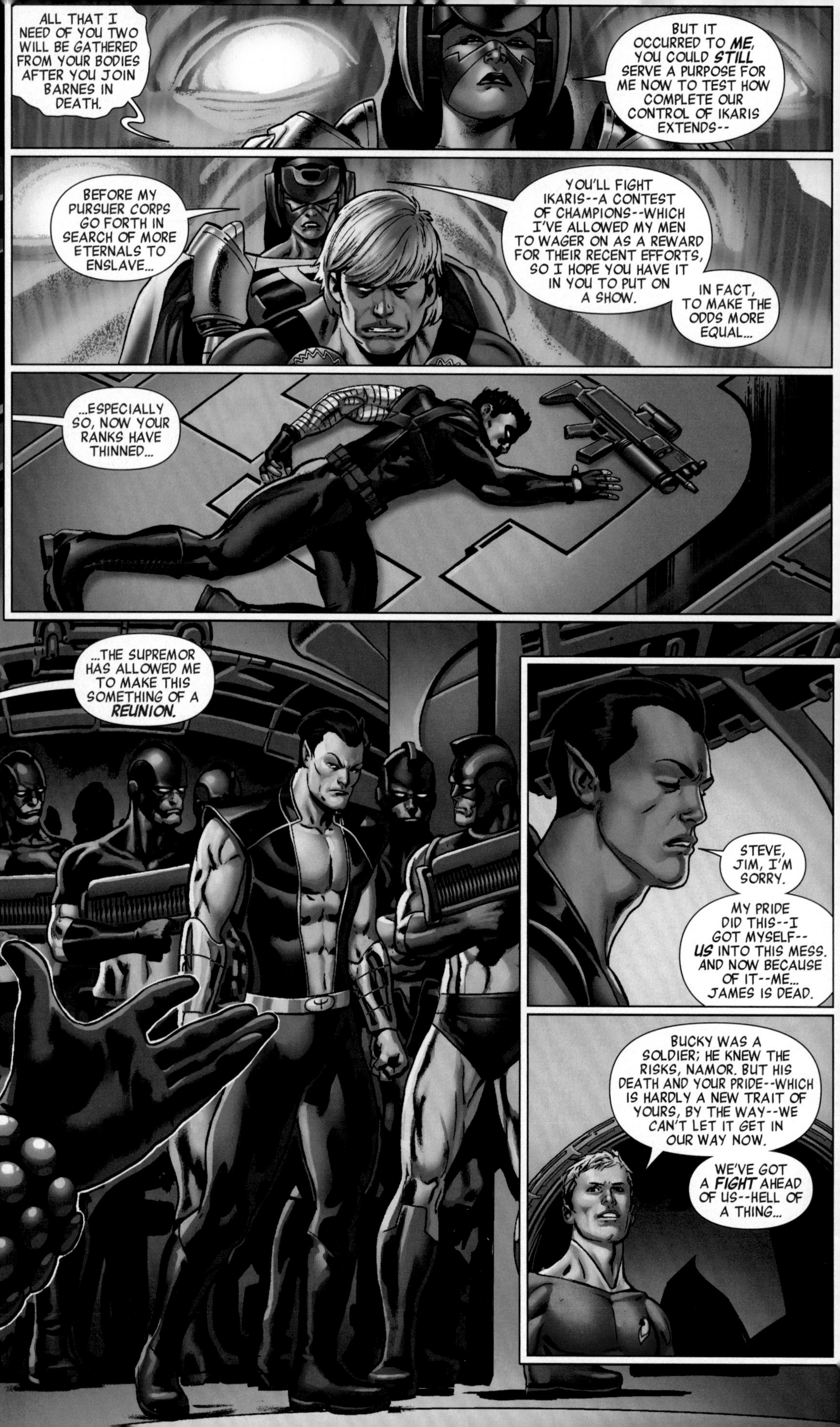
ALL THAT I NEED OF YOU TWO WILL BE GATHERED FROM YOUR BODIES AFTER YOU JOIN BARNES IN DEATH.
BUT IT OCCURRED TO ME, YOU COULD STILL SERVE A PURPOSE FOR ME NOW TO TEST HOW COMPLETE OUR CONTROL OF IKARIS EXTENDS--
BEFORE MY PURSUER CORPS GO FORTH IN SEARCH OF MORE ETERNALS TO ENSLAVE...
YOU'LL FIGHT IKARIS--A CONTEST OF CHAMPIONS--WHICH I'VE ALLOWED MY MEN TO WAGER ON AS A REWARD FOR THEIR RECENT EFFORTS, SO I HOPE YOU HAVE IT IN YOU TO PUT ON A SHOW.
IN FACT, TO MAKE THE ODDS MORE EQUAL...
...ESPECIALLY SO, NOW YOUR RANKS HAVE THINNED...
...THE SUPREMOR HAS ALLOWED ME TO MAKE THIS SOMETHING OF A REUNION.
STEVE, JIM, I'M SORRY.
MY PRIDE DID THIS--I GOT MYSELF-- US INTO THIS MESS. AND NOW BECAUSE OF IT--ME... JAMES IS DEAD.
BUCKY WAS A SOLDIER; HE KNEW THE RISKS, NAMOR. BUT HIS DEATH AND YOUR PRIDE--WHICH IS HARDLY A NEW TRAIT OF YOURS, BY THE WAY--WE CAN'T LET IT GET IN OUR WAY NOW.
WE'VE GOT A FIGHT AHEAD OF US--HELL OF A THING...

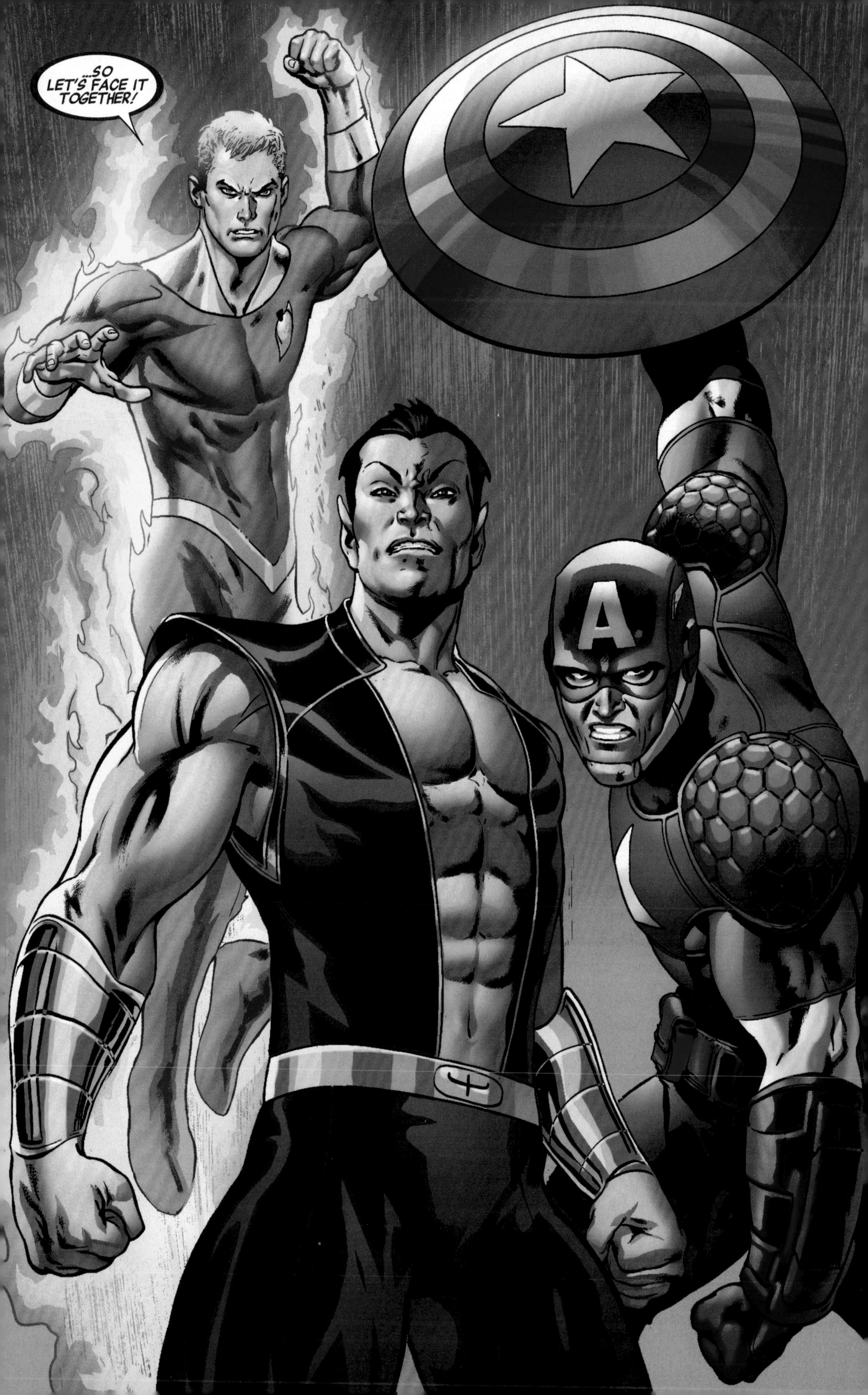
...SO LET'S FACE IT TOGETHER!

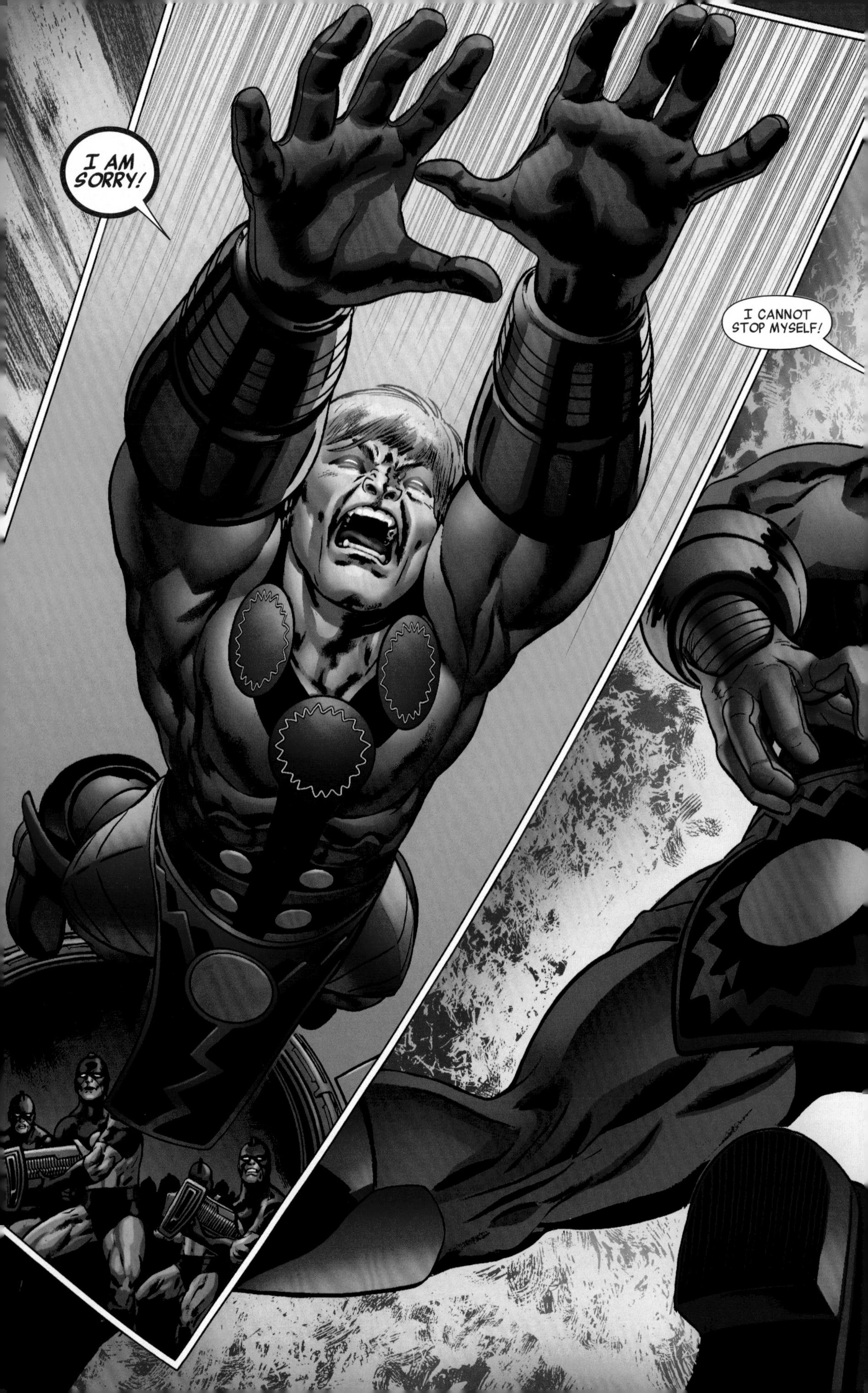
I AM SORRY!
I CANNOT STOP MYSELF!

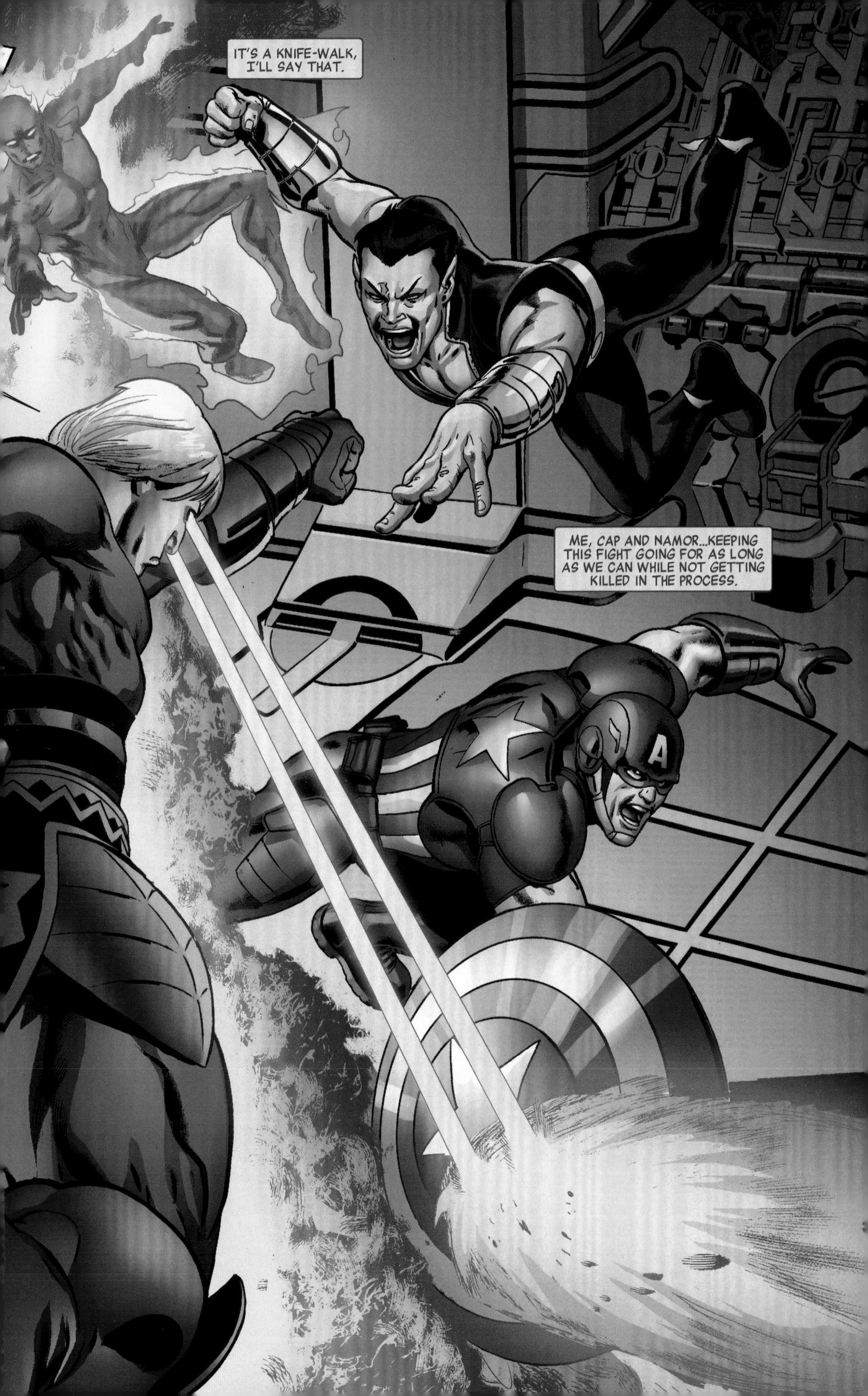
IT'S A KNIFE-WALK, I'LL SAY THAT.
ME, CAP AND NAMOR...KEEPING THIS FIGHT GOING FOR AS LONG AS WE CAN WHILE NOT GETTING KILLED IN THE PROCESS.

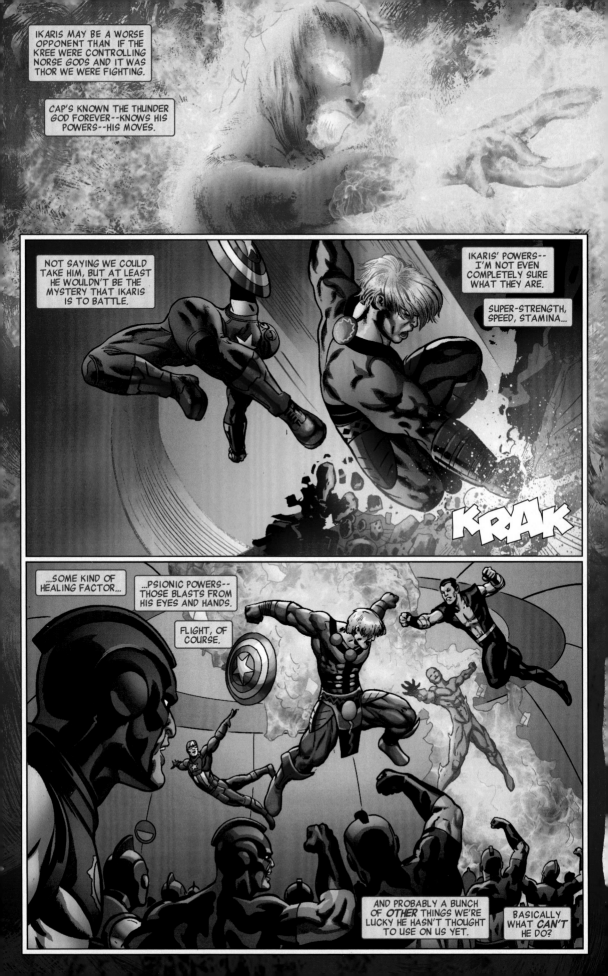

IKARIS MAY BE A WORSE OPPONENT THAN IF THE KREE WERE CONTROLLING NORSE GODS AND IT WAS THOR WE WERE FIGHTING.

CAP'S KNOWN THE THUNDER GOD FOREVER--KNOWS HIS POWERS--HIS MOVES.

NOT SAYING WE COULD TAKE HIM, BUT AT LEAST HE WOULDN'T BE THE MYSTERY THAT IKARIS IS TO BATTLE.

IKARIS' POWERS-- I'M NOT EVEN COMPLETELY SURE WHAT THEY ARE.

SUPER-STRENGTH, SPEED, STAMINA...

KRAK

...SOME KIND OF HEALING FACTOR...

...PSIONIC POWERS-- THOSE BLASTS FROM HIS EYES AND HANDS.

FLIGHT, OF COURSE.

AND PROBABLY A BUNCH OF OTHER THINGS WE'RE LUCKY HE HASN'T THOUGHT TO USE ON US YET.

BASICALLY WHAT CAN'T HE DO?

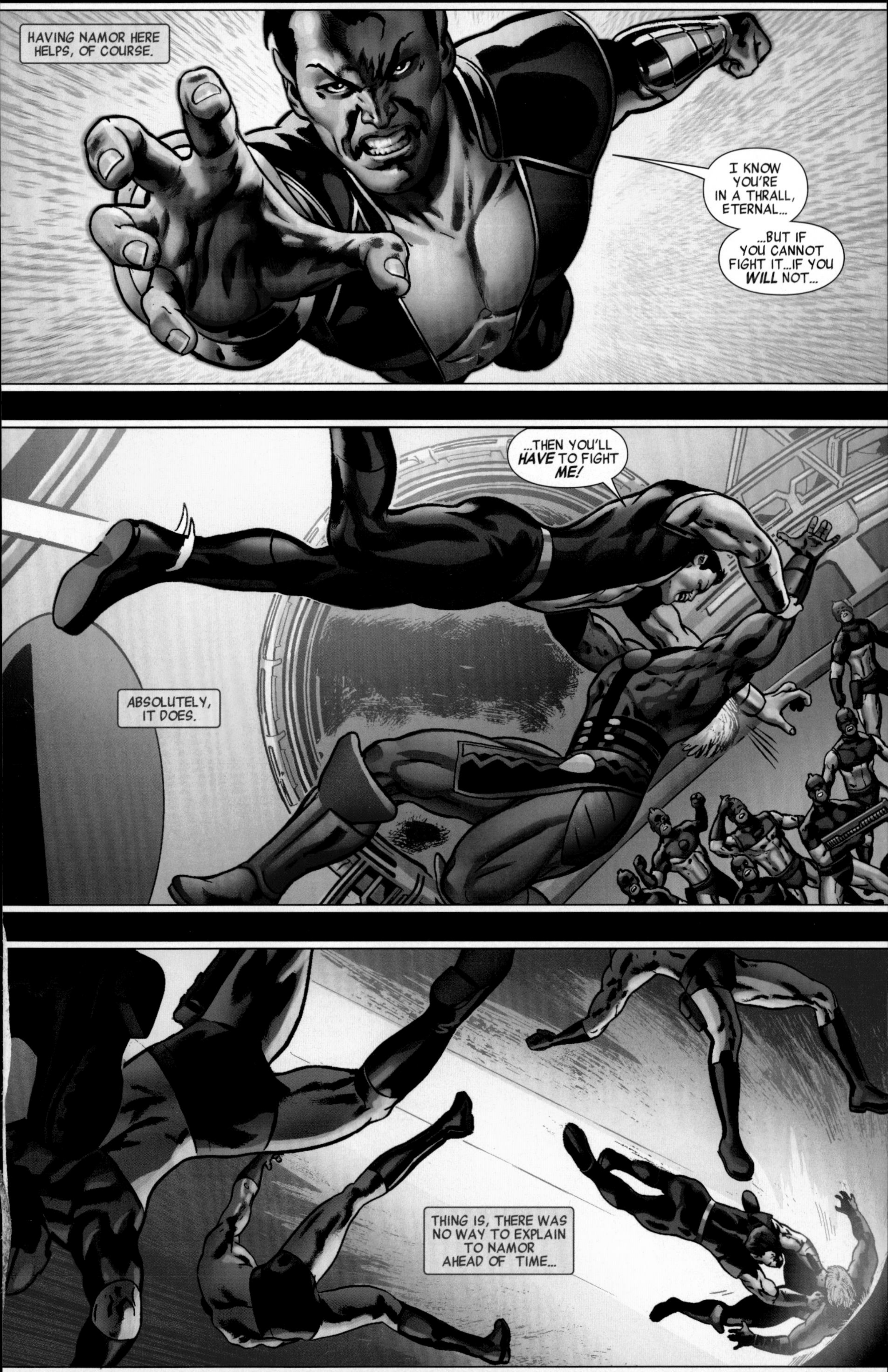
HAVING NAMOR HERE HELPS, OF COURSE.
I KNOW YOU'RE IN A THRALL, ETERNAL...
...BUT IF YOU CANNOT FIGHT IT...IF YOU WILL NOT...
...THEN YOU'LL HAVE TO FIGHT ME!
ABSOLUTELY, IT DOES.
THING IS, THERE WAS NO WAY TO EXPLAIN TO NAMOR AHEAD OF TIME...

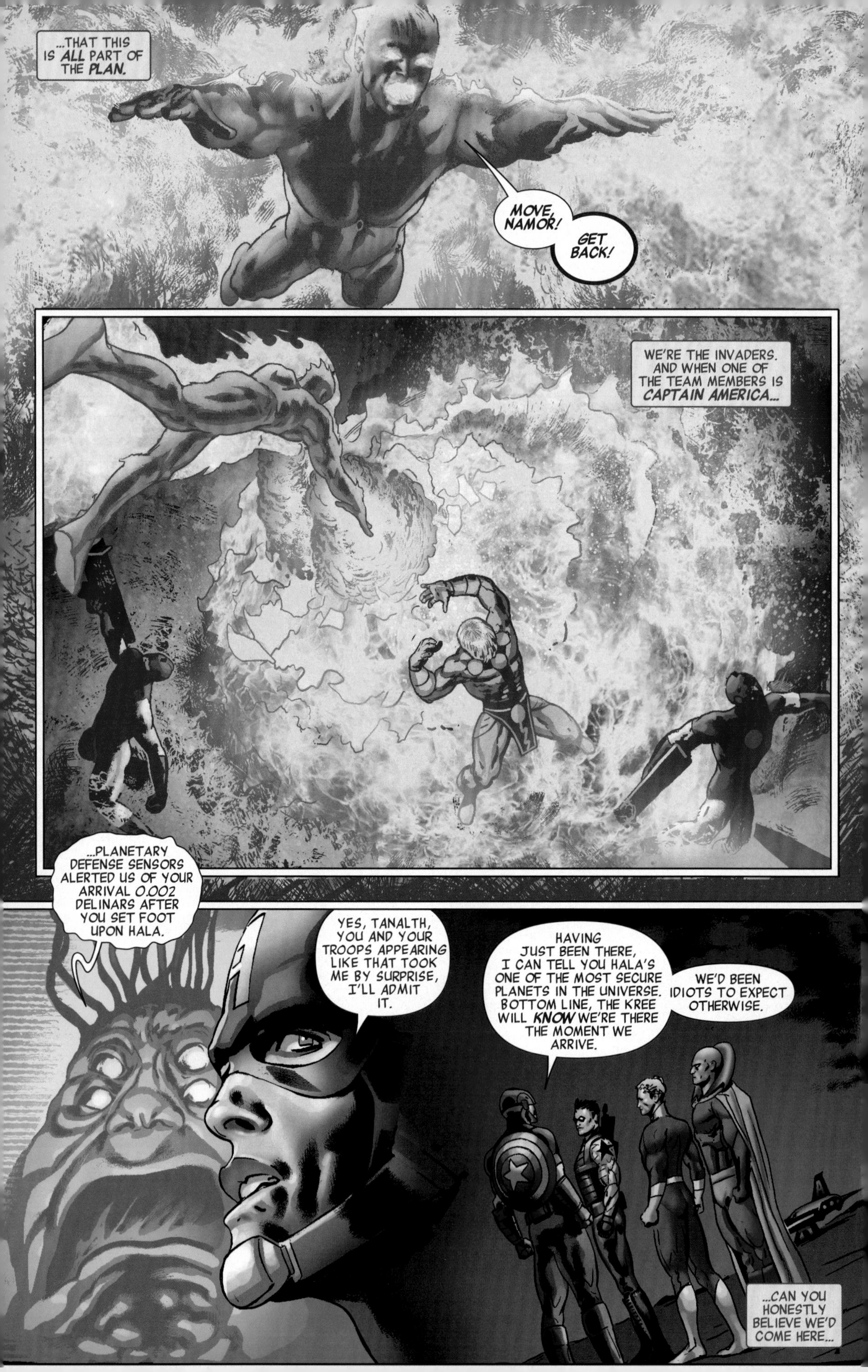
...THAT THIS IS ALL PART OF THE PLAN.
MOVE, NAMOR!
GET BACK!
WE'RE THE INVADERS. AND WHEN ONE OF THE TEAM MEMBERS IS CAPTAIN AMERICA...
...PLANETARY DEFENSE SENSORS ALERTED US OF YOUR ARRIVAL 0.002 DELINARS AFTER YOU SET FOOT UPON HALA.
YES, TANALTH, YOU AND YOUR TROOPS APPEARING LIKE THAT TOOK ME BY SURPRISE, I'LL ADMIT IT.
HAVING JUST BEEN THERE, I CAN TELL YOU HALA'S ONE OF THE MOST SECURE PLANETS IN THE UNIVERSE. BOTTOM LINE, THE KREE WILL KNOW WE'RE THERE THE MOMENT WE ARRIVE.
WE'D BEEN IDIOTS TO EXPECT OTHERWISE.
...CAN YOU HONESTLY BELIEVE WE'D COME HERE...

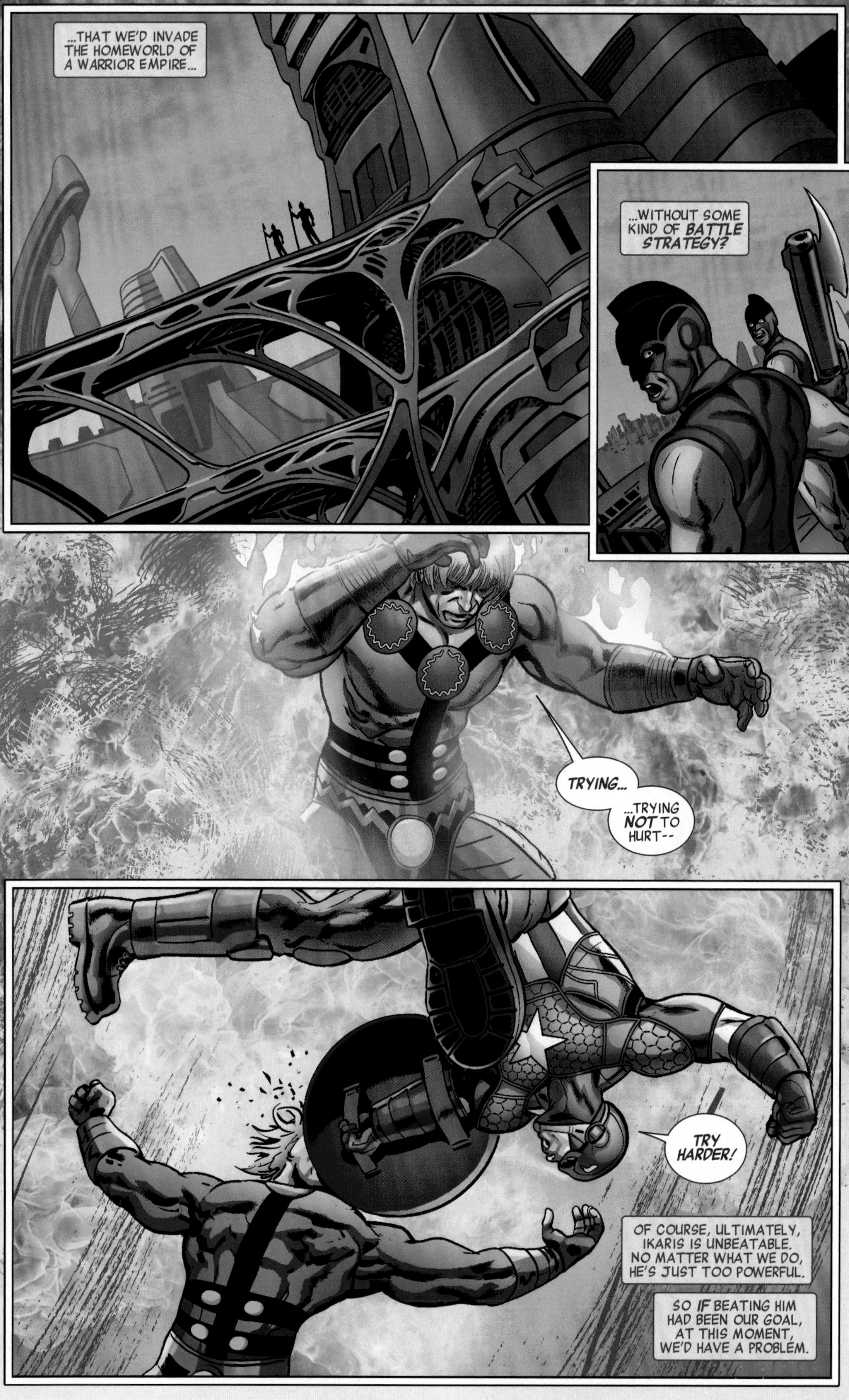
...THAT WE'D INVADE THE HOMEWORLD OF A WARRIOR EMPIRE...
...WITHOUT SOME KIND OF BATTLE STRATEGY?
TRYING...
...TRYING NOT TO HURT--
TRY HARDER!
OF COURSE, ULTIMATELY, IKARIS IS UNBEATABLE. NO MATTER WHAT WE DO, HE'S JUST TOO POWERFUL.
SO IF BEATING HIM HAD BEEN OUR GOAL, AT THIS MOMENT, WE'D HAVE A PROBLEM.

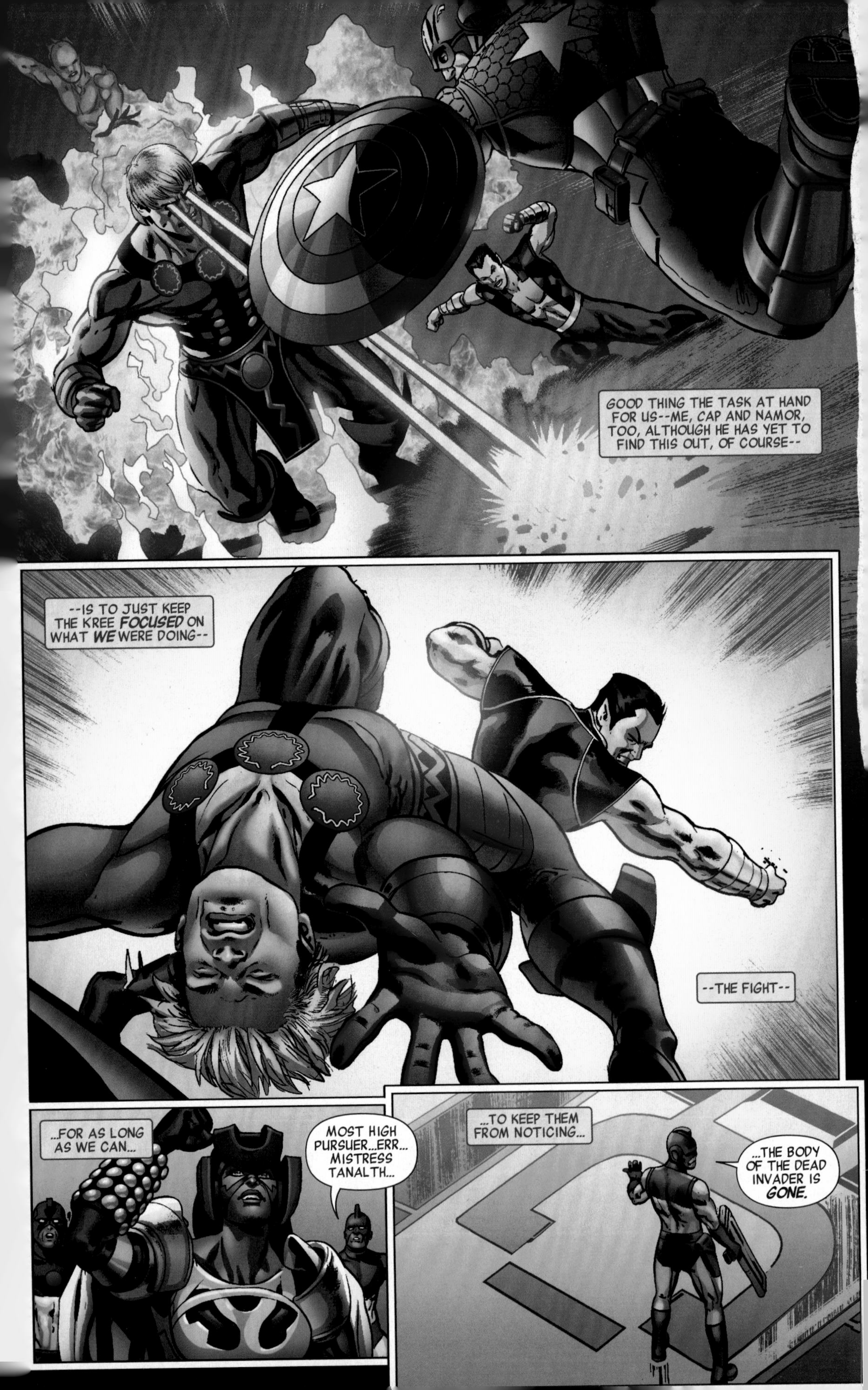
GOOD THING THE TASK AT HAND FOR US--ME, CAP AND NAMOR, TOO, ALTHOUGH HE HAS YET TO FIND THIS OUT, OF COURSE--
--IS TO JUST KEEP THE KREE FOCUSED ON WHAT WE WERE DOING--
--THE FIGHT--
...FOR AS LONG AS WE CAN...
MOST HIGH PURSUER...ERR... MISTRESS TANALTH...
...TO KEEP THEM FROM NOTICING...
...THE BODY OF THE DEAD INVADER IS GONE.

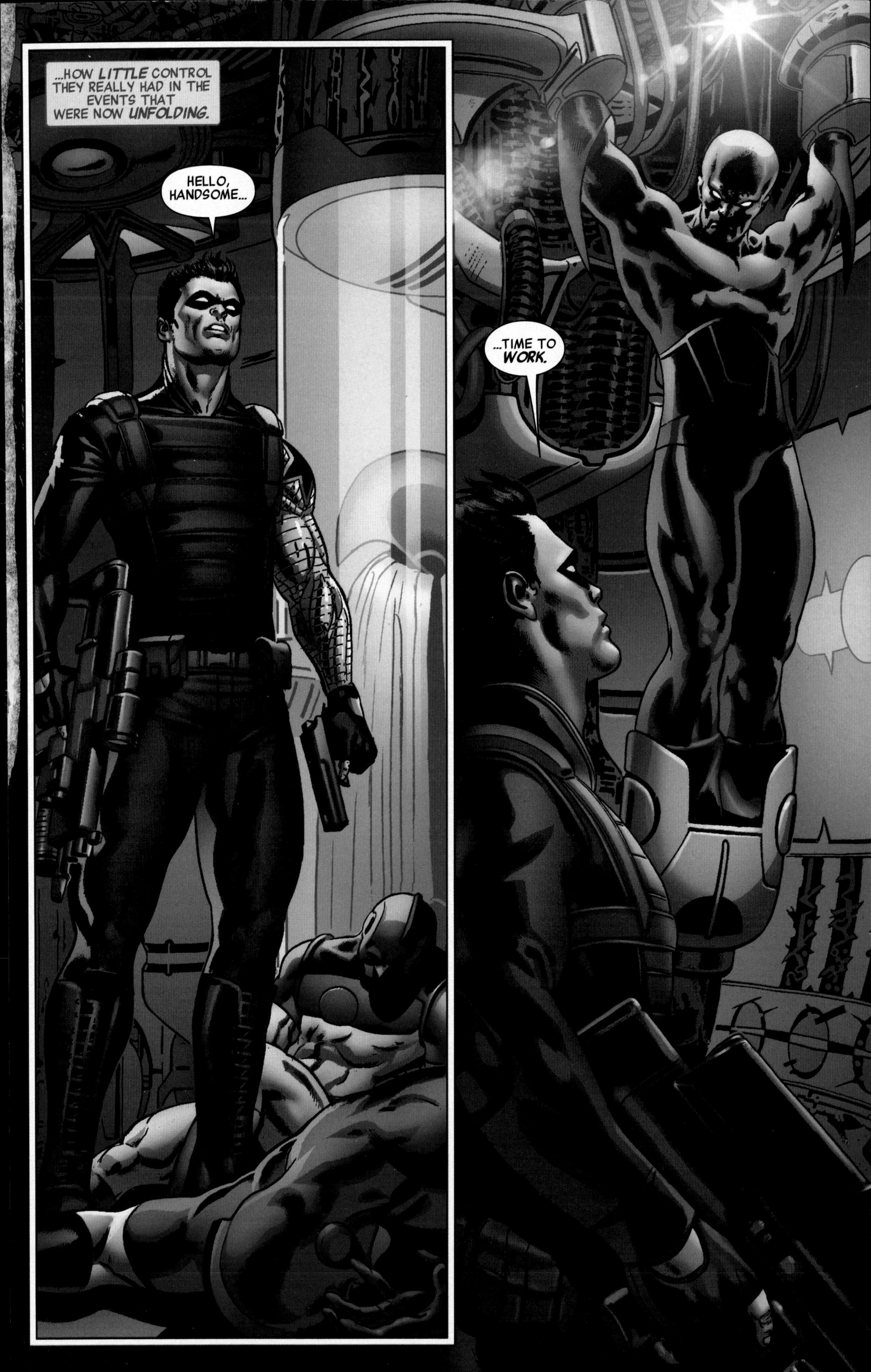
...HOW LITTLE CONTROL THEY REALLY HAD IN THE EVENTS THAT WERE NOW UNFOLDING.
HELLO, HANDSOME...
...TIME TO WORK.

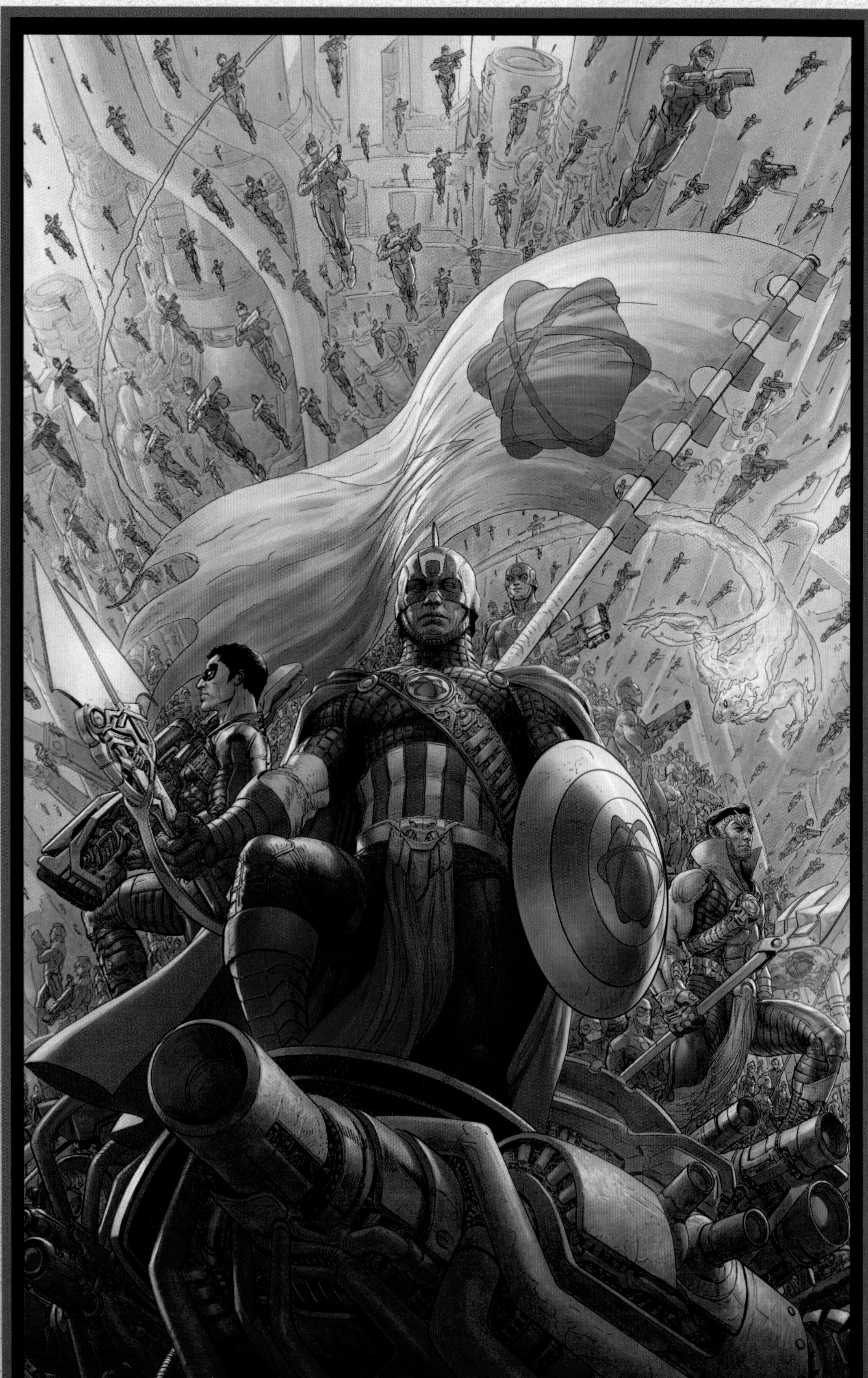

#5

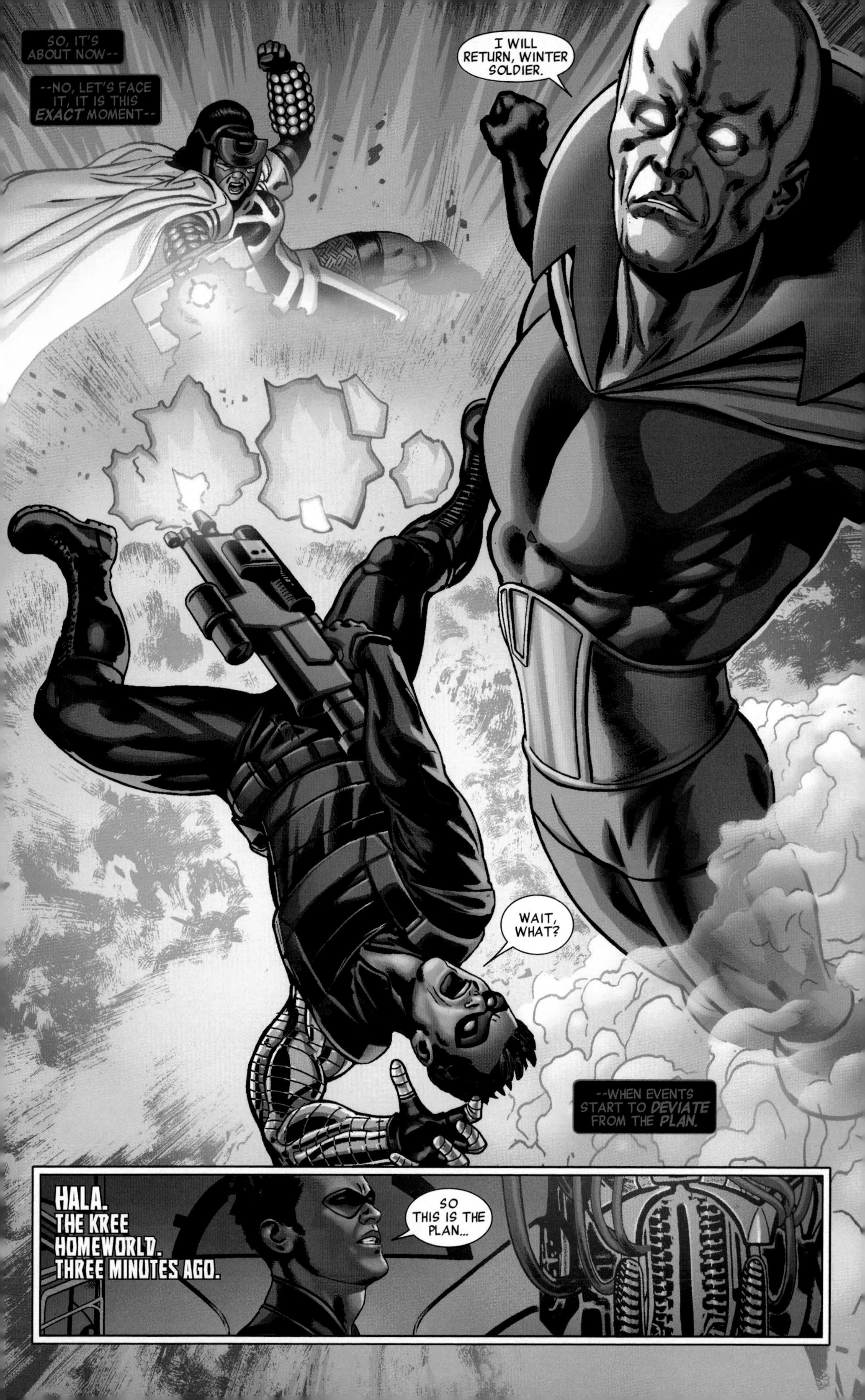
SO, IT'S ABOUT NOW--
--NO, LET'S FACE IT, IT IS THIS EXACT MOMENT--
I WILL RETURN, WINTER SOLDIER.
WAIT, WHAT?
--WHEN EVENTS START TO DEVIATE FROM THE PLAN.
HALA. THE KREE HOMEWORLD. THREE MINUTES AGO.
SO THIS IS THE PLAN...

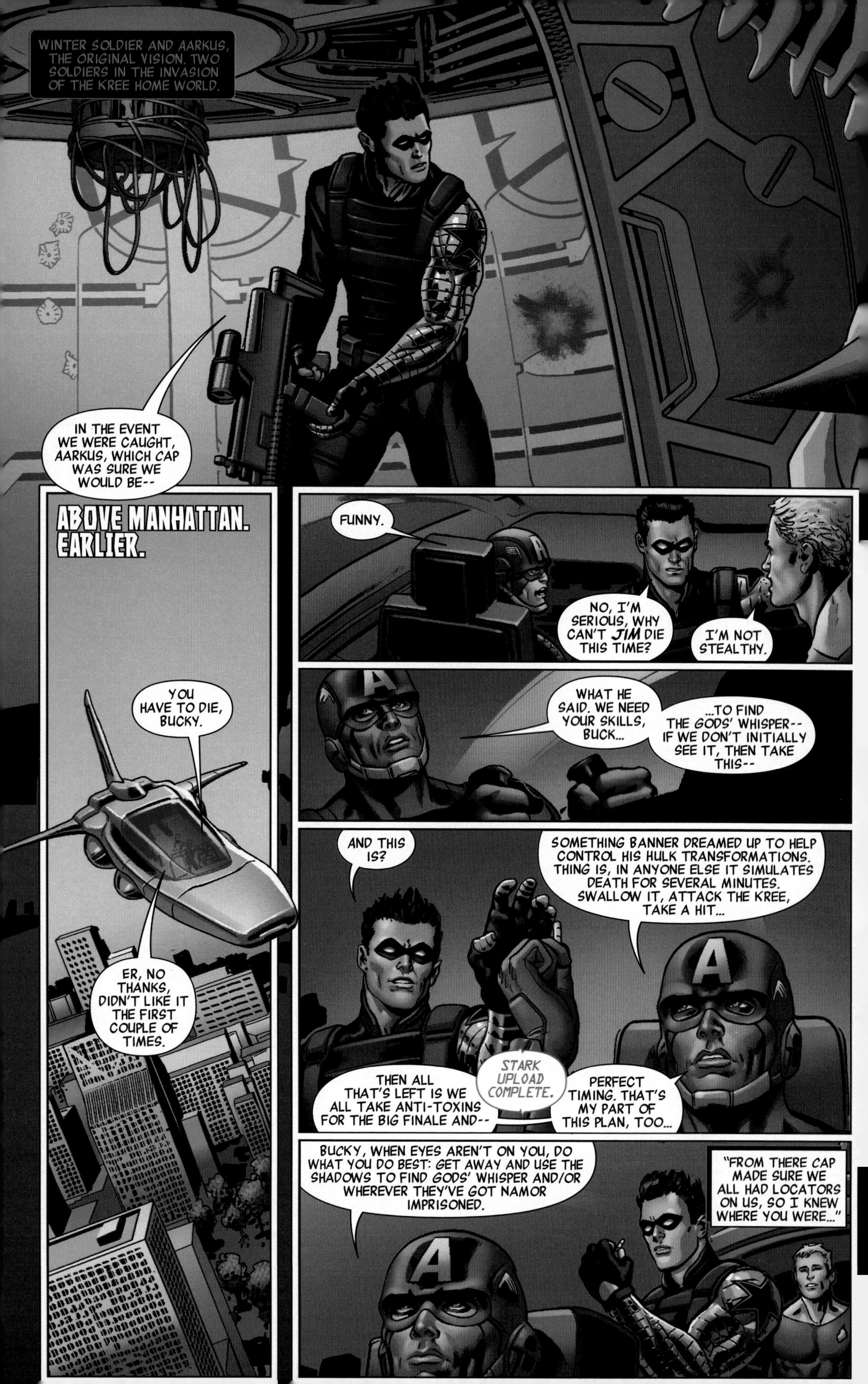
WINTER SOLDIER AND AARKUS, THE ORIGINAL VISION. TWO SOLDIERS IN THE INVASION OF THE KREE HOME WORLD.
IN THE EVENT WE WERE CAUGHT, AARKUS, WHICH CAP WAS SURE WE WOULD BE--
ABOVE MANHATTAN. EARLIER.
YOU HAVE TO DIE, BUCKY.
ER, NO THANKS, DIDN'T LIKE IT THE FIRST COUPLE OF TIMES.
FUNNY.
NO, I'M SERIOUS, WHY CAN'T JIM DIE THIS TIME?
I'M NOT STEALTHY.
WHAT HE SAID. WE NEED YOUR SKILLS, BUCK...
...TO FIND THE GODS' WHISPER-- IF WE DON'T INITIALLY SEE IT, THEN TAKE THIS--
AND THIS IS?
SOMETHING BANNER DREAMED UP TO HELP CONTROL HIS HULK TRANSFORMATIONS. THING IS, IN ANYONE ELSE IT SIMULATES DEATH FOR SEVERAL MINUTES. SWALLOW IT, ATTACK THE KREE, TAKE A HIT...
THEN ALL THAT'S LEFT IS WE ALL TAKE ANTI-TOXINS FOR THE BIG FINALE AND--
STARK UPLOAD COMPLETE.
PERFECT TIMING. THAT'S MY PART OF THIS PLAN, TOO...
BUCKY, WHEN EYES AREN'T ON YOU, DO WHAT YOU DO BEST: GET AWAY AND USE THE SHADOWS TO FIND GODS' WHISPER AND/OR WHEREVER THEY'VE GOT NAMOR IMPRISONED.
"FROM THERE CAP MADE SURE WE ALL HAD LOCATORS ON US, SO I KNEW WHERE YOU WERE..."

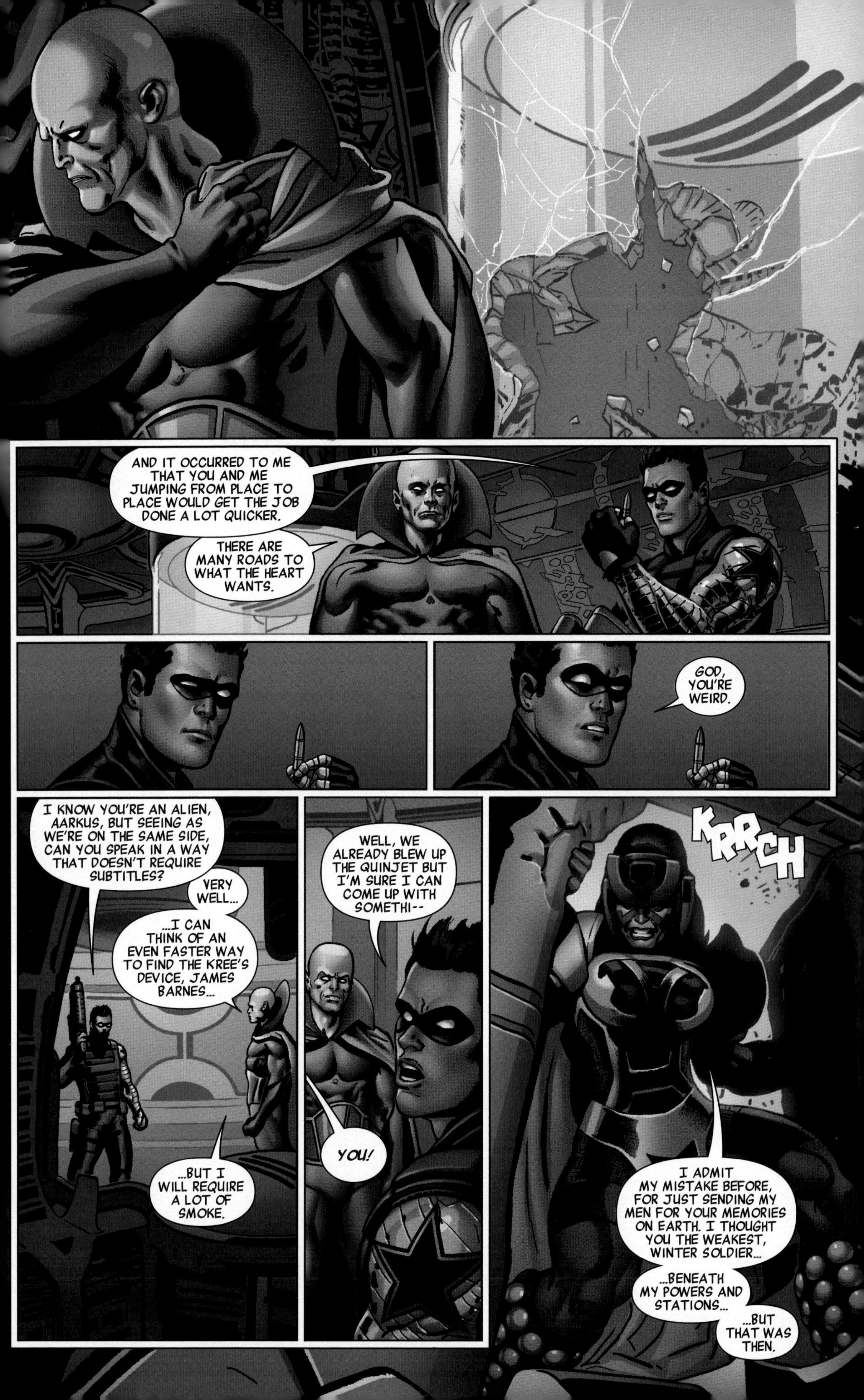
AND IT OCCURRED TO ME THAT YOU AND ME JUMPING FROM PLACE TO PLACE WOULD GET THE JOB DONE A LOT QUICKER.
THERE ARE MANY ROADS TO WHAT THE HEART WANTS.
GOD, YOU'RE WEIRD.
I KNOW YOU'RE AN ALIEN, AARKUS, BUT SEEING AS WE'RE ON THE SAME SIDE, CAN YOU SPEAK IN A WAY THAT DOESN'T REQUIRE SUBTITLES?
VERY WELL...
...I CAN THINK OF AN EVEN FASTER WAY TO FIND THE KREE'S DEVICE, JAMES BARNES...
...BUT I WILL REQUIRE A LOT OF SMOKE.
WELL, WE ALREADY BLEW UP THE QUINJET BUT I'M SURE I CAN COME UP WITH SOMETHI--
YOU!
KRRCH
I ADMIT MY MISTAKE BEFORE, FOR JUST SENDING MY MEN FOR YOUR MEMORIES ON EARTH. I THOUGHT YOU THE WEAKEST, WINTER SOLDIER...
...BENEATH MY POWERS AND STATIONS...
...BUT THAT WAS THEN.

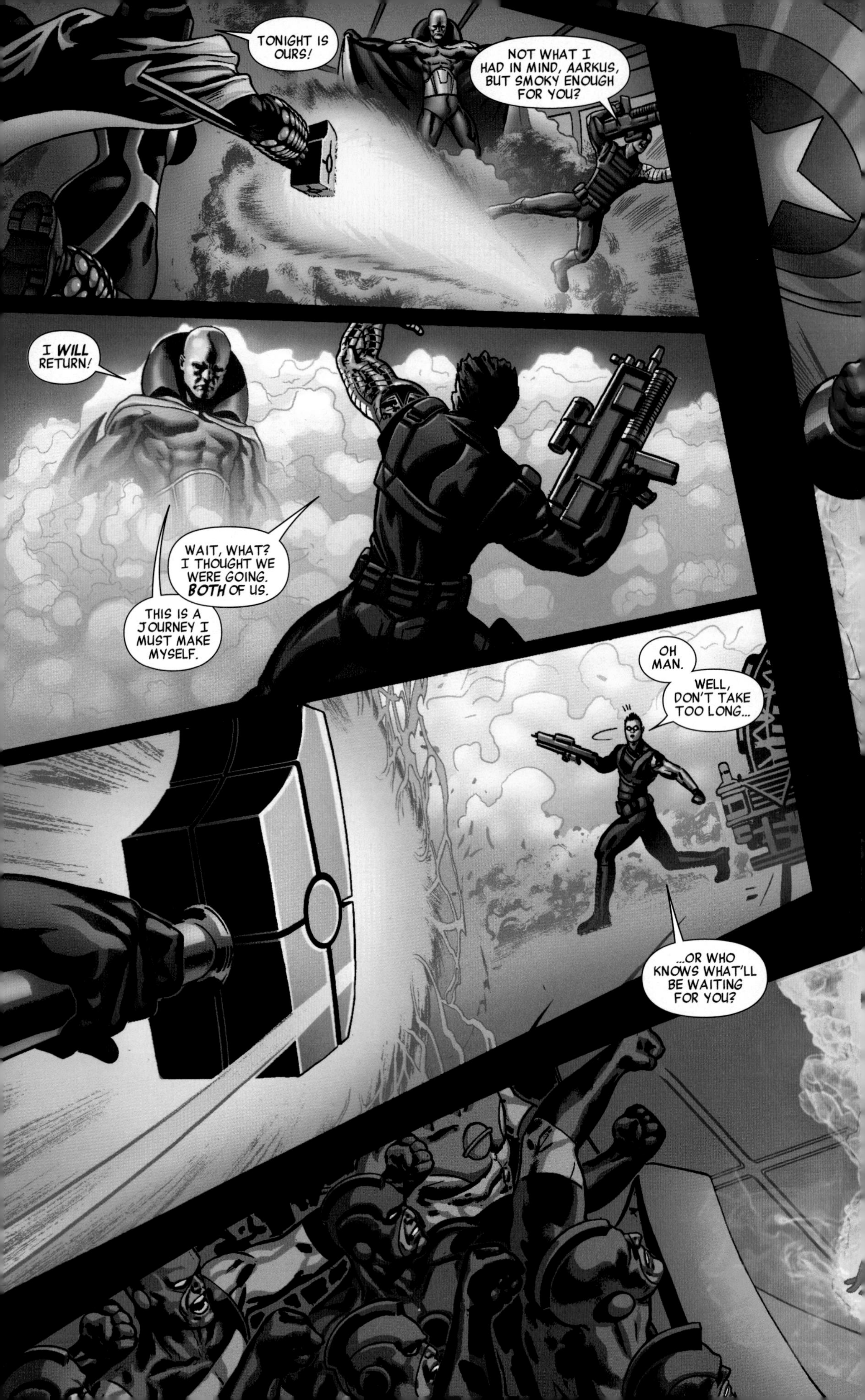
TONIGHT IS OURS!
NOT WHAT I HAD IN MIND, AARKUS, BUT SMOKY ENOUGH FOR YOU?
I WILL RETURN!
WAIT, WHAT? I THOUGHT WE WERE GOING. BOTH OF US.
THIS IS A JOURNEY I MUST MAKE MYSELF.
OH MAN.
WELL, DON'T TAKE TOO LONG...
...OR WHO KNOWS WHAT'LL BE WAITING FOR YOU?

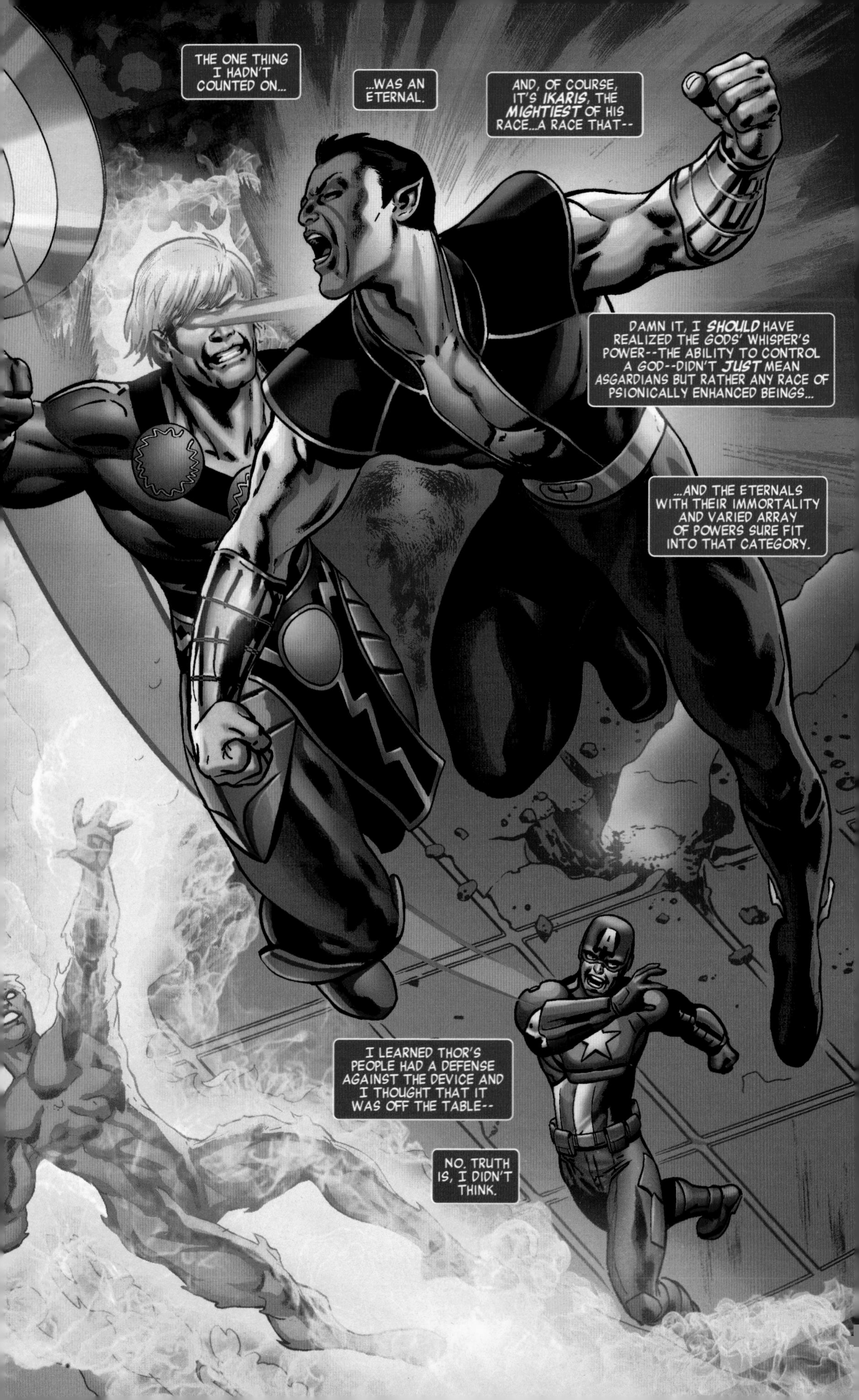
THE ONE THING I HADN'T COUNTED ON...
...WAS AN ETERNAL.
AND, OF COURSE, IT'S IKARIS, THE MIGHTIEST OF HIS RACE...A RACE THAT--
DAMN IT, I SHOULD HAVE REALIZED THE GODS' WHISPER'S POWER--THE ABILITY TO CONTROL A GOD--DIDN'T JUST MEAN ASGARDIANS BUT RATHER ANY RACE OF PSIONICALLY ENHANCED BEINGS...
...AND THE ETERNALS WITH THEIR IMMORTALITY AND VARIED ARRAY OF POWERS SURE FIT INTO THAT CATEGORY.
I LEARNED THOR'S PEOPLE HAD A DEFENSE AGAINST THE DEVICE AND I THOUGHT THAT IT WAS OFF THE TABLE--
NO. TRUTH IS, I DIDN'T THINK.

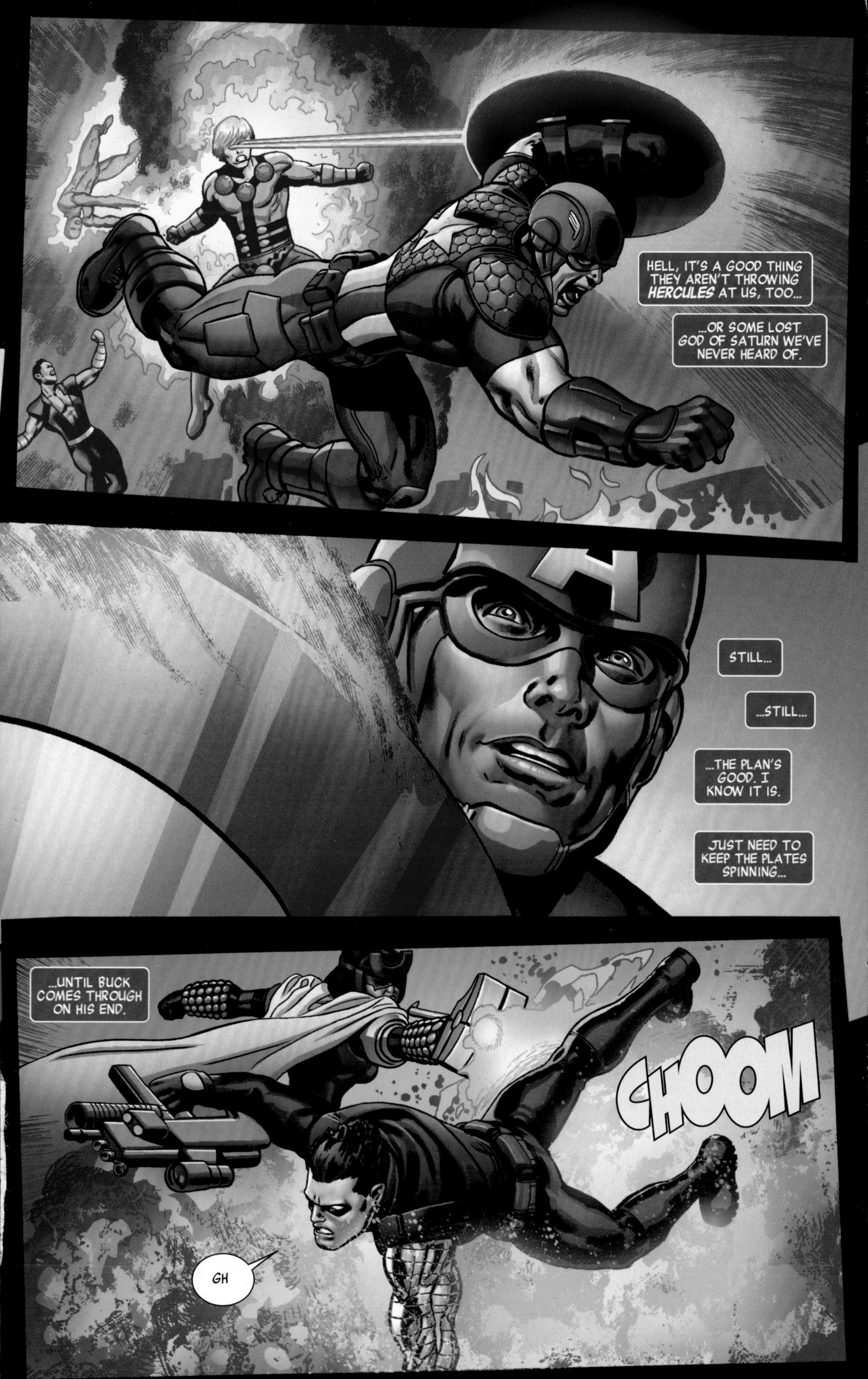
HELL, IT'S A GOOD THING THEY AREN'T THROWING HERCULES AT US, TOO...
...OR SOME LOST GOD OF SATURN WE'VE NEVER HEARD OF.
STILL...
...STILL...
...THE PLAN'S GOOD. I KNOW IT IS.
JUST NEED TO KEEP THE PLATES SPINNING...
...UNTIL BUCK COMES THROUGH ON HIS END.
CHOOM
GH

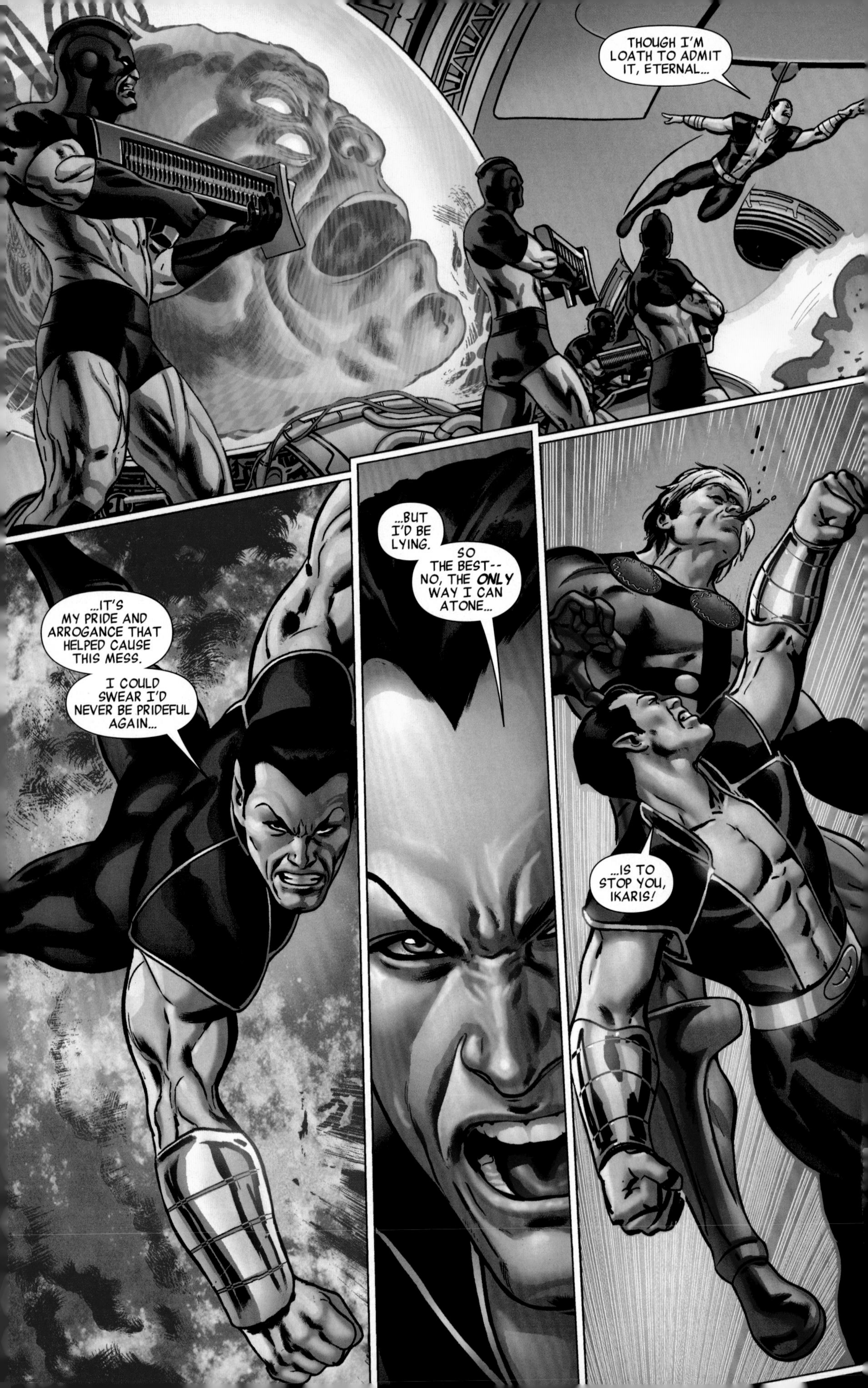
THOUGH I'M LOATH TO ADMIT IT, ETERNAL...
...IT'S MY PRIDE AND ARROGANCE THAT HELPED CAUSE THIS MESS.
I COULD SWEAR I'D NEVER BE PRIDEFUL AGAIN...
...BUT I'D BE LYING.
SO THE BEST-- NO, THE **ONLY** WAY I CAN ATONE...
...IS TO STOP YOU, IKARIS!

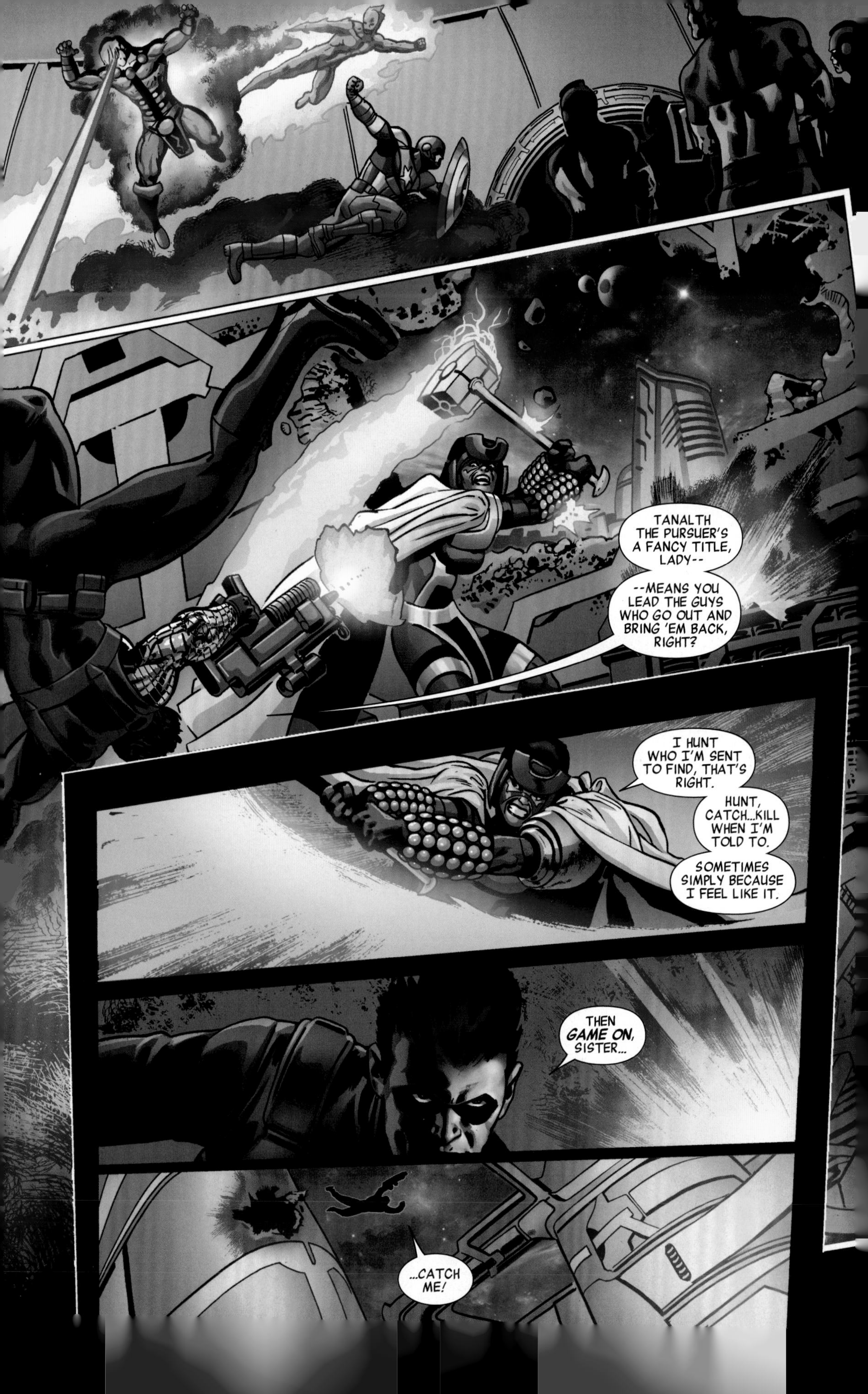

TANALTH THE PURSUER'S A FANCY TITLE, LADY--
--MEANS YOU LEAD THE GUYS WHO GO OUT AND BRING 'EM BACK, RIGHT?
I HUNT WHO I'M SENT TO FIND, THAT'S RIGHT.
HUNT, CATCH...KILL WHEN I'M TOLD TO.
SOMETIMES SIMPLY BECAUSE I FEEL LIKE IT.
THEN GAME ON, SISTER...
...CATCH ME!

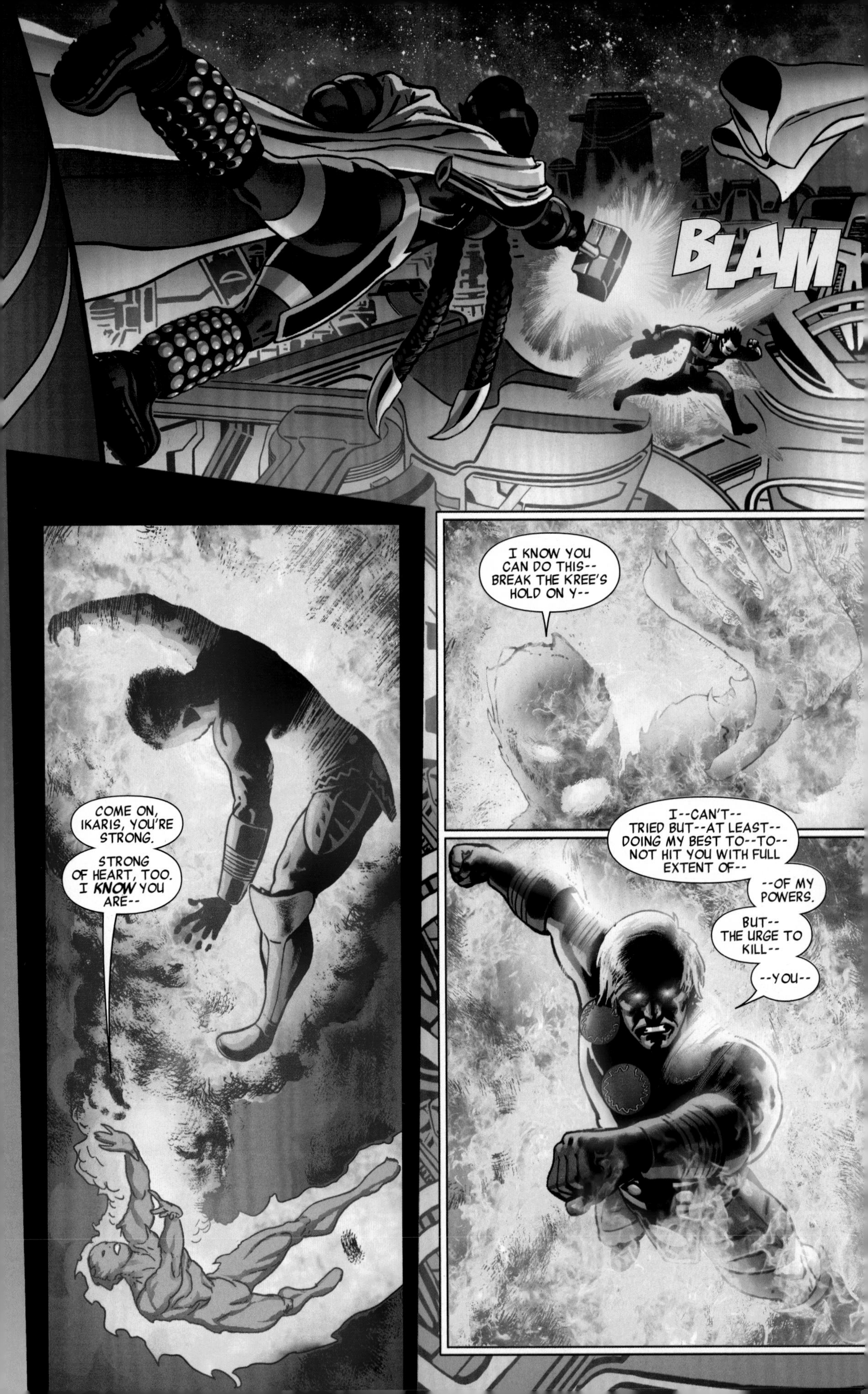
BLAM
COME ON, IKARIS, YOU'RE STRONG.
STRONG OF HEART, TOO. I *KNOW* YOU ARE--
I KNOW YOU CAN DO THIS-- BREAK THE KREE'S HOLD ON Y--
I--CAN'T-- TRIED BUT--AT LEAST-- DOING MY BEST TO--TO-- NOT HIT YOU WITH FULL EXTENT OF--
--OF MY POWERS.
BUT-- THE URGE TO KILL--
--YOU--

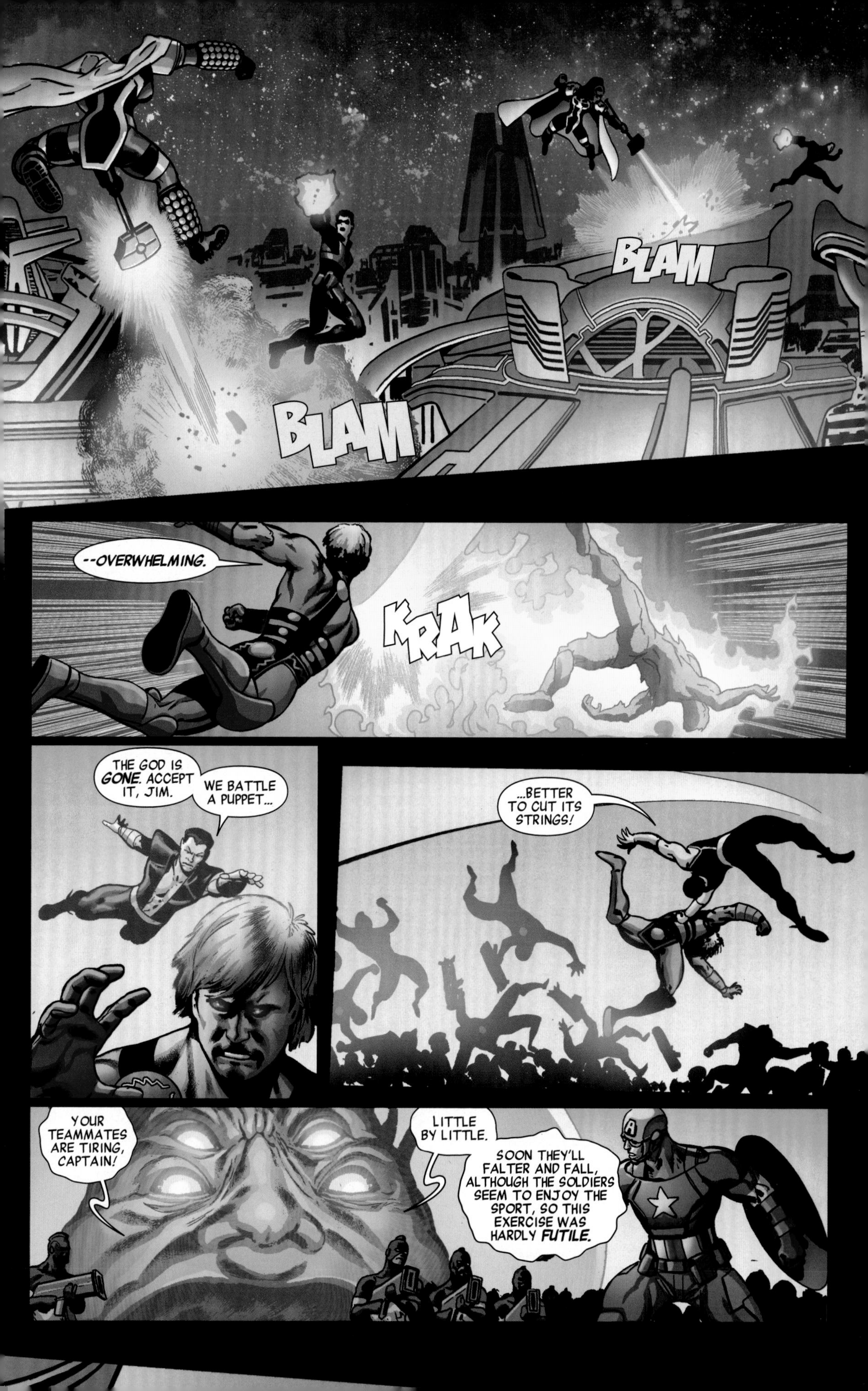
BLAM
BLAM
--OVERWHELMING.
KRAK
THE GOD IS GONE. ACCEPT IT, JIM.
WE BATTLE A PUPPET...
...BETTER TO CUT ITS STRINGS!
YOUR TEAMMATES ARE TIRING, CAPTAIN!
LITTLE BY LITTLE.
SOON THEY'LL FALTER AND FALL, ALTHOUGH THE SOLDIERS SEEM TO ENJOY THE SPORT, SO THIS EXERCISE WAS HARDLY FUTILE.

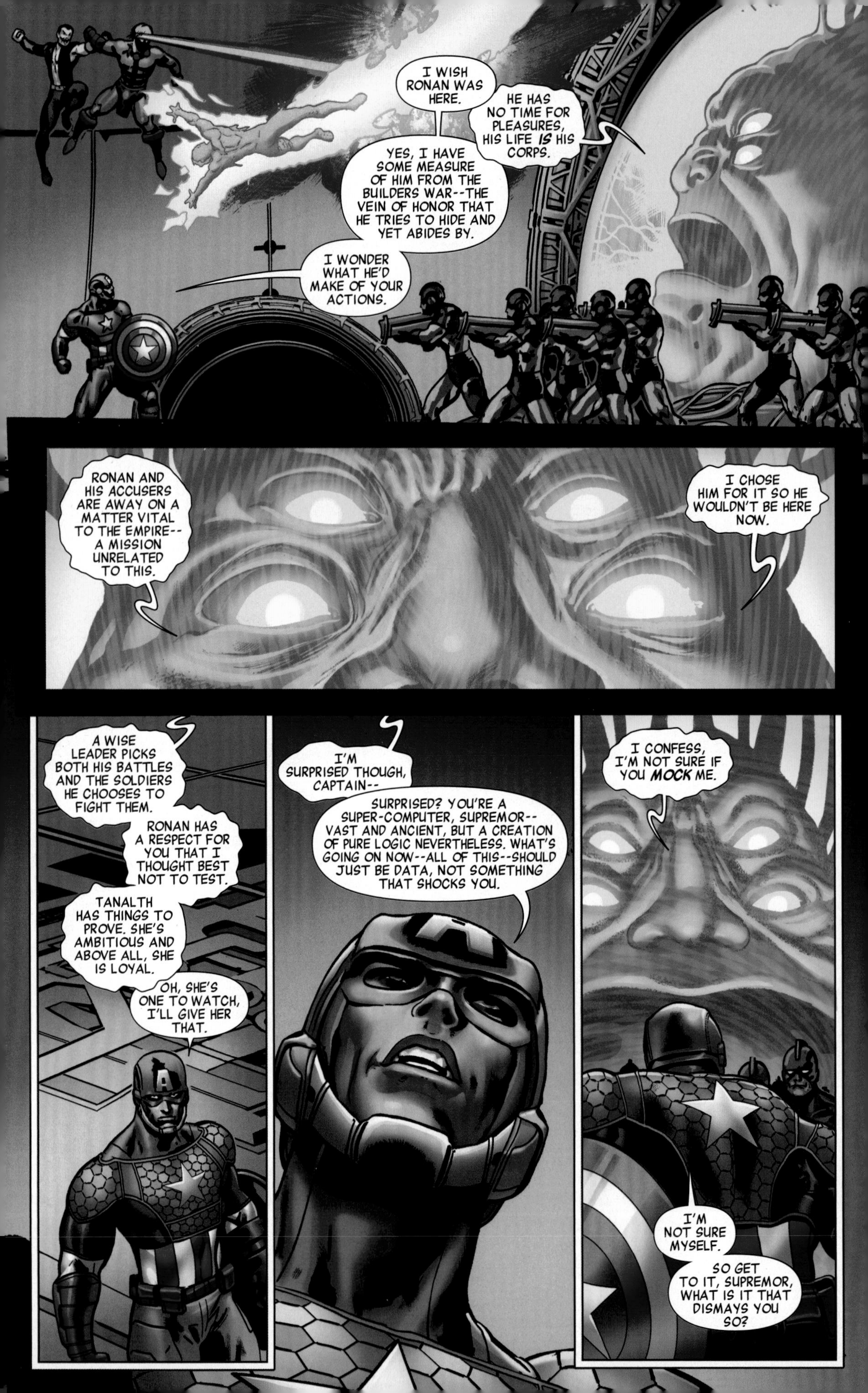
I WISH RONAN WAS HERE.
HE HAS NO TIME FOR PLEASURES, HIS LIFE IS HIS CORPS.
YES, I HAVE SOME MEASURE OF HIM FROM THE BUILDERS WAR--THE VEIN OF HONOR THAT HE TRIES TO HIDE AND YET ABIDES BY.
I WONDER WHAT HE'D MAKE OF YOUR ACTIONS.
RONAN AND HIS ACCUSERS ARE AWAY ON A MATTER VITAL TO THE EMPIRE--A MISSION UNRELATED TO THIS.
I CHOSE HIM FOR IT SO HE WOULDN'T BE HERE NOW.
A WISE LEADER PICKS BOTH HIS BATTLES AND THE SOLDIERS HE CHOOSES TO FIGHT THEM.
RONAN HAS A RESPECT FOR YOU THAT I THOUGHT BEST NOT TO TEST.
TANALTH HAS THINGS TO PROVE. SHE'S AMBITIOUS AND ABOVE ALL, SHE IS LOYAL.
OH, SHE'S ONE TO WATCH, I'LL GIVE HER THAT.
I'M SURPRISED THOUGH, CAPTAIN--
SURPRISED? YOU'RE A SUPER-COMPUTER, SUPREMOR--VAST AND ANCIENT, BUT A CREATION OF PURE LOGIC NEVERTHELESS. WHAT'S GOING ON NOW--ALL OF THIS--SHOULD JUST BE DATA, NOT SOMETHING THAT SHOCKS YOU.
I CONFESS, I'M NOT SURE IF YOU MOCK ME.
I'M NOT SURE MYSELF.
SO GET TO IT, SUPREMOR, WHAT IS IT THAT DISMAYS YOU SO?

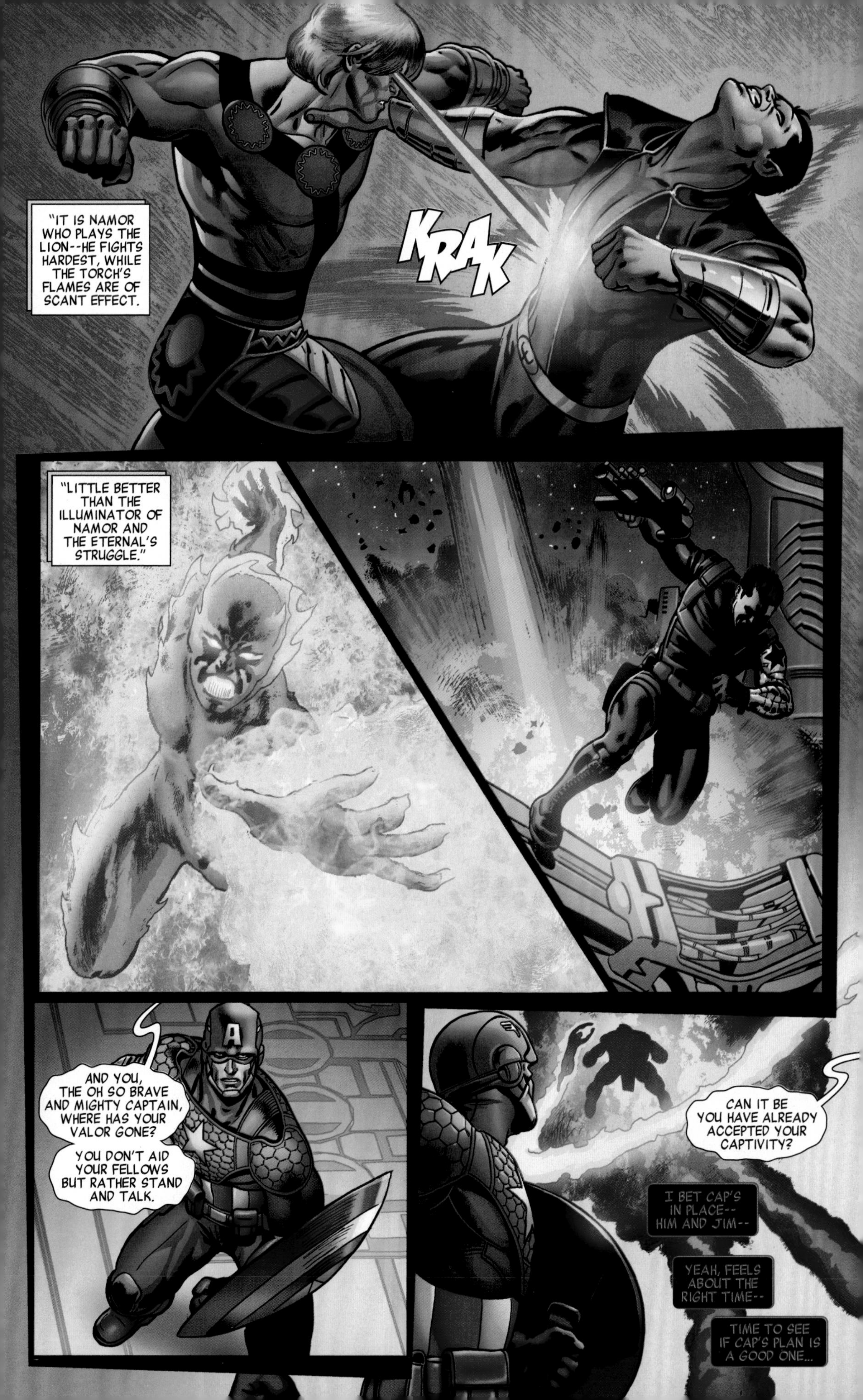
"IT IS NAMOR WHO PLAYS THE LION--HE FIGHTS HARDEST, WHILE THE TORCH'S FLAMES ARE OF SCANT EFFECT.
KRAK
"LITTLE BETTER THAN THE ILLUMINATOR OF NAMOR AND THE ETERNAL'S STRUGGLE."
AND YOU, THE OH SO BRAVE AND MIGHTY CAPTAIN, WHERE HAS YOUR VALOR GONE?
YOU DON'T AID YOUR FELLOWS BUT RATHER STAND AND TALK.
CAN IT BE YOU HAVE ALREADY ACCEPTED YOUR CAPTIVITY?
I BET CAP'S IN PLACE-- HIM AND JIM--
YEAH, FEELS ABOUT THE RIGHT TIME--
TIME TO SEE IF CAP'S PLAN IS A GOOD ONE...

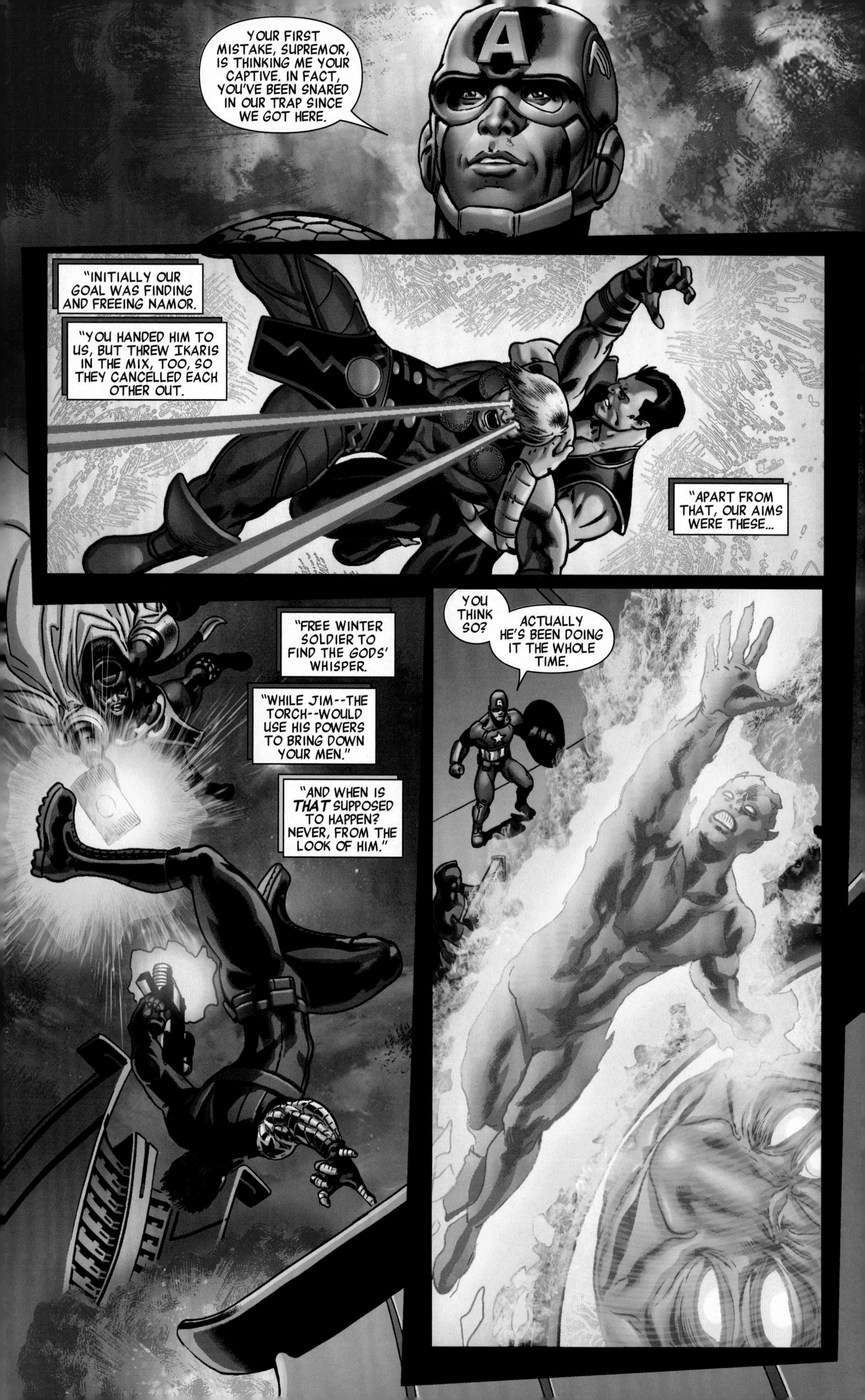

YOUR FIRST MISTAKE, SUPREMOR, IS THINKING ME YOUR CAPTIVE. IN FACT, YOU'VE BEEN SNARED IN OUR TRAP SINCE WE GOT HERE.
"INITIALLY OUR GOAL WAS FINDING AND FREEING NAMOR.
"YOU HANDED HIM TO US, BUT THREW IKARIS IN THE MIX, TOO, SO THEY CANCELLED EACH OTHER OUT.
"APART FROM THAT, OUR AIMS WERE THESE...
"FREE WINTER SOLDIER TO FIND THE GODS' WHISPER.
"WHILE JIM--THE TORCH--WOULD USE HIS POWERS TO BRING DOWN YOUR MEN."
"AND WHEN IS *THAT* SUPPOSED TO HAPPEN? NEVER, FROM THE LOOK OF HIM."
YOU THINK SO?
ACTUALLY HE'S BEEN DOING IT THE WHOLE TIME.

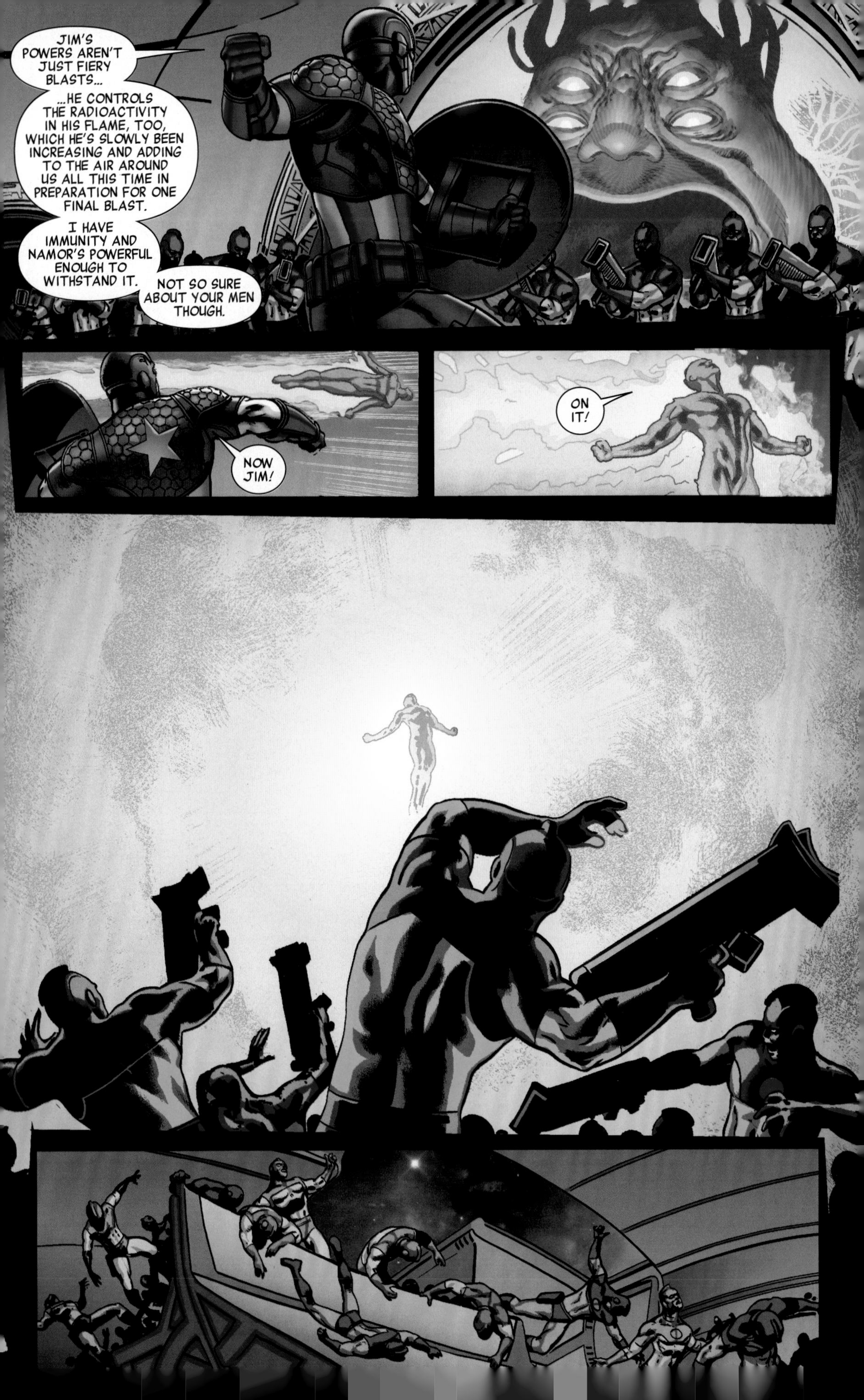
JIM'S POWERS AREN'T JUST FIERY BLASTS...
...HE CONTROLS THE RADIOACTIVITY IN HIS FLAME, TOO, WHICH HE'S SLOWLY BEEN INCREASING AND ADDING TO THE AIR AROUND US ALL THIS TIME IN PREPARATION FOR ONE FINAL BLAST.
I HAVE IMMUNITY AND NAMOR'S POWERFUL ENOUGH TO WITHSTAND IT.
NOT SO SURE ABOUT YOUR MEN THOUGH.
NOW JIM!
ON IT!

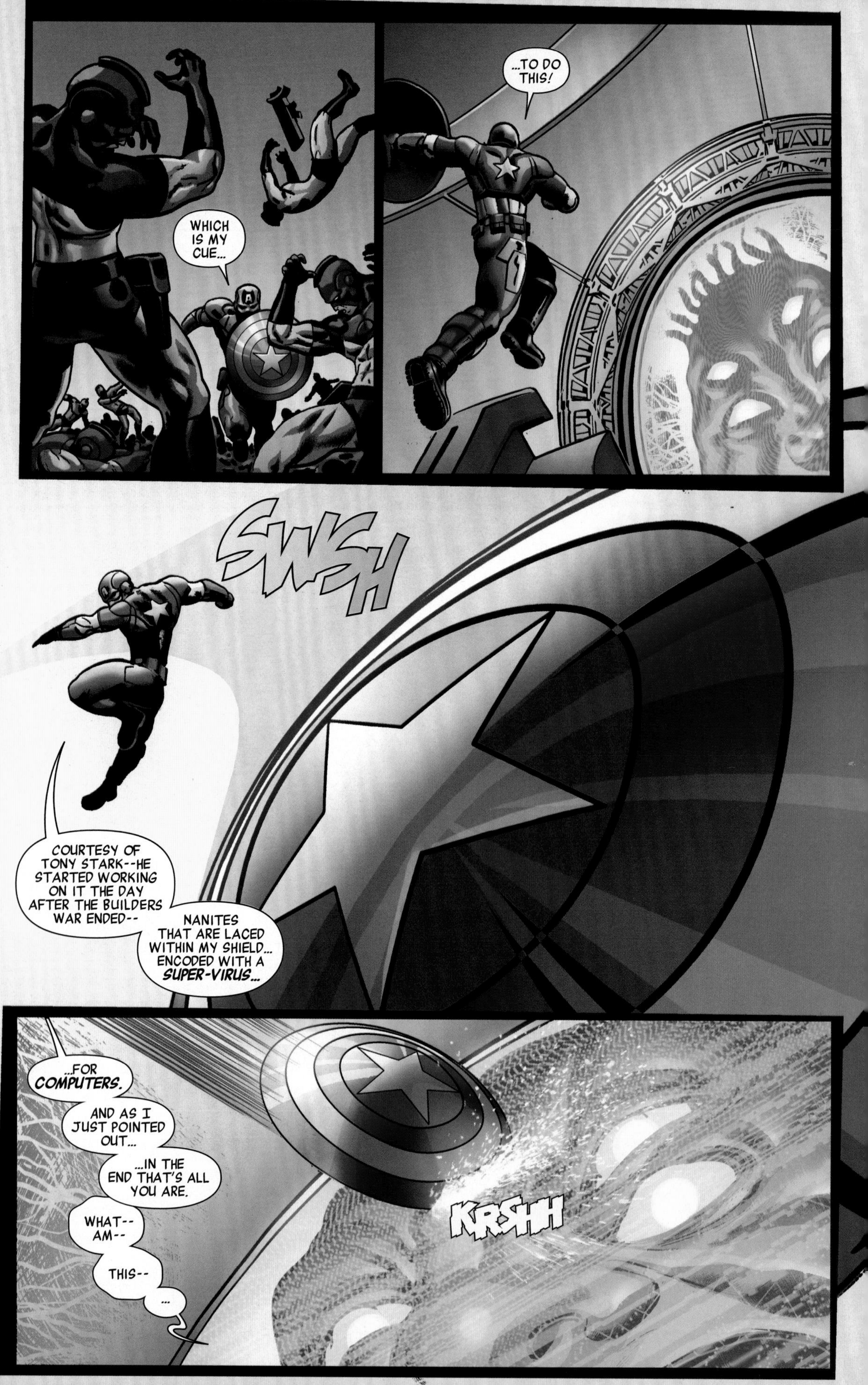
WHICH IS MY CUE...
...TO DO THIS!
SWISH
COURTESY OF TONY STARK--HE STARTED WORKING ON IT THE DAY AFTER THE BUILDERS WAR ENDED--
NANITES THAT ARE LACED WITHIN MY SHIELD... ENCODED WITH A SUPER-VIRUS...
...FOR COMPUTERS.
AND AS I JUST POINTED OUT...
...IN THE END THAT'S ALL YOU ARE.
KRSHH
WHAT--
AM--
THIS--
...

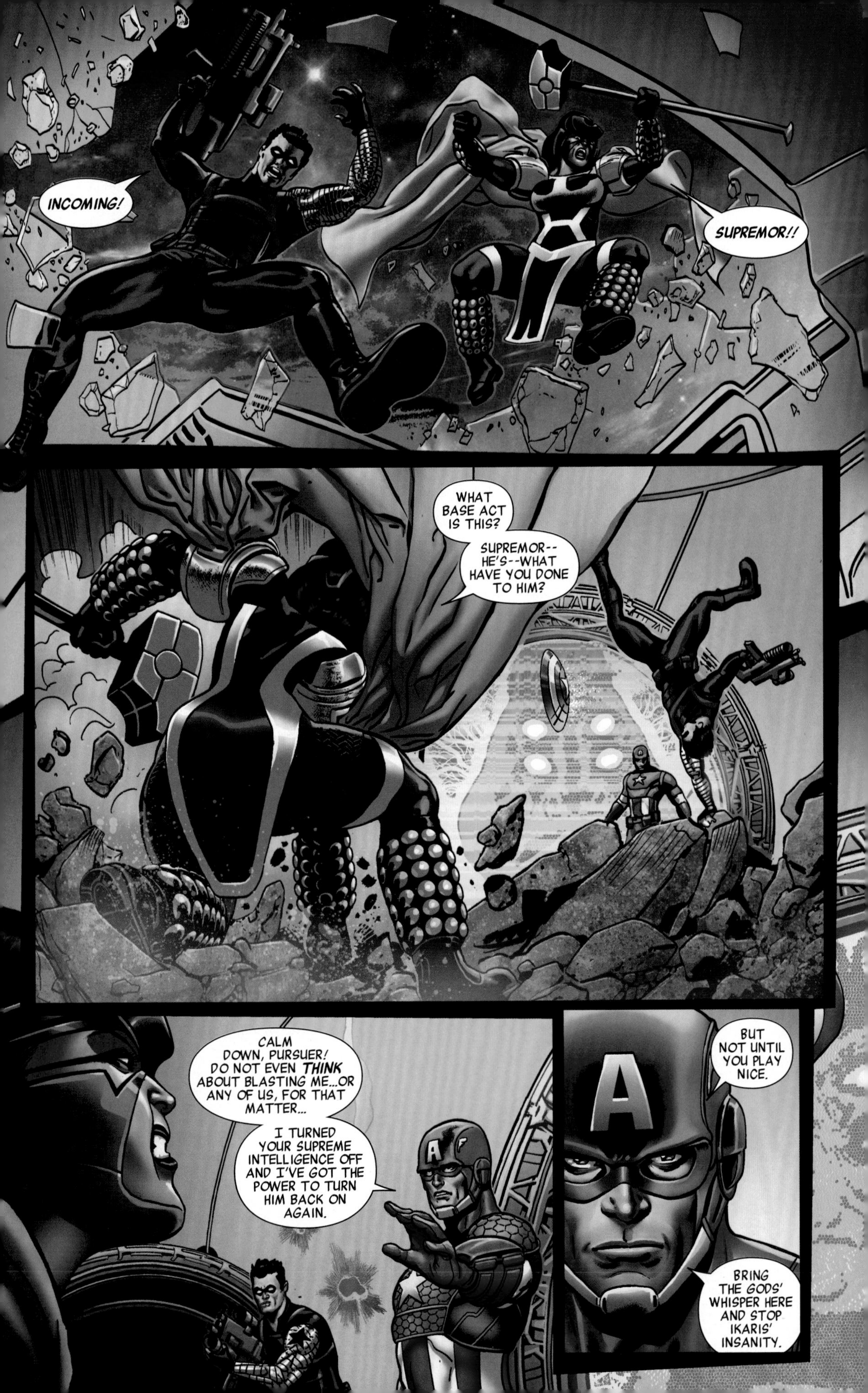
INCOMING!
SUPREMOR!!
WHAT BASE ACT IS THIS?
SUPREMOR-- HE'S--WHAT HAVE YOU DONE TO HIM?
CALM DOWN, PURSUER! DO NOT EVEN THINK ABOUT BLASTING ME...OR ANY OF US, FOR THAT MATTER...
I TURNED YOUR SUPREME INTELLIGENCE OFF AND I'VE GOT THE POWER TO TURN HIM BACK ON AGAIN.
BUT NOT UNTIL YOU PLAY NICE.
BRING THE GODS' WHISPER HERE AND STOP IKARIS' INSANITY.

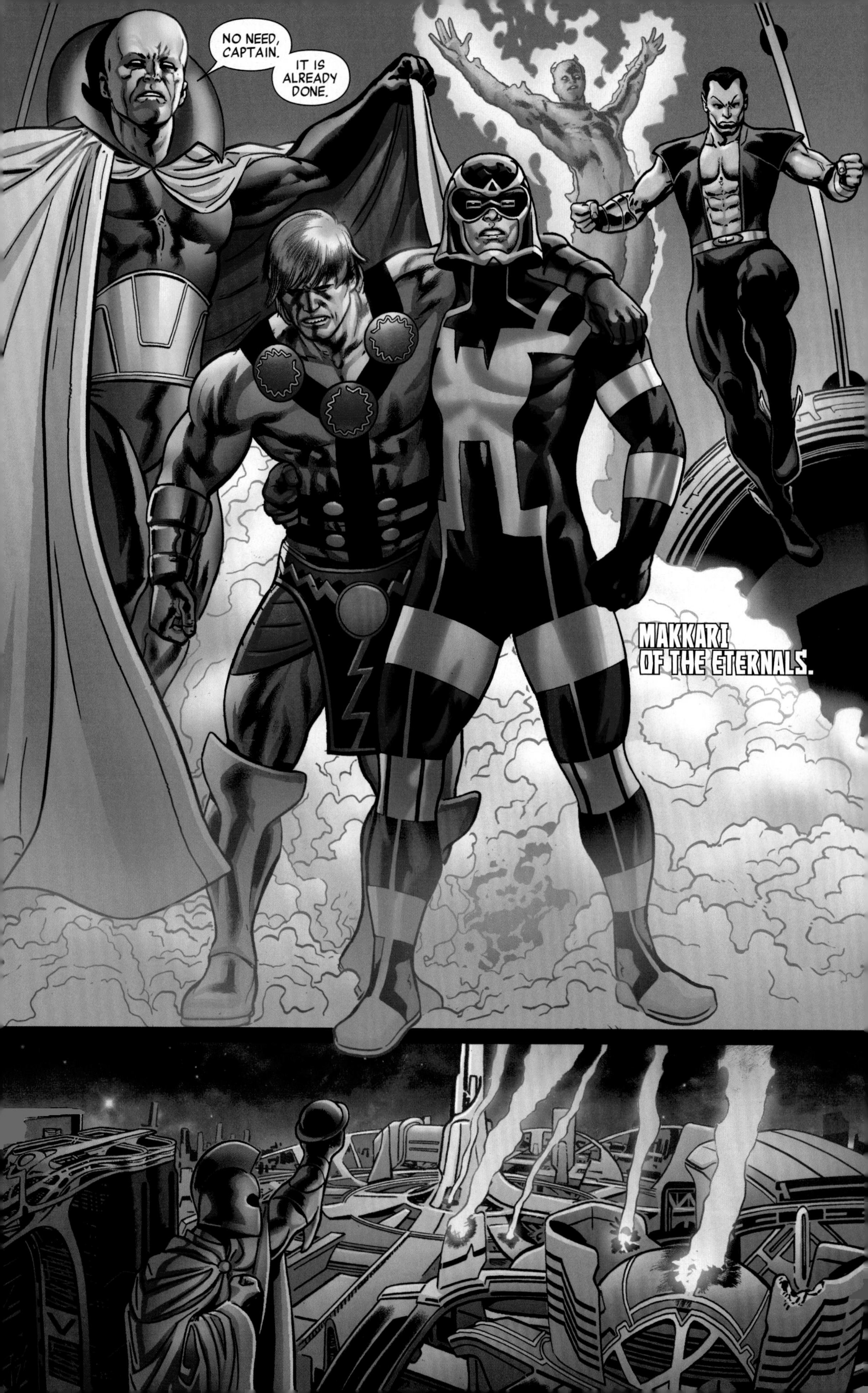
NO NEED, CAPTAIN.
IT IS ALREADY DONE.
MAKKARI OF THE ETERNALS.

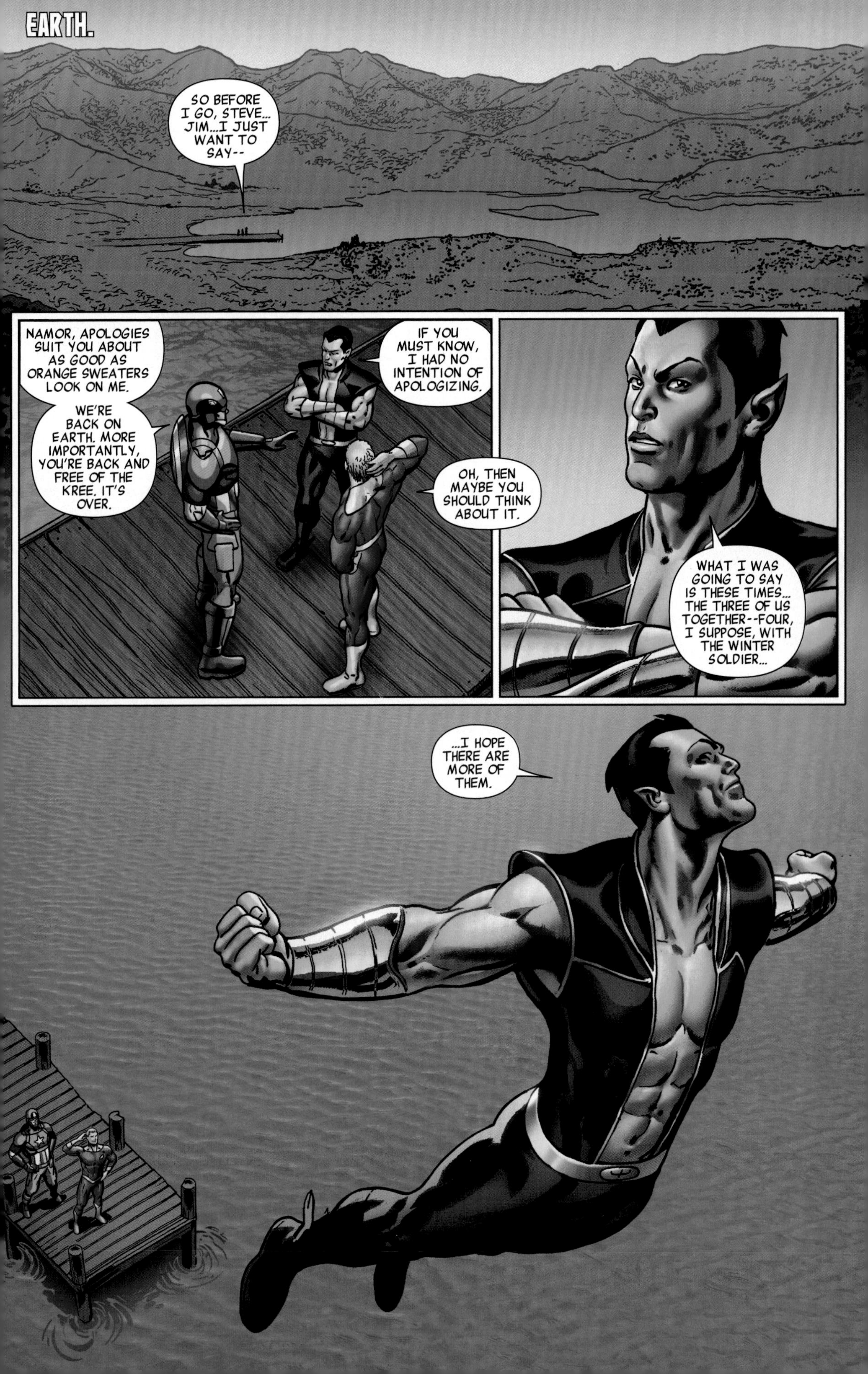
EARTH.
SO BEFORE I GO, STEVE... JIM...I JUST WANT TO SAY--
NAMOR, APOLOGIES SUIT YOU ABOUT AS GOOD AS ORANGE SWEATERS LOOK ON ME.
WE'RE BACK ON EARTH. MORE IMPORTANTLY, YOU'RE BACK AND FREE OF THE KREE. IT'S OVER.
IF YOU MUST KNOW, I HAD NO INTENTION OF APOLOGIZING.
OH, THEN MAYBE YOU SHOULD THINK ABOUT IT.
WHAT I WAS GOING TO SAY IS THESE TIMES... THE THREE OF US TOGETHER--FOUR, I SUPPOSE, WITH THE WINTER SOLDIER...
...I HOPE THERE ARE MORE OF THEM.

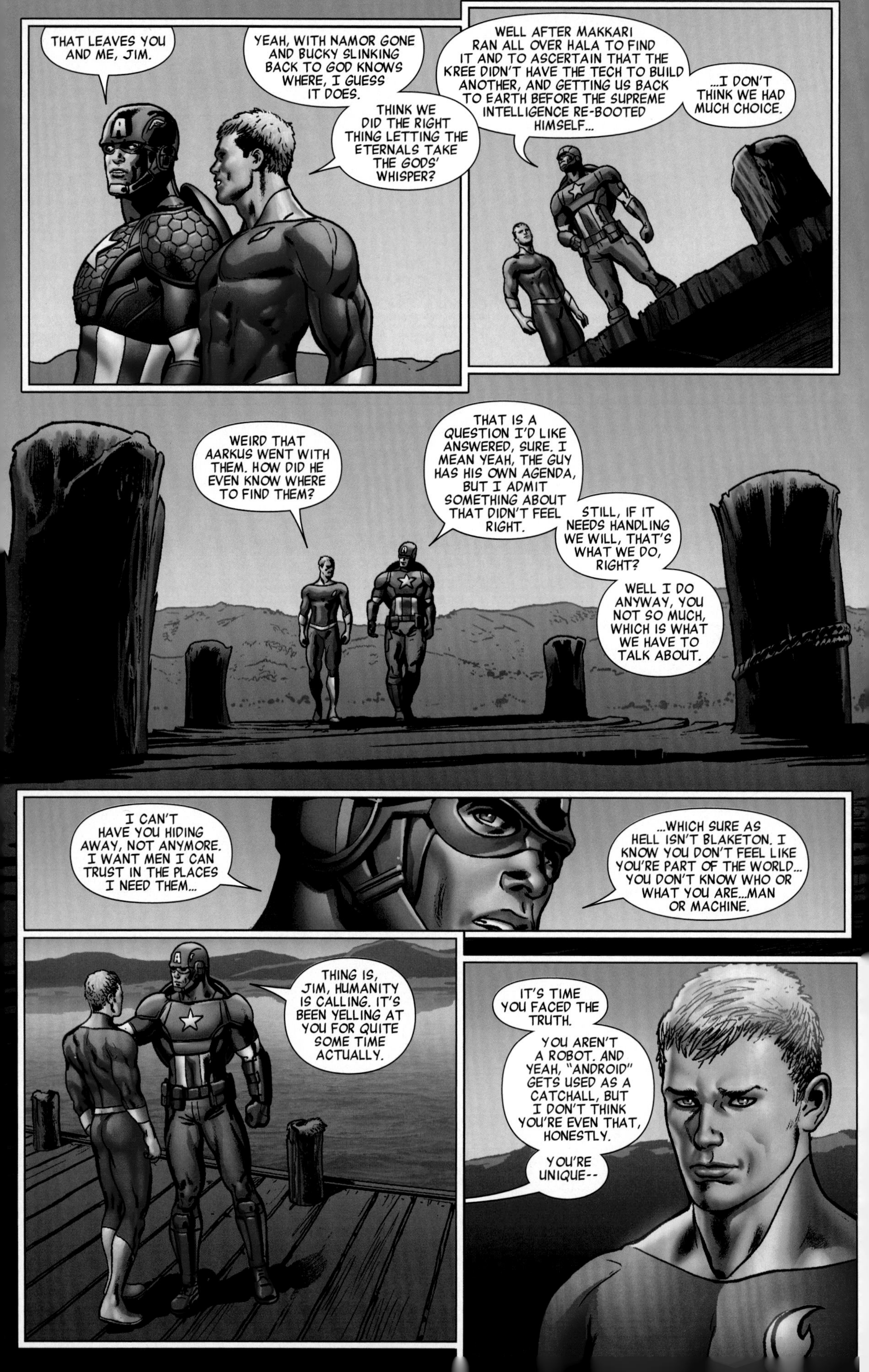
THAT LEAVES YOU AND ME, JIM.
YEAH, WITH NAMOR GONE AND BUCKY SLINKING BACK TO GOD KNOWS WHERE, I GUESS IT DOES.
THINK WE DID THE RIGHT THING LETTING THE ETERNALS TAKE THE GODS' WHISPER?
WELL AFTER MAKKARI RAN ALL OVER HALA TO FIND IT AND TO ASCERTAIN THAT THE KREE DIDN'T HAVE THE TECH TO BUILD ANOTHER, AND GETTING US BACK TO EARTH BEFORE THE SUPREME INTELLIGENCE RE-BOOTED HIMSELF...
...I DON'T THINK WE HAD MUCH CHOICE.
WEIRD THAT AARKUS WENT WITH THEM. HOW DID HE EVEN KNOW WHERE TO FIND THEM?
THAT IS A QUESTION I'D LIKE ANSWERED, SURE. I MEAN YEAH, THE GUY HAS HIS OWN AGENDA, BUT I ADMIT SOMETHING ABOUT THAT DIDN'T FEEL RIGHT.
STILL, IF IT NEEDS HANDLING WE WILL, THAT'S WHAT WE DO, RIGHT?
WELL I DO ANYWAY, YOU NOT SO MUCH, WHICH IS WHAT WE HAVE TO TALK ABOUT.
I CAN'T HAVE YOU HIDING AWAY, NOT ANYMORE. I WANT MEN I CAN TRUST IN THE PLACES I NEED THEM...
...WHICH SURE AS HELL ISN'T BLAKETON. I KNOW YOU DON'T FEEL LIKE YOU'RE PART OF THE WORLD... YOU DON'T KNOW WHO OR WHAT YOU ARE...MAN OR MACHINE.
THING IS, JIM, HUMANITY IS CALLING. IT'S BEEN YELLING AT YOU FOR QUITE SOME TIME ACTUALLY.
IT'S TIME YOU FACED THE TRUTH.
YOU AREN'T A ROBOT. AND YEAH, "ANDROID" GETS USED AS A CATCHALL, BUT I DON'T THINK YOU'RE EVEN THAT, HONESTLY.
YOU'RE UNIQUE--

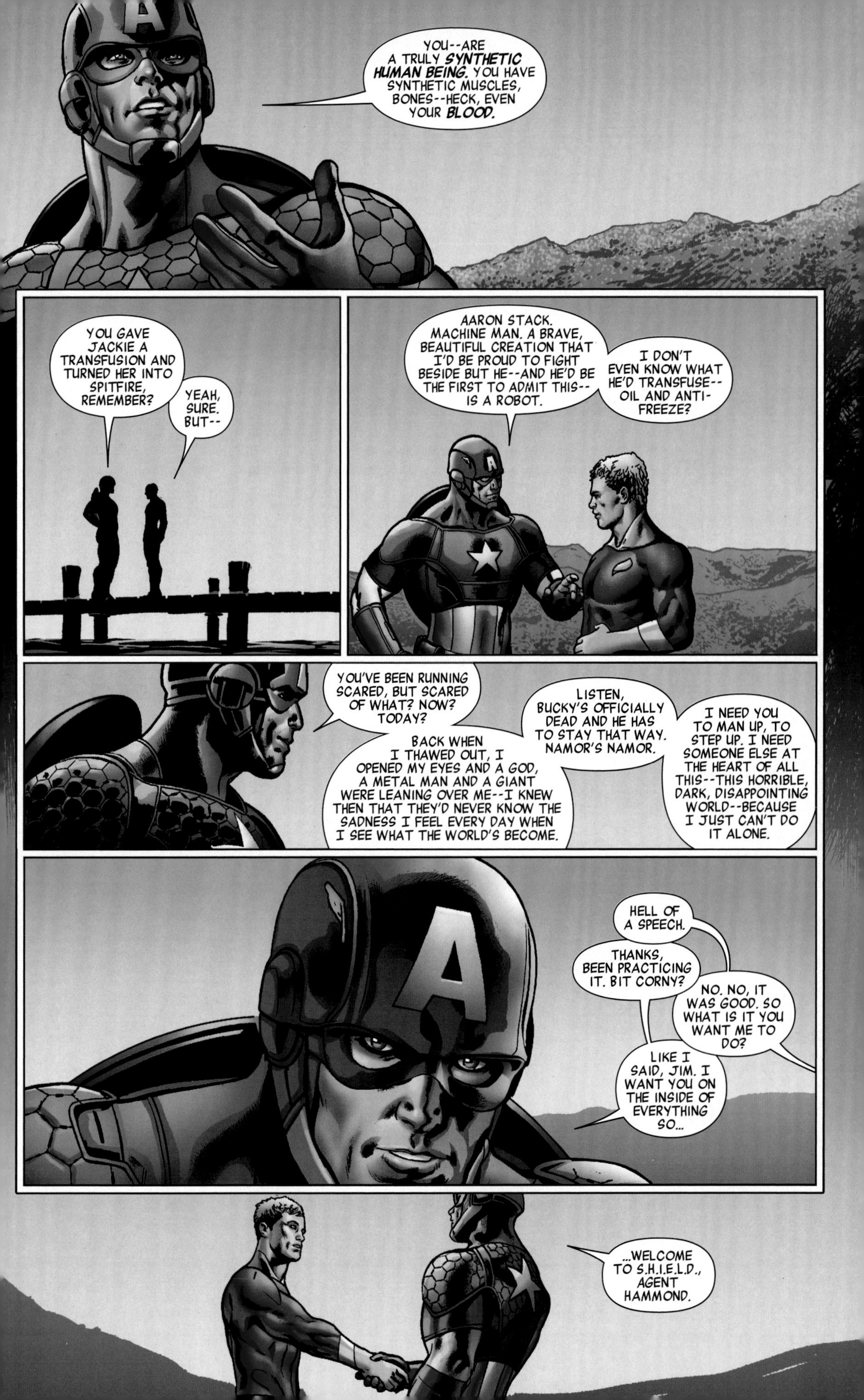
YOU--ARE A TRULY SYNTHETIC HUMAN BEING. YOU HAVE SYNTHETIC MUSCLES, BONES--HECK, EVEN YOUR BLOOD.
YOU GAVE JACKIE A TRANSFUSION AND TURNED HER INTO SPITFIRE, REMEMBER?
YEAH, SURE. BUT--
AARON STACK. MACHINE MAN. A BRAVE, BEAUTIFUL CREATION THAT I'D BE PROUD TO FIGHT BESIDE BUT HE--AND HE'D BE THE FIRST TO ADMIT THIS--IS A ROBOT.
I DON'T EVEN KNOW WHAT HE'D TRANSFUSE--OIL AND ANTI-FREEZE?
YOU'VE BEEN RUNNING SCARED, BUT SCARED OF WHAT? NOW? TODAY?
BACK WHEN I THAWED OUT, I OPENED MY EYES AND A GOD, A METAL MAN AND A GIANT WERE LEANING OVER ME--I KNEW THEN THAT THEY'D NEVER KNOW THE SADNESS I FEEL EVERY DAY WHEN I SEE WHAT THE WORLD'S BECOME.
LISTEN, BUCKY'S OFFICIALLY DEAD AND HE HAS TO STAY THAT WAY. NAMOR'S NAMOR.
I NEED YOU TO MAN UP, TO STEP UP. I NEED SOMEONE ELSE AT THE HEART OF ALL THIS--THIS HORRIBLE, DARK, DISAPPOINTING WORLD--BECAUSE I JUST CAN'T DO IT ALONE.
HELL OF A SPEECH.
THANKS, BEEN PRACTICING IT. BIT CORNY?
NO. NO, IT WAS GOOD. SO WHAT IS IT YOU WANT ME TO DO?
LIKE I SAID, JIM. I WANT YOU ON THE INSIDE OF EVERYTHING SO...
...WELCOME TO S.H.I.E.L.D., AGENT HAMMOND.

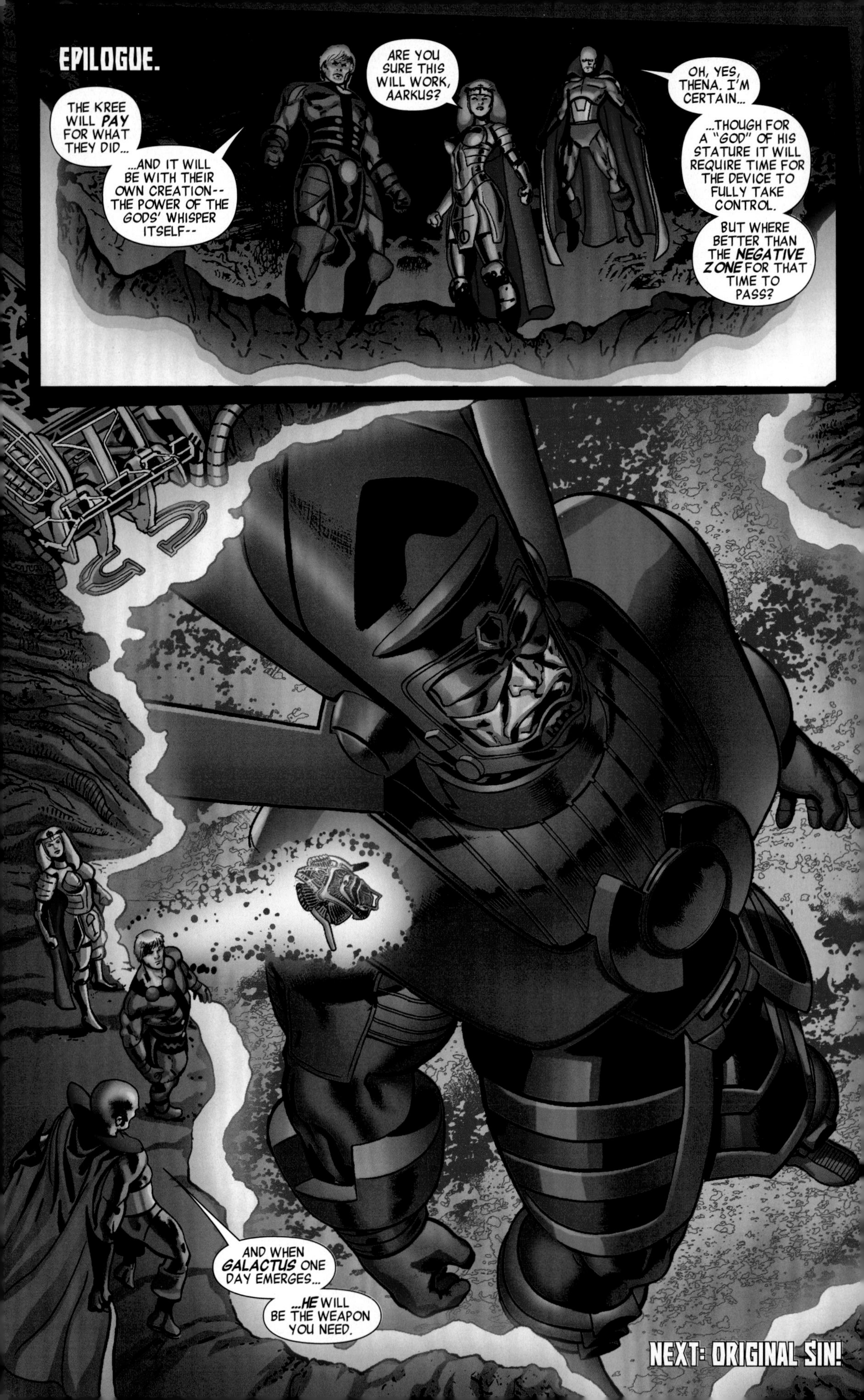
EPILOGUE.
THE KREE WILL PAY FOR WHAT THEY DID...
...AND IT WILL BE WITH THEIR OWN CREATION-- THE POWER OF THE GODS' WHISPER ITSELF--
ARE YOU SURE THIS WILL WORK, AARKUS?
OH, YES, THENA. I'M CERTAIN...
...THOUGH FOR A "GOD" OF HIS STATURE IT WILL REQUIRE TIME FOR THE DEVICE TO FULLY TAKE CONTROL.
BUT WHERE BETTER THAN THE NEGATIVE ZONE FOR THAT TIME TO PASS?
AND WHEN GALACTUS ONE DAY EMERGES...
...HE WILL BE THE WEAPON YOU NEED.
NEXT: ORIGINAL SIN!

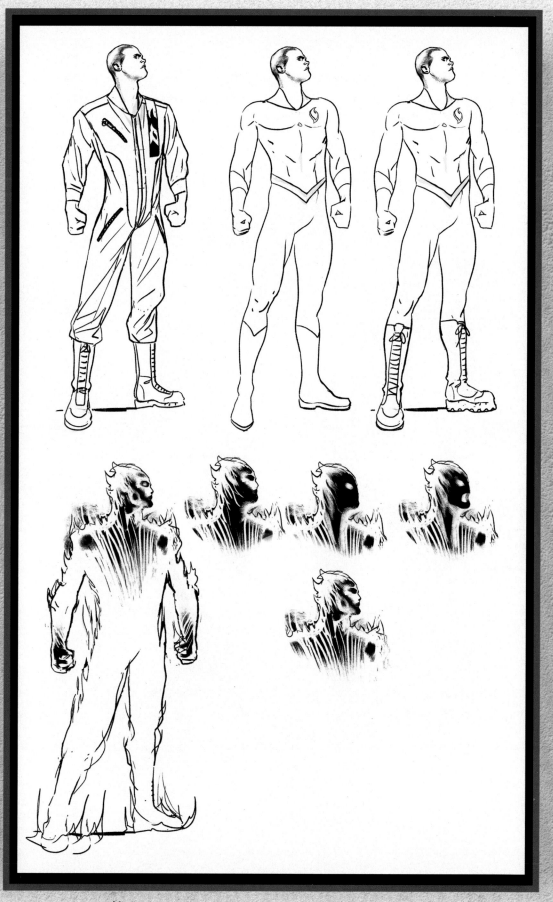

#1 Design Variant by Steve Pugh

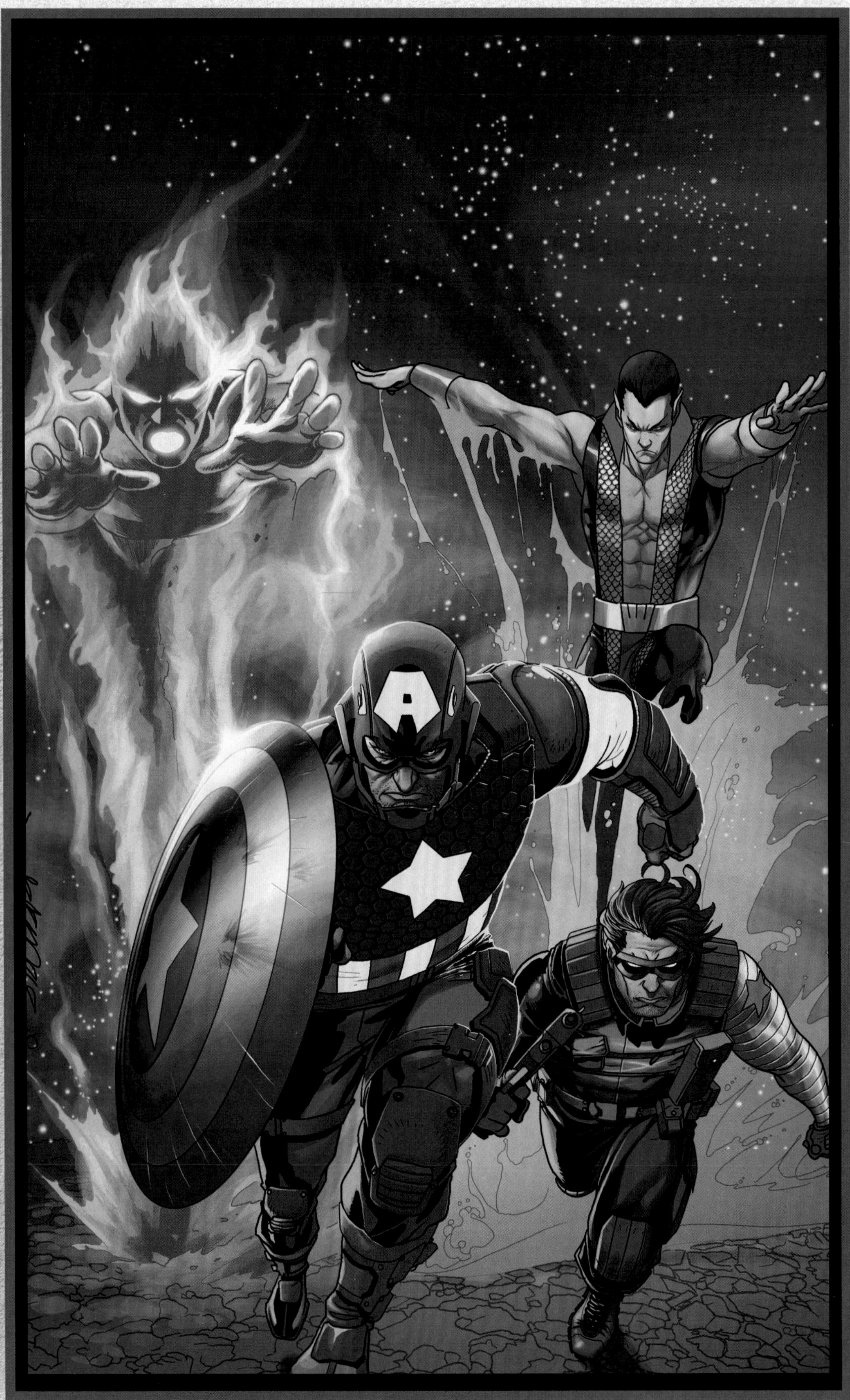

#2 Variant by Salvador Larroca & Frank Martin

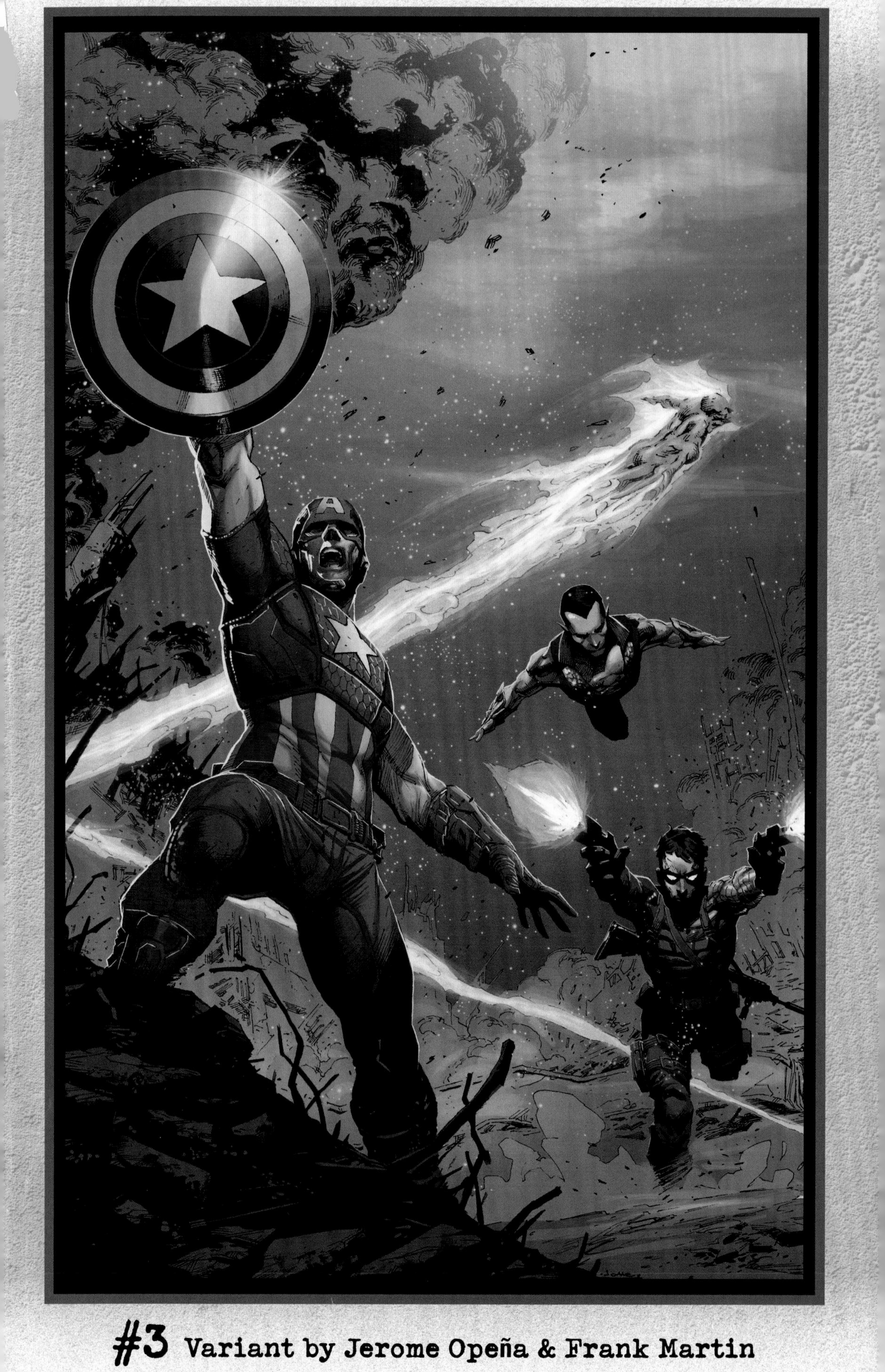

#3 Variant by Jerome Opeña & Frank Martin

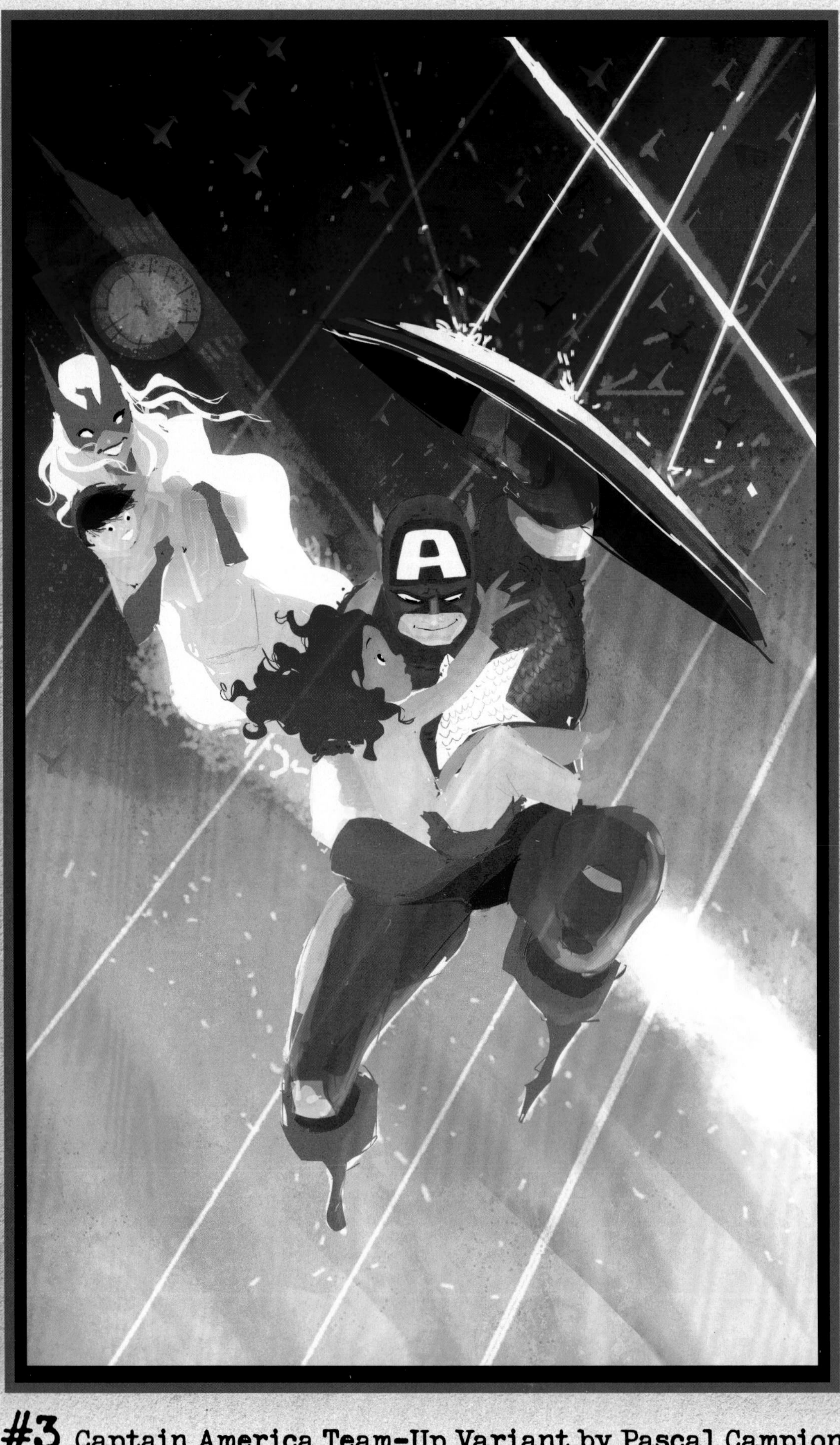

#3 Captain America Team-Up Variant by Pascal Campion